The RSS

100 Years of Service Dedication & Nation Building

Commemorating the Journey of the
Rashtriya Swayamsevak Sangh

CHINMAYA SAXENA

AYUSHMAN SINGH

Edited By – Jag Mohan Saxena

INDIA • SINGAPORE • MALAYSIA

ISBN

Hardcase 979-8-89186-920-2
Paperback 979-8-89133-962-0

"संघ शक्ति कलियुगे
भारत माता की जय"

Contents

Praise for the Book — 7

Acknowledgements — 17

Author's Profile — 21

Editor Profile — 25

Chronology | Timeline — 27

Introduction ~ The RSS — 53

Chapter – 1 How, When and Where ~ Dr. Hedgewar Ji and the Emergence, Background of the Sangh — 59

Chapter – 2 Fundamentals of the Sangh "Guruji Golwalkar" ~ Growth & Expansion — 75

Chapter – 3 The Organizational Structure of the Sangh & Constituents Units — 91

Chapter – 4 Beliefs, Notions & Philosophy of the Sangh — 116

Chapter – 5 Leadership & Impact ~ Sarsanghchalaks of the RSS — 140

Chapter – 6 RSS & The Hindutva Paradigm — 158

Chapter – 7 Contribution of Sangh in Nation Building & Challenges — 178

Chapter – 8 The Stalwarts of Hindutva & Sangh Parivar — 199

Chapter – 9 The Sangh Parivar ~ Affiliated Organizations & Contribution — 226

Chapter – 10 The 21st Century Bharat & The RSS Perspective ~ Kartavya Kaal — 256

Quotes & Sayings — 273

Praise for the Book

The book is an important study on the Sangh and is written with patience, perseverance, and clarity. To encompass hundred years of the Sangh in a book is a very daunting task. The book covers almost all aspect of the Sangh and I am sure it will prove to be an asset for readers who wish to get an insight into the Sangh, and its role in the Bharatiya society.

I congratulate the authors on writing a book on the Sangh as the organization will complete its 100 years of establishment in 2025, this book will be of significance and importance to understand the functioning and the growth of the Sangh over the decades.

– Sh. Om Prakash Mathur
Member, Central Election Committee, Bharatiya Janta Party
Former MP, Rajya Sabha, Former National Vice President, BJP

With a widespread network of thousands of shakas and millions of Swayamsevaks and volunteers across Bharat, the Sangh is a formidable and powerful organization working towards nation building with a spirit of Bharatiyata.

The book is written commemorating the historic journey of the Sangh, as the organization is on the cusp of completing 100 years of its establishment. I congratulate the authors for their effort and I am sure this book will serve as a very important narrative to understand the Sangh and its organizational functioning.

– Sh. Rajendra Singh Rathore
Leader of Opposition Rajasthan Legislative Assembly
Former Cabinet Minister, Government of Rajasthan

The Sangh follows the ideal of protecting "Jati Dharma Sanskriti" and works to make this pledge meaningful and to serve the society. The Sangh maintains spiritual brotherhood with all the communities; this is primarily because the Sangh's definition of Hindu is not linked to any religion but to a national identity of Bharat. It is an all-inclusive term that encompasses all communities and faith of the nation.

This is the reason that the Sangh has become an organisation of the ordinary people and has expanded over the years; it is related to the ordinariness and common simplicity of the people, it gives them confidence that they can bring about changes in the society and in the nation.

– Sh. Rajyavardhan Singh Rathore AVSM,
Hon'ble Member of Parliament (Lok Sabha)
National Spokesperson, Bharatiya Janta Party

The Sangh has evolved into a force for Hindu renaissance and nation-building, extending its reach beyond the confines of Sangh shakhas. The Sangh's most significant contribution lies in elevating the social and intellectual consciousness of ordinary citizens and creating an environment conducive to Hindu renaissance. In virtually every facet of Bharat's vast social, cultural, and political landscape, including the diaspora, the Sangh has an active and significant presence. I am very glad that this book has been written embarking the 100 years of the Sangh.

– Sh. Saurabh Srivastava
Member of Legislative Assembly, BJP
Varanasi Cantonment, Uttar Pradesh

The Rashtriya Swayamsevak Sangh (RSS) is one of the largest voluntary organizations working towards promoting Indian nationalism and patriotism. It believes in a vision of India is rooted in its ancient culture and traditions, the organization is committed towards nation building and service through wide range of activities in the field of healthcare, education disaster relief etc.

I hope that the book "The RSS: 100 Years of Service, Dedication and Nation Building" depicting the glorious journey of this organization will serve as a testament to the organization's endurance, resilience and ever evolving significance.

I believe that Ayushman Singh's ideological upbringing which has shaped his personality and his political outlook, would have helped in better shaping of the contents of the book.

I am sure this book will be a huge success. My Best Wishes to Ayushman Ji and Chinmaya Ji

– Sh. Nand Gopal Gupta 'Nandi'
Minister
Industrial Development, Export Promotion,
NRI & Invest Promotion
Government of Uttar Pradesh

As an organization, the Sangh is unique. No other organisation has shown such enormous voluntary service for the nation. For decades, generation after generation it has instinctively chosen austerity and devoted itself to the national cause. The Sangh is committed to Vyakti Nirman & Rashtra Nirman. The Book will be of importance to readers and the academicians in understanding the journey of the Sangh since its inception.

– Sh. Abhinav Prakash
National Vice President
Bhartiya Janta Yuva Morcha (BJYM)
& Assistant Professor, University of Delhi

The Sangh is an organization built on the principles of service and sacrifice, it reflects discipline, purity of purpose and unflinching commitment to national rejuvenation.

The Sangh's primary objective is to awaken Hindu society and strengthen to serve the cause of the Nation which is "Param Vaibhav", and achieving the same with having our ancient vision of life, brotherhood, social harmony, sustainable development in connotation to the environment and build the ideal citizens.

The Sangh aspires to achieve this objective by fostering amity and brotherhood among people and communities within the nation. What binds the volunteers and Swayamsevaks of the Sangh is not loyalty to any cult figure or supreme leader but an unspoken commitment to nation-building and unwavering loyalty towards Bharat Mata, while reviving and nurturing the civilizational values encapsulated in the term Hindutva. The Book Provides an Bird eye view of the ocean of Sangh, & it's vision in action.

Writing a book reflecting upon the journey of 100 years of the Sangh, is indeed a very significant task, I congratulate the authors for their dedication and perseverance in writing the book.

– Sh. Gurcharan Singh Gill
Senior Advocate
National President, Rashtriya Sikh Sangat
Former Additional Advocate General, Government of Rajasthan

Condensing nearly a century of an organization's life of this magnitude within the confines of a single book is no easy feat. Nonetheless, the authors have strived to keep it concise and engaging by interweaving interesting anecdotes and recounting critical historical junctures in the Sangh's journey. The book provides a comprehensive overview of the Sangh's evolution from a tightly-knit cadre-based organization to a mass movement.

The book is an endeavour to comprehend the ideals and philosophy that propel the Sangh, its formation and organizational principles, structure, and the diverse range of activities it undertakes

For an organization not only to endure but to thrive over such a prolonged period is a testament to its unwavering sense of purpose. Today, we can proudly affirm that the Sangh is the sole organization tirelessly dedicated to the future of Bharat.

*– **Prof Dr. Sh. Kaushal Kumar Sharma***
Dean, School of Social Sciences &
Chairperson, Special Centre for Disaster Research
Jawaharlal Nehru University, New Delhi

Vande Mataram!

The RSS is an organisation which is based on the principles of service and sacrifice, it reflects discipline and purity of purpose. The idea of nation above self reflects the true patriotic character of this organisation.

The life and journey of every swayamsevak is in itself an inspiration for the youth. The relentless effort of the Sangh towards nation building and betterment of society has motivated many young ones to join this organisation and become a full time pracharak.

I congratulate the authors of 'The RSS : 100 years of Service, Dedication and Nation Building' who have made an attempt to collect and reproduce an account of this organisation highlighting its glorious journey. My best wishes for the book!

*– **Sh. Rahul Singh***
President, Seva Bharti ~ Kashi Prant

The Sangh has always been a historic and magnificent organization, since its establishment in 1925 till now the Sangh has been inspiring millions of people. The Sangh's commitment to Hindutva and Bharat has been unparalleled. It is no exaggeration to say that, with its numerous affiliated associations, millions of dedicated Swayamsevaks, the Sangh stands as the nation's most significant & influential organization. The Book manifests the slogan "Sanghe Shakti Kaliyuge"

*– **Sh. Pramod Kr. Chaturvedi***
Renowned Vastu - Astro Advisor &
Life Coach

I am feeling immense pleasure and pride that two bright and young brains of our nation, Mr. Ayushman Singh Ji and Mr. Chinmaya Saxena Ji have come up with a detailed and illuminative account on Rashtriya Swayamsevak Sangh in the form of a book, at the time when the organization is gearing up for centenary celebrations of its historic, illustrious and enviable journey fueled by the indefatigable spirit of its founders and volunteers.

Books have always been revered as one and only all-weather friend of mankind sans any sort of discrimination. Quite convincingly, this book will familiarize the readers especially our ambitious youth with evolutinary journey, traditions and organizational processes of RSS. I am confident that by the time our readers wind up the chapters, they will be self-motivated to forge bonds of friendship and partnership to put up collaborative efforts towards the formation of empowered and prosperous Bharat.

I wish both the budding writers brimming with waves of patriotism great success in all their future endeavors. Jai Sri Ram.

*– **Pujya Acharya Shantanu Ji Maharaj***
Founder, Ramayanam Foundation

Understanding the origins and history of the Sangh is essential for understanding Bharat today, and how its influence continues to shape the nation. The book is written at a very important time as the Sangh completes its 100 years of establishment in 2025, the book commemorates the journey of the Sangh and provides an excellent and detailed overview of the organization.

*– **Sh. Dhananjay Sharma***
National Office Member
Bhartiya Janta Yuva Morcha (BJYM) &
BJYM, Magazine Team Member.

The aims and objectives of the Sangh are to weld together the various diverse groups within the Hindu Samaj and to revitalise and rejuvenate the same based on its Dharma and Sanskriti, that it achieves an all-round development of Bharatvarsh. The Sangh believes in the orderly evolution of society and adheres to peaceful and legitimate means of realisation of its ideals.

The Book provides an excellent and detailed examination of the development and growth of the Sangh over the years, it will be a very valuable addition of the study of the Sangh and will contribute immensely to a better understanding of the organization.

– Dr. Saurabh Ji
Deputy Proctor, University of Delhi,
Assistant Professor, Department of Sanskrit,
Faculty of Arts, University of Delhi

This Small but rich in text and taste, document does possess the intrinsic worth of describing, depicting and directing the comprehensive chronological trajectory of inception, upsurge and efficacy of a national cultural organization i.e., the Rashtriya Swayamsevak Sangh (RSS).

It is certainly the fruit of the unfathomable intelligence, diligence and brilliance of the authors duo Sh. Chinmaya Saxena and Sh. Ayushman Singh and the most adequate editing of Sh. Jag Mohan Saxena. I observe and feel that this precious piece of scholarly significance will enlighten the vision and version of the readers and enrich them with the perspectives and prospects of the ideologically par excellent contribution of the largest cultural organization of the world dedicated and devoted to the noblest cause of human beings and humanity. The words fail to applaud their merit, matter and mindfulness. May god further equip these authors with wisdom to bring out such valuable publication in future too.

– Prof Sh. Harikesh Singh
Ex- Vice Chancellor, Jai Prakash University
Chapra (Saran.), Bihar

I highly appreciate the efforts of the young writers who had put lot of labour and collected almost all relevant material about the 100-year dedicated long journey of RSS. The dedicated life of thousands of Pracharaks and millions of Swayamsevaks had changed the course of country's future and Hindu society in particular.

I wish that this book will reach to all the youngsters for enriching their knowledge and thinking about RSS and it's activities in making a just and sanatan society. Please accept my best wishes for the timely publication of this much needed book.

– Sh. Kavindra Pratap Singh, IPS (Retd)
President, Vishwa Hindu Parishad ~ Kashi Prant

Acknowledgements

Writing an acknowledgment is like looking back with a heart full of gratitude for those who believed in you, stood by you, and walked with you. But every journey which reaches its destination has blessings of supreme power, that protective energy which surrounds yet remains elusive. We bow down with all gratitude for its protection and blessings.

Writing this book has been an enriching experience of learning, both with regards to the research, discussions and interactions that happened during the course of writing the book. While we interacted and learned from each of our discussions, we also deeply appreciate few of the closest individuals to our project that require special mentions.

Sh. Jag Mohan Saxena, our esteemed editor and guide, we owe a debt of gratitude for his meticulous guidance and unflagging dedication. His wisdom and encouragement have been instrumental in shaping the book.

Prof. Smt Manika Mohan, Mrs. Vidya Singh, Sh. Rahul Singh, Smt.Vandana Singh, Ms. Smiti Saxena Sh. Atman Singh as part of our families, your affectionate support and constant encouragement enriched our journey, whose support and compassion have nurtured us, we bow in gratitude. Your contributions are immeasurable and we hope to make you proud.

Sh. Dharmendra Pareek, Sh. Sudesh Saini for their unwavering commitment that breathed life into our vision, your dedication is truly commendable. Sh. Aditya Vardhan Pancholi, for his immense support in sculpting this book is deeply appreciated. We also thank Sh. Sanjeev Singhal for his valuable support to the project.

We extend our heartfelt gratitude to all those mentioned above and countless others who have contributed in various ways. This book stands as a testament to the power of collaboration and the strength of a supportive community. We would also like to thank Sangh Pracharaks and post holders who helped in reviewing the content of the book. None of this would have been possible without their support.

The idea to write this book came to us in October 2022 and we had set a goal to dedicate this book to The Rashtriya Swayamsevak Sangh to mark the completion of 100 years of the organization. The Sangh will be completing 100 years in 2025, and has emerged as the largest voluntary organization in the nation working constantly to promote and instil cultural identity and pride amongst masses.

We decided to keep the book factual. Primary reliance was placed on various available literature on Sangh and its affiliated organizations.

As we commemorate the impending centenary of the Sangh in 2025, we are humbled by its enduring purpose and ideals. This book is our endeavour to understand and celebrate the Sangh's remarkable journey. The Sangh has faced trials and tribulations but remains resolute in upholding its values. It is more than an organization; it is a way of life and a symbol of a resurgent Bharat. This book is not just the story of the Sangh; it closely resonates with the story of our nation.

We humbly pay our respects to the senior Swayamsevak's of the Sangh, who have laboured tirelessly and selflessly, without expecting any personal rewards, to establish a robust foundation for the Sangh in the face of formidable challenges.

We deeply acknowledge and give credit to the webpages and social media links and sources which have provided us with the images used in the book, that have been taken from the webpages and social media links of organizations affiliated to the Rashtriya Swayamsevak Sangh, we duly acknowledge the credits of the images which have been used in the book and we deeply appreciate the sources for making the images available to us.

We hope that the book brings value to our readers and look forward to receiving their feedback and wishes, which will be a significant encouragement to us.

Chinmaya Saxena

Ayushman Singh

Author's Profile

Chinmaya Saxena

Mr. Chinmaya Saxena is a third generation Lawyer. He received his Bachelors (Hons.) in Political Science and Governance from Kirori Mal College, University of Delhi and LL. B (Law) from the Faculty of Law, University Law College. He has been associated with the Sangh since his adulthood days.

He is also the founder of the Jaipur Youth Parliament & the Kirori Mal Youth Parliament, He has formerly worked with the National Human Rights Commission (NHRC), National Commission for Women (NCW), PUCL, CLRA, Lok Sabha, which has enriched his experience in public policy, planning and legal issues.

Even with his regular schedule in the legal profession, his passion for reading and learning continues, he also holds various accreditations in Law, Public Policy, Business and Finance from Yale, Columbia University, University of Michigan, University of Virginia, London Business School, (Micro Masters) IIM-Bangalore and IMF.

His debut book "India Post Independence: The Making of a Nation" written and published in 2021, is forwarded by Dr. Kiran Bedi Ex-Lieutenant governor, Puducherry. The book was written commemorating the 75 years of independence of the nation, on the occasion of the 'Azadi ka Amrut Mahotsav', the book attempts to cohesively build a complete narrative of major events in the nation, since independence till the recent times and is a collection of articles and essays written over time. The book is one of the best sellers in the UPSC academic book segment.

It is a matter of great pride for the author to refer about his great grandfather late Shri Radha Krishna Rastogi, an eminent lawyer who served as the Advocate General for the State of Rajasthan. All through his life he remained actively associated with the Sangh while dedicating himself selflessly to carry forward the work assigned to him, He remained Prant Sanghchalak in the Sangh.

Writing a book on the Sangh is a dream come true moment for him, he believes that the Sangh is a dynamic and wonderful organization committed to service of the society and the nation. He is deeply influenced and inspired by the ideals and philosophy of the Sangh, and he feels immense pride in writing a book dedicated to the Sangh as the organization is on the verge of completing 100 years of its establishment in the year 2025.

In his word's "The Book will be of special interest to readers who want to understand the Sangh as an organization and to value its phenomenal journey since its establishment in 1925 till the present times." The Sangh is more than an organization; it is a way of life and a vehicle for uniting a resurgent Bharat.

Ayushman Singh

Mr. Ayushman Singh, a young, bright mind always beaming with organic ideas and accompanying an insatiable appetite for contemplation has graduated from the prestigious Delhi University. A seasoned and bilingual debator, he has won numerous awards at state and district level competitions since childhood. His double graduation degrees in Law and English literature have bestowed upon him the skill of eloquence and articulation, much sought-after trait in a wordsmith.

Beyond honing Mr. Singh's understanding in textual and contextual complexities of social and global issues, the admirable academic profile has further equipped the author with logical clarity interlaced with humanitarian or compassionate dimensions, a prerequisite to undertake socio-scientific analysis of matters spanning the barricades of man-made and natural nature. The author's decision to pen a comprehensive account on Rashtriya Swayamsevak Sangh (RSS) world's largest multifaceted voluntary organization with its societal and political intent, stemmed from his firm belief in writing being one of the most noble pursuits and harbinger of constructive change that new India demands for universal progress and peace but without loosing its originality.

His spiritually, academically and culturally enriched upbringing has motivated and capacitated him to conduct rigorous research and explore enormous resources while navigating through the multi-directional functional zones of RSS since its inception in 1925 so as to present to our readers an unbiased narrative of the endeavours of brothers in saffron following the enduring trials of opportunities, challenges and accomplishments.

Lastly, it is evident that though there is an abundance of hagiographic literature on RSS and its volunteers in regional languages, limited visibility of RSS in English writings does restricts its accessibility and popularity to some extent. In that light, the present body of work being an illuminative and engrossing account certainly comes across as an unostentatious effort with a neutral and fresh perspective to wedge the gaps created due to paucity of encylopediac and fair description in English language about RSS and its evolution from an organization to a movement.

Editor Profile

Jag Mohan Saxena

Jagmohan Saxena is a senior lawyer with over four decades of practice in the field of law. He has practiced in the Rajasthan High Court and the Supreme Court of India. He had the honour of serving twice as the Additional Advocate General and has been standing counsel for various departments of the State of Rajasthan.

His association with the Sangh dates back to his college days in 1976-77 when he interacted with Shri Eknath Ji Ranade, which left a lasting impression on him and motivated him to commit himself to the organisation. His dedication to the organisation is evident in his continuous service and commitment to its philosophy of serving the nation.

He expresses his deep respect and admiration for the contributions of Param Pujianye Dr. Hedgewar Ji and Guruji Golwalkar in establishing and building the Sangh. He believes that their roles in the organization's development have been historical and inspirational.

The editor also expresses gratitude towards his father and mentor late Sh. Hirde Narain Saxena, an eminent Lawyer and an ardent follower of the philosophy of Sangh and deep respect to Late Sh. Suraj Narain Ji Pareek, a senior and renowned Lawyer with whom the editor remained associated during his profession in law, he was also very inspirational because of his profound ideology which he followed to propagate the philosophy of the Sangh.

Overall, his involvement in the book as its editor reflects his strong commitment to the Sangh's philosophy and his desire to contribute to the preservation and dissemination of the organization's significant history and principles. He believes that the book will serve as a tribute to the Sangh's extraordinary journey over the decades. It delves into the fundamental values, principles, and profound significance the organization holds within the Bharatiya culture.

Chronology | Timeline

The Rashtriya Swayamsevak Sangh
1925-2023

1925

On September 27, 1925, Param Punjaniye Doctor Ji Sh. Keshav Baliram Hedgewar, the esteemed founder of the Sangh, declared during the Vijayadashami (Dusshera) celebration, "Today, we are inaugurating the Sangh." He emphasized the importance of physical, intellectual, and all-around self-improvement to achieve the cherished goals of independence of the nation & spreading Hinduvta.

The formal inception of the Sangh took place at Doctor Ji's residence in Sukravari, Nagpur. The Sangh adopted the Khaki shirt and shorts as its uniform (Ganvesh), along with military-style ankle-length black boots. Sunday sessions focused on drill and marches, while Thursdays and Saturdays were reserved for discussions on important national issues.

1926

On April 17, 1926, during a meeting at Dr. Sh. Hedgewar's Ji's house, the name "Rashtriya Swayamsevak Sangh" was chosen from a list of four options (Jaripatka Mandal, Bharat Uddharak Mandal, Hindu Swayamsevak Sangh, and Rashtriya Swayamsevak Sangh).

Daily gatherings, known as Nitya shakhas, commenced on May 28, 1926 at the Mohite Wada ground in Nagpur. The introduction of the "Danda" (lathi) and new commands like Dakhsa and Aaram marked an important milestone. The practice of saluting the Bhagwa Dhwaj and concluding sessions with the Prarthana (prayer) in Hindi and Marathi became a tradition.

1927

In 1927, the first Sangh shiksha varg, initially called the officer's training camp (O.T.C.), was held in Mohite Wada, Nagpur. It included 17 participants (Shiksharthis) who underwent a 40-day training program.

During the Nagpur riots, Sangh organized its cadres into 16 shakhas across the city to protect the Hindu community. This display of commitment and courage during the Nagpur riots significantly boosted the Sangh's popularity and influence, leading to a surge in its membership across the nation.

1928

The first Guru Dakshina Utsava took place, collecting a total contribution (Samarpana) of 84 Rupees. Sh. Vitthalbhai Patel, elder brother of Sh. Sardar Patel, visited the Mohite Wada Shakha in Nagpur. The first initiation ceremony (Pratignya), involved 99 selected Swayamsevaks. By the end of the year, 18 shakhas were actively established in Nagpur. Additionally, the first winter camp of the Sangh and the first route march with a band (Ghosh) were conducted.

1929

In a meeting held on November 9-10 at Doke Math, Nagpur, Doctor Ji Sh. Hedgewar was designated as the Sarsanghachalak, Balaji Huddar as the Sarkaryavah (General secretary), and Martandrao Jog as Chief Trainer (Sarsenapati). This marked the beginning of Sangh's expansion in the state of Maharashtra.

1930

Instructed by Doctor Ji, all shakhas celebrated January 26 as Independence Day. Doctor Ji participated in the Jungle Satyagraha and was imprisoned, receiving six months of rigorous imprisonment and three months of simple imprisonment. Before his participation, he designated Dr. Laxman Vasudev Paranjape Ji as the Interim Sarsanghchalak.

The Khaki cap was replaced by the black cap (Topi) as part of the Sangh uniform (Ganvesh).

1931

Doctor Ji and other Sangh cadres were transferred to Akola jail, where he started a shakha within the jail premises, giving birth to the Vidarbha unit of the Sangh. He was released from prison on February 14, 1931.

Upon his release, Dr. Hedgewar Ji received numerous public felicitations during his stay in Akola and Wardha. On February 17, upon returning to Nagpur, a massive crowd gathered at the railway station to welcome him, and he resumed his role as the Sangh Sarsanghchalak.

1932

The first batch of full-time workers, known as "Pracharaks," were introduced in the organizational structure of the Sangh. Pracharaks included Dadarao Parmarth, Babasaheb Apte, Rambhau Jamgade, and Gopalrao Yerkuntwar. In the latter half of 1932, they became full-time workers and were dispatched to different parts of Maharashtra to advance the Sangh's work.

1934

A Sangh camp was held in Wardha, and Sh. Mahatma Gandhi Ji paid a visit. Impressed by the discipline and absence of untouchability within the Sangh, he stated, "I am convinced that any organization inspired by the high ideal of service and self-sacrifice is bound to grow in strength."

1935

In 1935, the first and second Sangh shiksha varg were organized in Pune. Since then, Sangh shiksha vargs have been conducted across the nation for the past 98 years.

1936

Almost eleven years after the Sangh's formation in 1925, Laxmibai Kelkar of Wardha approached Dr. Hedgewar Ji with the idea of involving women in the Sangh activities. A decision was made to establish the Rashtra Sevika Samiti, a women's organization with the same principles and conduct as the Sangh, though operating independently. Rashtra Sevika Samiti was founded on Vijayadashami Day, focusing on cultural, moral values, and patriotism.

1937

Sh. M.S. Golwalkar (Guruji), the second Sarsanghchalak of the Sangh, renamed the training camps as Sangh shiksha varg. Traditional cultural programs in Sangh camps on Saturday evenings and Sundays were discontinued after 1938, as they were deemed to affect the training program. The duration of the camps was also reduced from 40 to 30 days.

1938

In 1938, Sangh shiksha vargs were introduced in Lahore (Undivided India). The Sangh camps emphasized equality, irrespective of class, creed, or caste.

1939

The white shirt replaced the Khaki shirt of the uniform (Ganvesh) of the Sangh. The Sangh cadre strength was assessed as nearly 1,50,000, spread among various age groups across the nation, in the Home Department's 1939 to 1940 report on volunteer organizations.

An important meeting of senior Sangh functionaries was convened in February 1939 at Sindi, around 50 km from Nagpur. It was organized at the residence of a senior Sangh functionary Sh. Nanasaheb Talatule. Sangh founder Dr. Sh, Hedgewar Ji, Guruji, Sh. Bala Saheb Deoras, Sh.Appaji Joshi, Sh.Vithal Rao Patki, Sh. Babaji Salodkar participated in the meeting. The meeting conducted a detailed review of the way Sangh had functioned from 1925 to 1939 and it was decided to bring uniformity. Sanskrit replaced Marathi and English as a medium of instruction, and it was decided that the instructions issued at the Sangh shakhas would be in Sanskrit henceforth.

The issue of developing a Sangh prayer in Sanskrit was also discussed. The essence of the Sangh prayer was initially penned in Marathi, the then 'Karyavah' (Head) of Mohite shakha at Nagpur, Narayanrao Bhide, who was known to be an expert in Sanskrit, was entrusted with the responsibility of converting the Marathi prose into a Sanskrit prayer. He did his job so well that, with hardly any changes, all in the Sangh accepted the Sanskrit translation.

This Sanskrit prayer was recited in the next Sangh camp held at Pune in the presence of Dr. Hedgewar Ji and Guruji Golwalkar for the first time. The same Sanskrit prayer is recited even today in the Sangh shakhas without any change.

Dr. Bhimrao Ambedkar visited Sangh shiksha varg in Pune in 1939. When Dr. Ambedkar asked Dr. Hedgewar whether there were any untouchables in the camp, the Sangh founder replied that there were neither touchable nor untouchables, but only Hindus. Dr. Ambedkar said, "I am surprised to find the Swayamsevaks working in absolute equality and brotherhood without even caring to know the caste of the others."

1940

Dr. Syama Prasad Mukherjee met Dr. Hedgewar to discuss the challenges faced by Hindus in Bengal. The British government banned the Sangh uniform (Ganvesh) and route marches. On June 21, 1940, Param Pujaniye Doctor Ji, the founder of the Sangh, passed away. Madhav Sadashiva Golwalkar Ji (Sh. Guruji) was appointed as the Second Sarsanghchalak on July 3.

1941

Under the leadership of Sh.Guruji Golwalkar, the Sangh experienced unprecedented expansion, particularly in villages and rural areas across the nation.

1942

The Quit India agitation, demanding British withdrawal from India, saw active participation from several Sangh workers. In the Ashti and Chimur regions of Maharashtra, some Swayamsevaks sacrificed their lives. This growing integration of the Sangh with the movement raised concerns among the British Government.

1944

Guruji, Sh.Babasaheb Apte, and Sh. Balasaheb Deoras embarked on extensive tours around the country to propagate the ideas and philosophy of the Sangh and enlighten the people.

1947

On June 3, the congress accepted partition, resulting in massive loss of life among Hindus in Punjab and Bengal. The Sangh organized over three thousand relief camps across the nation.

India achieved independence on August 15. Gandhi Ji addressed a gathering of 500 Swayamsevaks in Delhi on September 14. Sh. Guruji Golwalkar travelled to Srinagar on October 17 to advise the Maharaja of Kashmir to accede to India. In Kenya, Swayamsevaks established the "Bharatiya Swayamsevak Sangh." The Bharat Prakashan Trust began publishing the Organiser weekly on July 3, 1947.

1948

Gandhi Ji was assassinated on January 30. The Sangh expressed its deepest condolences. Sh. Guruji Golwalkar was illegally imprisoned. The government allegedly blamed the Sangh for Mahatma Gandhi's assassination and arrested 17,000 Swayamsevaks. On February 4. Sh. Guruji announced the closure of Sangh shakhas. After the failure of talks with the government, Swayamsevaks launched Satyagraha, demanding the removal of the ban on the Sangh.

1949

The Sangh constitution was drafted. The government unconditionally lifted the ban on the Sangh on July 12. Sh. Guruji was released from Jail on July 13. A rousing welcome was given to him all over Bharat during his whirlwind tour.

The Akhil Bhartiya Vidyarthi Parishad (ABVP) was established for nation-building through student power. It was founded by the initiative of senior Sangh ideologue Sh. Balraj Madhok and was formally registered on July 9, 1949. Sh. Yashwant Rao Kelkar played an important role in establishing the structure of the Akhil Bhartiya Vidyarthi Parishad (ABVP).

1950

India became a Republic on January 26. Sh. Guruji Golwalkar instructed Swayamsevaks to celebrate this occasion. Freedom from British colonial rule was celebrated across Sangh offices (Karyalayas) around the nation.

The first-ever Akhil Bhartiya Pratinidhi Sabha was held in March, and Bhaiyya Ji Dani was elected Sarkaryavah (General secretary). The Vastuhara Sahayata Samiti was started to help Hindu refugees from Pakistan.

Senior Sangh Pracharak Sh. Nanaji Deshmukh established the nation's first Saraswati Shishu Mandir at Gorakhpur in 1950.

1951

The origin and the seed of the Bhartiya Janta Party were sowed as the Bhartiya Jana Sangh was established on October 21 with the support of Hindu Mahasabha and Sangh; Sh.Syama Prasad Mukherjee was the first President of the BJS.

1952

The cow protection movement, known as the Gauraksha Andolan, was launched by the Sangh, demanding the prohibition of cow slaughter in the country. Swayamsevaks collected 1,75,39,813 signatures covering every part of the country from 85,000 cities and villages. All these signatures were presented to the President, Dr. Rajendra Prasad, on December 8.

The Vanvasi Kalyan Asharam was established, Sh. Guruji participated in the concluding ceremony of 'Abhinav Bharat,' an organization that Sh. Veer Savarkar founded for the freedom of Bharat.

1953

The sudden demise of Sh. Syama Prasad Mukherjee in Kashmir on June 23, who was the Founder and President of the Bhartiya Jana Sangh, occurred while he was protesting against the special status given to Kashmir, leading to his arrest and mysterious death during detention.

The Chinmaya Mission was founded and established in 1953. The Mission is a worldwide non-profit organization dedicated to spreading the knowledge of Advaita Vedanta, the Bhagavad Gita, the Upanishads, and other ancient Hindu scriptures. Through the Mission, Swami Chinmayananda spearheaded a global Hindu spiritual and cultural renaissance that popularized these spiritual texts and values.

1954

The Sangh played a vital role in the liberation of Dadar and Nagar Haveli from Portuguese control. Sangh leaders Raja Wakankar, Nana Kajrekar, and Sudhir Phadke led a troop of 200 Sangh workers who fought against armed Portuguese soldiers; many Sangh workers were martyred. Ultimately, the Portuguese surrendered and flew, and on August 2, the region was handed over to the central government.

1955

Swayamsevaks took a leading part in the all-party struggle for the liberation of Goa from the control of the Portuguese. In 1955, the Jana Sangh leader, Jagannath Rao Joshi, who was inspired by the ideology of the Sangh, led 3,000 protesters, including women and children, from Maharashtra state through the Goa border, where many Sangh volunteers were martyred and injured.

Sh. Guruji Golwalkar wrote to Prime Minister Nehru, urging the government to respond to the inhuman firing on citizens and take measures to free the part of the motherland that was still languishing in the slavery of foreigners. The Rashtra Sevika Samiti also participated in the Goa liberation movement led by Saraswati Apte 'Tai'

Senior Sangh ideologue Sh.Dattopant Thengadi founded the Bhartiya Mazdoor Sangh (BMS), the labour wing of the Sangh, which is also one of the largest labour organizations in the world.

1956

On November 21, 1956, the Sangh in Mysore discussed the language issue, which was an important issue at that time. K.C Cariappa, the first commander in chief of the Indian army, was very much impressed by Sh. Guruji's frank and patriotic views on the issue.

1958

The Shishu Shiksha management committee was formed in 1958 for children's direction and planned development, and Shishu Mandirs were established in many other states.

1959

In 1959, the Sangh passed a resolution stating that the Sh. Ram Janmabhoomi, Krishna Janmabhoomi and Kashi Vishwanath are essential symbols of Hindu identity and should be returned to the Hindus for regular prayers. The resolution was passed in the Sangh's Akhil Bharatiya Pratinidhi Sabha (ABPS) Baithak.

1960

In the 1960s, Sangh volunteers joined different social and political movements in the nation, including Bhoodan, a land reform movement led by Vinoba Bhave, and Sarvodaya, led by Jayaprakash Narayan. The Sangh also supported the formation of organizations like Lok Bharati and Deendayal research institute, among others.

These organizations, started and supported by Sangh volunteers, came to be known collectively as the Sangh Parivar. The next few decades saw steady and influential growth of the Sangh Parivar in Bharat's social and political space.

1961

Goa was liberated from Portuguese rule in December by Operation Vijay, conducted during 17-19 December. The Sangh, since 1955, had been vocal about eradicating the Portuguese from Goa.

1962

The India-China war occurred. The role of Sangh in helping the Indian army during the War of 1962 is undisputed by facts. Sangh Swayamsevaks organized relief camps and provided ration for the army and for the people. They worked at traffic signals too during that time of crisis.

The long boots and brown leather belt were introduced in the Sangh uniform (Ganvesh).

1963

Sangh was invited to the republic day parade by the then Prime minister Jawaharlal Nehru in recognition of volunteer work done by the Sangh during the war of 1962. It was a moment to cherish as the Sangh's service to the nation was recognized. More than three thousand Swayamsevaks with full uniform (Ganvesh) and band participated in this parade on January 26, 1963.

Swami Vivekananda centenary celebrations began. The Sangh passed a resolution to construct a grand memorial for Swami Vivekananda in Kanyakumari.

The Bharat Vikas Parishad was founded in 1963 on the birth anniversary of Swami Vivekananda and was registered as a society on July 10, 1963. Its primary purpose is to organize citizens for philanthropic work. BVP is a member of the Sangh Parivar.

1964

The Vishwa Hindu Parishad (VHP) was established in 1964 by Guruji Golwalkar and S.S. Apte in collaboration with Swami Chinmayananda. Its objective is "to organize, consolidate the Hindu society and to serve and protect the Hindu Dharma." It was established to construct and renovate Hindu temples and deal with cow slaughter and religious conversion. The VHP is a member organization of the Sangh Parivar.

1965

Pakistan attacked India, and Lal Bahadur Shastri, the then Prime minister, invited Sh. Guruji Golwalkar to the all-leaders conference in New Delhi. At the conference, Sh. Guruji extended complete cooperation and support on behalf of the Sangh. The Sangh was also hailed by the Prime minister and General Khushwant Singh of the Indian army for its contribution to relief and support during the Indo-Pak war.

Sh. Madhukar Dattatreya Deoras (Babasaheb) was elected as General Secretary (Sarkaryavaha) of the Sangh. The Integral humanism doctrine, drafted by Pt. Sh. Deen Dayal Upadhyaya as a political program, was adopted in 1965 as the official doctrine of the Jan Sangh.

1966

Sh. Vinayak Damodar Savarkar passed away on February 26 and left a profound legacy of leadership and contribution to the nation. Before his death, he had written an article titled "Atmahatya Nahi Atmaarpan," in which he argued that when one's life mission is over and the ability to serve society is no longer present, it is better to end life at will rather than waiting for death. Sh. Savarkar fasted unto death; he was a true Karm Yogi, legendary Hindutva leader, stalwart, and pioneer statesman whose contribution will always be cherished and remembered by future generations.

1967

Pt. Deen Dayal Upadhyaya became the 10th President of the Bhartiya Jana Sangh. He played a vital role in expanding the base of the Bhartiya Jan Sangh. Sh. Upadhyay joined the Sangh in 1937 and came under the influence of Sh. Nanaji Deshmukh and Bhau Jugade. He was a lifelong Pracharak of the Sangh and later became the general secretary of the BJS from its inception in 1951 till 1967.

Pt. Deendayal Upadhyay Ji was a historic personality who wanted Bharat and the ideals and ethos of Hindutva to flourish.

1968

The 10th President of Bhartiya Jana Sangh, Pt.Sh. Deendayal Upadhyay Ji, was murdered on board a train at Mughalsarai. As a Sangh pracharak, he was regarded as an ideal Swayamsevak of the Sangh, essentially because his discourse reflected the pure thought current of the Sangh. He was also the founder of the integral humanism philosophy.

In memory of the great leader, the Deendayal Research Institute (Deendayal Shodh Sansthan) was founded by Sh. Nanaji Deshmukh in 1968. The institute has been striving to validate the principles enunciated by the late Sh. Upadhyaya through his philosophy of *'Integral Humanism'*

1971

War with Pakistan broke out for the third time. The Sangh volunteered in the war, and Swayamsevaks actively participated in providing relief and ration supplies. The Sangh was the first organization to donate blood during the war.

1972

The Vivekananda Rock Memorial in Kanyakumari was inaugurated by the then President of India, Sh. V.V. Giri. During the 1963 – 72 period, Sh. Eknath Ramakrishna Ranade Ji, a senior pracharak of the Sangh, played an instrumental role in constructing the Vivekananda Rock Memorial in Kanyakumari, Tamil Nadu.

The Vivekananda Kendra, was established on January 7, 1972, by Sh. Eknath Ranade Ji. The organization is based near the Vivekananda Rock Memorial in Kanyakumari and works in the field of social service.

1973

Sh. Guruji Golwalkar passed away on June 5, leaving behind a glorious legacy of leadership, sacrifice, and commitment towards the goal of serving the people and the philosophy of Hindutva. He was a visionary par excellence, a memoir of Sh. Guruji in front of Dr. Hedgewar Smruti Mandir was established in Nagpur.

Sh. Balasaheb Deoras was designated as the third Sarsanghchalak on June 6. Sh. Madhavrao Muley was elected as Sarkaryavah.

1974

Tri-centenary celebrations of the coronation of Chhatrapati Shivaji Maharaj were organized by the Sangh. The black shoes replaced the military-style boots of the Sangh uniform (Ganvesh).

The Akhil Bhartiya Gharak Panchayat was founded in 1974 as a forum and organization working for bringing consumer awareness in all spheres of society. It is affiliated with the Sangh and forms a part of the Sangh Parivar.

1975

The Sangh completed 50 years of its establishment by Param Pujnaiye Sh. Dr. Hedgewar Ji. The Sangh had devoted itself for the past 50 years to the task of making Bharat strong and prosperous while preserving its great cultural values. The Sangh had always been unfailing in discharging its duty towards society under every problematic situation, whether arising from foreign aggression or natural calamity.

Prime minister Indira Gandhi imposed the illegal emergency in the country on June 25. The government allegedly used power to suppress independent voices across the nation.

The Sangh was banned illegally for the second time on July 4. The Akhil Bharatiya Lok Sangharshana Samiti was launched to fight against the emergency. Sangh Sarsanghchalak Sh. Balasaheb Deoras Ji was arrested, and many Sangh leaders worked underground. Commendable work was done during the emergency by the Sangh in mobilizing cadres against the Emergency. The Sangh established an underground network and communication system to continue the organization's work despite the ban.

1977

In 1977, the Bharatiya Jana Sangh merged into the newly formed Janata Party, which won the elections and came to power. On March 22, the government lifted the illegal ban on the Sangh.

That same year, a cyclone had hit the coastal areas of Andhra Pradesh in December, resulting in significant human loss. Swayamsevaks worked tirelessly in relief operations under adverse conditions. The Sangh distributed 2,40,000 items of clothing and 32,000 utensils.

Sh. Rajendra Singh Ji (Rajju Bhaiya) was designated as Sah Sarkaryavaha (Joint general secretary). The Vidya Bharati (Vidya Bharati Akhil Bhartiya Shiksha Sansthan), the educational wing of the Sangh, was established.

1978

In 1978, Sh. Madhava Rao Muley, Sarkaryavaha, passed away on September 30. Subsequently, Sh. Rajendra Singh (Rajju Bhaiya) was elected as Sarkaryavaha.

Madhya Bharat Prant Shivir was held in Indore, attended by 6,000 Swayamsevaks. Furthermore, the Akhil Bharatiya Itihas Sankalan Yojana (ABISY), an affiliated organization of the Sangh, was founded in 1978-79. This visionary initiative, conceived in 1973 by Sh. Moropant Pingley Ji, aimed to correct the biases introduced by the British Raj in Bharat's history.

1979

On April 8, 1979, the then Sangh Sarsanghachalak Sh. Balasaheb Deoras addressed a mammoth gathering of volunteers at Ambedkar stadium, Delhi. In his address, he called for initiating service activities among the weaker sections of society, marking the inception of Seva Bharati. The Seva Bharati was formally established on October 2 in Delhi.

1980

The year 1980 witnessed the launch of the Sangh's mass public contact programme – Jana Samparka Abhiyan – which covered 95,000 villages and approximately 1 crore families.

The Bharatiya Janta Party was formed on 6th April 1980 by Sh. Atal Bihari Vajpayee Ji & Sh. L.K Advani Ji.

1981

In February 1981, an alleged mass conversion of about 800 Hindus occurred in Meenakshipuram, Tamil Nadu. In response, the Sangh and other Hindu organizations protested against these conversions & conducted awareness campaign against religious conversions in parts of Tamil Nadu.

The concept of Sanskar Bharti, first developed in 1954, led to the establishment of its first institute in Lucknow in 1981. Sanskar Bharti is an organization dedicated to promoting Bharatiya art, fine arts, and culture, with contributions from intellectuals like Sh. Bhaurao Deoras, Sh. Haribhau Wakankar, and Sh. Nanaji Deshmukh.

Additionally, the Samskrita Bharati was founded in 1981 as a movement dedicated to preserving, developing, and propagating the Sanskrit language, its literature, traditions, and knowledge systems.

1982

In 1982, the Karnataka Prantik Shivir was held in Bangalore and was attended by more than 25,000 Sangh volunteers and Swayamsevaks.

The Bhartiya Vichara Kendra was established in 1982, and it was inaugurated by senior Sangh ideologue Sh. Dattopant Thengadi Ji on Vijayadashami.

1983

In 1983, the Vishwa Hindu Parishad launched the Ekatmata Yajna with active support from Swayamsevaks to strengthen people's faith and devotion to Bharat Mata and Ganga Mata.

Maharashtra Prantik Shivir was held in Pune, with more than 35,000 participants. Sh.Ashok Singhal Ji came to the forefront of the Vishwa Hindu Parishad and was made in charge of its affairs.

1984

In October 1984, there was massive human and property loss to the Sikh community in Delhi following the assassination of Smt. Indira Gandhi. Hundreds of Sikh families found protection in the homes of Swayamsevaks, relief camps were set up, and necessary services were rendered in Delhi and other parts of the country.

1985

In 1985, the Sangh celebrated its 60 years of establishment. Nationwide awareness programs were conducted, including visits to villages and cities to inform people about the Sangh's working, ideology, and functioning.

1986

In November 1986, the Rashtriya Sikh Sangat was officially formed in Amritsar by Sh. Shamsher Singh. Its goals included strengthening bonds between Sikhs and Hindus and promoting national unity, awareness, and patriotism. The Rashtriya Sikh Sangat has 500 branches across the nation and publishes the "Sangat Sandesh" magazine.

The Ekal Vidyalaya Foundation was founded in Gumla district, Jharkhand, in 1986. This initiative, was conceptualized by Sh. Bhaurao Deoras, the younger brother of the third Sarsanghachalak Sh. Balasaheb Deoras, EVF aims to provide free, accessible education to children in tribal areas, it now has a presence in over 75,000 villages, providing education to more than 2 million children across the nation.

In 1986 the 'Samkalp Foundation' was established to groom students to take up the administrative services as a career with a nationalistic spirit and a commitment towards basic human values. Since 1986 the Sangh has been grooming UPSC aspirants. The Samkalp Foundation is headquartered in R.K. Puram, Delhi.

1987

Sh. H.V. Sheshadri Ji was elected Sangh Sarkaryavah. Sh. Balasaheb Deoras Ji, Sarsanghchalak visited Chaitya Bhoomi on December 6 to pay his homage to late Dr. B.R Ambedkar Ji

1988

The Jan Sampark Abhiyan was launched on the eve of the centenary celebrations of Dr. Sh. Hedgewar Ji. Swayamsevaks contacted 1,50,000 families, conducted 76,000 meetings, and collected a sum of 11 crore rupees towards the Seva Nidhi.

1989

The Sangh celebrated the centenary year birth anniversary of Param Pujaniye Dr. Sh. Hedgewar Ji; across the Nation, celebrations took place. Many significant service projects were also announced under the aegis of the Seva Bharti by the Sarsanghchalak Sh. Babasaheb Deoras.

The Friends of Tribals Society (F.T.S.), or Vanbandhu Parishad, a volunteer organization was formed in 1989 with the goal of improving literacy and health among the Adivasi, rural tribal people in the nation. The society operates one teacher schools in the villages, led by trained members of the local community. The F.T.S. is associated with the Ekal Vidyalaya Foundation.

1990

The ***Ram Rath Yatra*** was held as a political and religious rally from September to October 1990. On October 30, thousands of Karsevaks moved towards the

Ram Janmabhoomi and were led by Mahant Sh. Nritya Gopal Das Ji, Sh. Ashok Singhal Ji.

Karseva was held in Ram Janmabhoomi in Ayodhya on October 30, daring restrictions imposed by the Mulayam Singh government; many innocent Karsevaks were martyred in the police firing. The Sangh condemned the killings. The Akhil Bhartiya Pratinidhi Sabha demanded that an inquiry be entrusted to the Supreme court of India.

1991

The Government of India implemented the liberalization, privatization, and globalization reforms to open the Indian economy; the Akhil Bhartiya Karykarni Mandal passed a resolution for encouraging the use of Swadeshi, and the Sangh expressed its deep concern at opening the doors for foreign and multinational companies in the name of economic liberalization. In 1991 the Swadeshi Jagran Manch, was founded by Sh. Dattopanth Thengadi Ji.

The Durga Vahini the women's wing of the Vishva Hindu Parishad (V.H.P.), was also founded in 1991 by Sadhvi Rithambara, the purpose of the Durga Vahini is to empower women and encourage them to participate in spiritual and cultural activities. It is headquartered in Delhi.

1992

Sh.Bhaurao Deoras Ji, Senior pracharak and the younger brother of Sarsanghchalak Sh. Balasaheb Deoras Ji passed away on May 14. Sh.Yadav Rao Joshi, senior Pracharak who worked extensively to establish the Sangh in Karnataka, passed away on August 20 for heavenly adobe.

Kar Sevaks removed the Babri structure on the Sh. Ram Janmabhoomi on December 6; the Government of India allegedly banned the Sangh for the third time on December 10; the Vishwa Hindu Parishad and the Bajrang Dal were also banned.

The Akhil Bharatiya Adhivakta Parishad (ABAP), the organization of lawyers associated with the Sangh Parivar, was founded in 1992 by Senior Sangh ideologue Sh. Dattopant Thengadi Ji.

1993

The government of India formed a tribunal for investigating the Babri Masjid dispute and demolition, Retd. Justice PK Bahri headed it. The Bahri tribunal found the ban on Sangh unjustified, and the ban was lifted on June 4; also, the ban on the Bajrang Dal was removed, but the alleged ban on the V.H.P. continued until it was removed in 1994.

1994

Prof. Rajendra Singh Ji (Rajju Bhaiya) was designated the 4th Sarsanghchalak of the Sangh on March 11. The Akhil Bhartiya Pratinidhi Sabha demanded the government that the ban on Vishwa Hindu Parishad be lifted without delay. At the same time, the Sabha also called upon all Hindu organizations to arouse public opinion against this unconstitutional act of the government.

In 1994, the Sampark Vibhag of the Sangh was set up to identify and connect with social achievers and, make them aware of Sangh's vision, and collaborate on areas of mutual interest. Sh. M.G Vadiya became the first Akhil Bharatiya Prachar Pramukh.

1995

The Akhil Bhartiya Karyakari Mandal of the Sangh welcomed the historic judgment of the Supreme court in the matter of Sarla Mudgal V/s. Union of India, emphasizing the urgent national need to take immediate legislative steps to enact the law on the uniform civil code in accordance with the letter and spirit of Article 44 of our Constitution.

1996

Sh. Balasheb Deoras Ji passed away on June 17. 1996. He lived to see Sh. Atal Bihari Vajpayee become the nation's Prime minister in May 1996, the first adherent of the Hindutva philosophy affiliation and former Sangh pracharak to become Prime minister.

1997

Sarsanghchalak Sh. Rajendra Singh Ji (Rajju Bhaiya) toured Kenya at the invitation of the Hindu council of Kenya from January 10 to 17th. During his visit, he addressed many gatherings of Indian families, university students and met senior government officials.

1999

The most devastating cyclone of the century had hit the coast of Orissa on October 28, causing a life loss of approximately 10,000 people and an Rs.1800 crore property loss. Sangh played an important role under the banner of Utkal Bipanna Sahayata Samiti in relief and rehabilitation activities. The Sangh extensively volunteered in the 1999 Kargil war. On July 26, 1999, India emerged victorious in the Kargil War.

2000

Sh. K.S Sudarshan Ji became the fifth Sarsanghachalak of the Sangh on March 10, 2000. He succeeded Sh. Rajendra Singh Ji (Rajju Bhaiya), who had stepped down on health grounds.

2001

Sangh Swayamsevaks served as volunteers in Gujarat and extensively helped the people and victims affected by the severe Bhuj earthquake of 2001; the massive earthquake killed approximately 20,000 people; the Sangh organized medical and relief camps in Bhuj and supplied medical aid, food, and ration to the victims

2003

The Akhil Bhartiya Karykarni Mandal of the Sangh reiterated its unqualified support to the just demand of the Hindu society for the restoration of the holy shrines of Ayodhya, Mathura, and Kashi. It emphasized that Bhagwan Ram, Bhagwan Krishna, and Bhagwan Shankar symbolize Bharat's age-old civilization, cultural and spiritual identity.

2004

Thousands of Swayamsevaks and Sangh volunteers helped victims and those affected by the tsunami disaster that shook the nation in 2004. Sh. Dattopant Thengadi Ji passed away for heavenly abode, he was a senior Sangh ideologue and pracharak of the Sangh; he was a legendary figure of the Sangh Parivar.

2007

Swayamsevaks celebrated the 150th year of the 1857 revolt across the nation; the third world Hindi conference was held in the United States of America and senior ideologues of the Sangh participated. The concluding ceremony of Sh. Guruji's Janmashatabdi was held in Delhi. Approximately 1 crore 60 lakh people, 13,000 saints, and 1,80,000 social activists participated in Sammelans throughout the year.

2008

Multiple bomb blasts occurred across the nation in Jaipur, Delhi, Uttar Pradesh, Bangalore, and Ahmedabad, and the gruesome 26/11 attack in Mumbai; the Akhil Bhartiya Karykarni Mandal expressed serious concern over the situation arising out of the serial bomb blasts taking place in various parts of the country. It highlighted the government of India's failure to intercept the terrorists and prevent such attacks from killing hundreds of innocent people nationwide.

2009

Pujaniye Sarsanghachalak K.S. Sudarshan Ji named Dr. Mohan Bhagwat Ji as the next Sarsanghchalak of the Sangh. Sh.Suresh Ji Joshi (Bhaiya Ji Joshi) was elected as the Sarkaryavaha of the Sangh.

2010

During the north Karnataka floods, Sangh deployed relief material for 180 villages and more than 2400 Swayamsevaks were involved in relief activities. Sangh resolved to build 1680 houses in 9 villages under the auspices of "Seva Bharati" as part of its rehabilitation activity.

Param Pujaniye Sarsanghachalak Ji's tour across the country received a mammoth response, in a few programs the number of Swayamsevak's attending the event touched 90,000 in places like Kerala, Mangalore, and Mahakaushal. The canvas brown belt replaced the brown leather belt in the uniform (Ganvesh).

2012

The three-day Akhil Bhartiya Karyakarni Mandal Baithak was concluded at Chennai. Sangh Passed an important resolution for the need of comprehensive response to the security challenge of China. A resolution concerning the rampant migration of illegal migrants from Bangladesh was also taken up. A save the cow campaign (Gau Gram Yatra) was concluded at the Reshim Bagh ground of Nagpur; noted Yog Guru Baba Ramdev explained the importance and essence of the holy Gau Mata in the national ethos of Bharat.

2013

Sangh extended its support to Swami Vivekananda's 150th birth anniversary celebrations that took the message of Swami Vivekananda to every nook and corner of the country. Working actively with Vivekananda Kendra, Sangh coordinated the momentous efforts made by spiritual organizations such as Ramakrishna Mission, Gayatri Parivar, Sharada Matham, Chinmaya Mission in nation building and ably carried the message of Swami Vivekananda to all sections of the society.

Unprecedented floods and cloudbursts had hit Uttarakhand, Sangh Swayamsevaks were the first to engage in relief activities and actively cooperated with the Indian Army and the NDRF in its rescue operations. Swayamsevaks also organized camps for rehabilitation and supplied medical aid and ration.

2014

At the Akhil Bhartiya Pratinidhi Sabha of the Sangh, the annual report of the present status of the number of shakas, among other works, was presented. A 13% increase in the number of shakhas was registered across the country between July 2012 and July 2014. During the Period, 4,635 shakhas were started. In 2012, Sangh had 49,761 active shakhas in the country. In the next one year, it went up to 52,125.

The B.J.P. emerged victorious in the 2014 Lok Sabha elections, and the 16th Lok Sabha was formed in the nation. Sh. Narendra Modi Ji became the 14th Prime Minister of India.

2015

Massive floods occurred in Chennai; Swayamsevaks actively cooperated with the NDRF personnel in the rescue operations, and nearly 10,000 food packets were distributed across the city of Chennai.

The Akhil Bhartiya Karyakarni Mandal passed a resolution concerning and urging the Government of India to reformulate the national population policy, and to prevent the illegal migration from across the borders. The Akhil Bhartiya Pratinidhi Sabha also passed a resolution welcoming the international yoga day, which was proclaimed by the 69th general assembly of the United Nations to observe June 21 of every year as international yoga day.

The Sangh completed 90 years of its foundation; the Sangh was founded in 1925 by Param Pujaniye Dr. Hedgewar Ji, The Sangh annual nationwide training camp (Tritiya Varsh) was concluded on June 4 at Reshim Bagh ground in Nagpur at the valedictory ceremony Param Pujaniye Sarsanghchalak Mohan Bhagwat Ji stated that 'Bharat is emerging as a powerful and strong nation'.

2016

The first Shrung Shivir "Swaranjali" took place in Bengaluru in January 2016. A total of 2195 Swayamsevaks from every region of the country participated in the event.

It was decided in the ABPS 2016, which was held from 11-13 March in Nagaur, Rajasthan, that the ninety-year-old Sangh Ganvesh "Khaki Knicker" was to be replaced by the "Full brown pants." The Ganvesh of Sangh was formally changed on October 11, the Vijayadashami Day (Dusshera), the foundation day of the Sangh.

2018

The annual Akhil Bhartiya Pratinidhi Sabha was held, and the Sangh reflected upon the steady work that the organization completed over 93 years of its existence; the Pratinidhi Sabha passed a resolution that stated that there is an urgent need to protect and promote the Bhartiya languages. During 2018 there were major floods in the state of Kerela and the Seva Bharti, helped in the rescue operation, and more than one lakh Swayamsevaks and Karyakartas of the Sangh were engaged in relief work in the state of Kerela.

2019

The Akhil Bhartiya Pratinidhi Sabha was held in Gwalior for the first time. The Tritiya Sangh shiksha varg was held in Nagpur in June, and 828 selected Swayamsevaks from across the nation participated.

The Akhil Bharatiya Karyakari Mandal of the Sangh wholeheartedly welcomed the extension of the Constitution of India to the state of Jammu and Kashmir, followed by the decision to make article 370 ineffective through the constitutional orders by the Hon'ble President and approval of the same by both the houses of the Parliament. The decision to reorganize the state into two union territories, namely Jammu-Kashmir and Ladakh, was also appreciated.

The B.J.P again formed the Government at the centre, and the 17th Lok Sabha was constituted. Sh. Narendra Modi Ji became the Prime minister for the second term.

2020

The major disease epidemic Corona was detected in the nation. The government of India, for the safety and security of the people, had to impose a lockdown in the nation; Swayamsevaks distributed rations and necessary items for livelihood of people across 92,700 Seva Kendra's which were distributed then to 73.81 lakh families across the nation.

In Pune, the Sangh started a covid centre where more than 2000 patients were treated and cured. The Sangh distributed more than one crore corona masks across the nation.

In August the Ram Mandir Bhoomi Pujan was held at the holy place of the Sh. Ram Janmabhoomi at Ayodhya, Param Pujyaniya Sarsanghchalak Sh. Mohan Bhagwat Ji, Hon'ble Prime Minister Sh. Narendra Modi Ji, and Chief Minister of Uttar Pradesh Sh. Yogi Adityanath Ji participated in the Bhoomi Pujan. It was a day to cherish, and a dream come true moment for every Hindu & Bharatiya.

2021

The Corona epidemic had again hit the nation in 2021; approximately 375,000 migrant workers were served food at 1978 centres organized by the Sangh nationwide. The Sangh passed the resolution in 2021 for uniting the nation against the Covid-19 pandemic. The Sangh national body also elected Sh.Dattatreya Hosabale Ji as its new general secretary (Sarkaryavaha).

The Akhil Bhartiya Pratinidhi Sabha passed a resolution for the construction of the Sh.Ram Mandir at the Ram Janma Bhoomi; the manifesto showcased the innate strength of the unity of Hindutva and the unity of Bharat.

2022

The nation completed 75 years of its independence, and the government of India initiated the campaign of 'Azadi ka Amrit Mahotsav'. Sangh also celebrated 97 years of its establishment.

The Akhil Bhartiya Pratinidhi Sabha was held in Gujarat, and approximately 1252 senior-level Karyakarta's of the Sangh participated from all the states of the nation.

2023

The ABPS (Akhil Bhartiya Pratinidhi Sabha) was held in the month of March at Panipat in Haryana; increasing women into the fold of the Sangh & their participation in the Sangh activities was discussed; 1464 senior level functionaries from across the nation were present.

As the Sangh is going to complete 100 years of its establishment in 2025. A team of 3,000 Swayamsevaks and volunteers has been formed, which is known as 'Shatabdi Varsh Vistarak,' who will take the work of the Sangh to the masses.

The third Sewa Sangam was held at Jaipur in April; it included 3,000 representatives of more than 800 voluntary service organizations from 45 provinces and 11 regions of the country. The Sangh route march (Path Sanchalan) was held in April across 45 places in Tamil Nadu, and thousands of Swayamsevaks participated from across the state and the nation.

On June 2, a passenger train and a freight train collided in the Balasore district of Odisha, killing more than 290 people and injuring hundreds; within just 40 minutes of the accident, hundreds of Swayamsevaks reached the location and initiated the relief operation. 250+ volunteers provided food, water, and assistance to affected families. 400+ units of blood was donated by the Sangh Swayamsevaks.

The Akhil Bharatiya "Prant Pracharak Baithak" of the Sangh was held at Ooty near Coimbatore, to discuss the ways to make Sangh shakhas more aligned with their social responsibilities and encourage them to be more proactive. This Annual Baithak was held from 13th to 15th July, 2023.

The annual Akhil Bharatiya Sangh Samanvya Baithak was held in Pune from 14-16 September, it discussed issues based on social harmony, environment conservation and technology.

Introduction ~ The RSS

Introduction

The Rashtriya Swayamsevak Sangh, founded in 1925 by the revered Dr. Keshav Baliram Hedgewar Ji, is on the cusp of completing a remarkable century in 2025. This book serves as a tribute to the Sangh's extraordinary journey over the decades. It delves into the fundamental values, principles, and profound significance the organization holds within the Bharatiya culture.

At its core, the Sangh thrives on fostering strong personal bonds, teamwork, brotherhood, and fraternity. These principles serve as the bedrock of the Sangh. It is only natural that countless Hindu families find resonance with the Sangh's ethos, as spirituality and Hindutva lie at the heart of our rich family traditions. Millions of Hindu families embrace spirituality as an integral part of their daily lives, placing paramount importance on unity with the world.

The Sangh stands as a wellspring of motivation and inspiration for the people of Bharat. This organization, with an estimated membership exceeding 10 million, quite possibly ranks as the largest voluntary organization globally. Every day, across the length and breadth of the nation, more than 60,000 shakhas or gatherings of Sangh members convene, with numerous others happening in various parts of the world.

The Sangh remains unwavering in its commitment to the Bharatiya nation, echoing Sri Aurobindo's concept of *"Bharat Shakti"* as the bedrock of our culture. Perhaps more than any other institution, the Sangh has fervently advocated for Hindutva and national unity. This emphasis finds its most succinct expression in the slogan: *"Sanghe Shakti Kaliyuge."* It's no exaggeration to proclaim that, with its myriad primary and auxiliary associations, millions of dedicated volunteers and a multitude of prominent leaders, the Sangh stands as the nation's most significant & influential organization.

This book is an ambitious undertaking, aiming to encapsulate the century-long journey of the Sangh and delve into its internal organizational dynamics. It seeks to elucidate how the organization has reached its current stature. Interestingly, many proponents and critics of the Sangh engage in debates without an in-depth understanding of the organization itself. This book strives to bridge that knowledge gap, shedding light on how the Sangh operates and detailing its evolution from 1925 to the present day.

The Sangh communicates in a language that resonates with every Bharatiya. It addresses all facets of society, including humanity, politics, economy, governance, religion, and social upliftment, assigning equal importance to each. Service and devotional dedication to Bharat Mata lie at the core of the Sangh philosophy.

Even the Sarsanghchalak, the highest-ranking official within the Sangh, is a humble and dedicated Swayamsevak committed to serving Bharat. This commitment, shared by all members across the country, fuels the Sangh's growth. With this ethos, the Sangh undertakes noble social responsibilities and contributes significantly to the society and the world. The Sangh views society as the primary instrument of change, firmly believing that societal transformation can only occur through individual preparedness and change. This aligns with the teachings of Swami Vivekananda, emphasizing the harmonious development of the mind, body, and soul, and underscores that true and enduring transformation hinges on societal change.

Change permeates the Sangh's literature and philosophy. The Sangh is inherently forward-looking and future-oriented, particularly among the youth. It fosters an environment of ideological awakening and facilitates debates on Hindutva, governance, the Hindu Rashtra, globalization, nationalism, social justice, and equality for all castes and communities.

The Sangh has steadfastly focused on these issues, contributing to the maturity of these societal discussions and paving the way for transformation. It has evolved into a force for Hindu renaissance and nation-building, extending its reach beyond the confines of Sangh shakhas. The Sangh's most significant contribution lies in elevating the social and intellectual consciousness of ordinary citizens and creating an environment conducive to Hindu renaissance. In virtually every facet of Bharat's vast social, cultural, and political landscape, including the diaspora, the Sangh has an active and significant presence.

The journey has not been without its challenges. The Sangh cadre is exceptionally well-trained, highly motivated, and undaunted, possessing a combination of intellect, purpose, and clarity of vision. As one of Bharat's oldest organizations, the Sangh operates selflessly, constantly adapting to changing times. Moreover, the organization has demonstrated resilience, surviving relentless vilification and harsh criticism.

The Sangh has faced three bans in independent Bharat's history. However, each time, the government had to lift the ban due to a lack of concrete evidence or justifiable reasons to sustain it. This demonstrates the Sangh's unwavering character and unyielding resolve. The Sangh stands as a timeless organization, destined to endure for eternity.

What sets the Sangh apart is its remarkable creativity, which manifests in its ability to establish a multitude of nearly autonomous organizations spanning across various aspects of life. Many Sangh affiliated organizations work tirelessly in diverse fields, such as Vidhya Bharti, focused on establishing schools aligned with the philosophy of the Sangh. Other noteworthy institutions, such as Samkalp, a Sangh – affiliated organization which provides affordable coaching to civil service aspirants preparing for UPSC and State service commissions.

These initiatives underscore the Sangh's commitment to the nation and societal well-being.

This also illustrates that the Sangh aspires to be more than just another organization in society; it seeks to contribute in every conceivable way to the nation's betterment and development. The Sangh is a unique organization, entirely voluntary in nature. In the Sangh shakhas, every Swayamsevak is equal; there are no rigid hierarchies. The Sangh operates as a decentralized and autonomous organization, fostering collaboration and coordination in spirit. It embodies the dynamic nature of Bharatiya society, and its vision stands as distinctive and unparalleled.

The unheralded heroes, the Sangh Swayamsevaks, have made immense sacrifices since the organization's inception in 1925, a testament to their mission and dedication. Without compromising its core vision of a strong Bharat and the preservation of the nation's Hindu cultural identity. The Sangh remains adaptable, responding to society's evolving needs.

The Sangh's primary objective is to serve Hindu society and Hindutva devoutly. It aspires to achieve this objective by fostering amity and brotherhood among people and communities within the nation. What binds the volunteers and Swayamsevaks of the Sangh is not loyalty to any cult figure or supreme leader but an unspoken commitment to nation-building and unwavering loyalty towards Bharat Mata, while reviving and nurturing the civilizational values encapsulated in the term Hindutva.

The Sangh is, perhaps, a fascinating case study for management students seeking to understand a unique organization. With its open architecture and organic growth, it possesses a robust network and a self-renewing nervous system, ensuring its continued healthy growth. It contributes significantly to Bharat's renaissance on the path to re-establishing the nation as the Vishwa Guru.

Condensing nearly a century of an organization's life of this magnitude within the confines of a single book was no easy feat. Nonetheless, the authors have strived to keep it concise and engaging by interweaving interesting anecdotes and recounting critical historical junctures in the Sangh's journey. The book provides a comprehensive overview of the Sangh's evolution from a tightly-knit cadre-based organization to a mass movement.

For an organization not only to endure but to thrive over such a prolonged period is a testament to its unwavering sense of purpose. Today, we can proudly affirm that the Sangh is an organization tirelessly dedicated to the future of Bharat.

This book is an endeavour to comprehend the ideals and philosophy that propel the Sangh, its formation and organizational principles, structure, and the diverse range of activities it undertakes. It also provides brief profiles of the Sangh Parivar organizations and prominent personalities associated with Hindutva and the Sangh.

This book is penned on the occasion of the Sangh's impending centenary in 2025, celebrating and commemorating its remarkable journey throughout the years.

The path from the Sangh's inception in 1925 to the present day has been far from smooth, marked by numerous trials and tribulations. Yet, the organization has remained unwavering in upholding its values and ethos. The Sangh is more than an organization; it is a way of life and a vehicle for uniting a resurgent Bharat. This is not just the story of the Sangh; it is the story of the nation's future.

CHAPTER - 1

How, When and Where Dr. Hedgewar Ji and the Emergence, Background of the Sangh

Introduction

Every morning at sunrise, groups of men in military style khaki uniforms gather outdoors in community halls and parks before saffron flags in all parts of the nation to participate in a common set of physical exercises, Dhwaj Pranam, and lessons about the Bharatiya society and Hindutva, they are taught to think of themselves as a family, a brotherhood with a mission to transform the Hindu society; they are the members of the Rashtriya Swayamsevak Sangh, the world's largest and one of the most influential organizations committed to Hindutva and Hindu revivalism.

The Sangh was established in 1925 in Nagpur, Maharashtra, on the auspicious occasion of Vijayadashmi by Param Pujaniye Dr. Keshav Baliram Hedgewar Ji, a doctor by profession.

The foundation of the Sangh is based on an understanding which was influential in pre-independent India; the political parties at the time of independence did not properly protect the Hindu community and its interests. The Sangh's objective was to train Hindu men who, based on their character-building experience in the Sangh work and would unite the Hindu community so that Bharat could again become united in nature, independent, and a creative society.

The roots of the Sangh are embedded in the soil of Maharashtra; its initial membership was mostly Maharashtrian, and its discipline and ideological framework were shaped almost entirely by Sh. Hedgewar, who left his potentially lucrative medical practice in his struggle against British rule.

Dr. Hedgewar was convinced that a fundamental change in social attitude was a necessary precondition to revive the spirit of Bharat and Hindutva, and that the properly trained cadre of the Sangh would prove to be a catalyst of change. He emphasized that "the Hindu culture is the life-breath of Hindustan. It is, therefore, clear that if Hindustan is to be protected, we should first nourish the Hindu culture.[1] Every Hindu must do his best to consolidate the society.

Dr Hedgewar envisioned an organization that would look beyond immediate gains, which would be non-political. Its only work would be to create extraordinary human beings out of ordinary members of society, who would be selflessly dedicated to the cause of nation-building and service to society; people who would lead a highly disciplined life based on high thinking and simple living, moulded with great character.

The Formative Years - Dr. Hedgewar Ji

Dr. Hedgewar was born on 1st April 1889 in Nagpur, he was educated at the Rashtriya Vidyalaya in Yavatmal, Pune, and as a young man, he was affirmative and showed exemplary leadership qualities. He avidly read Sh. Lokmanya Bal Gangadhar Tilak's 'Kesari' a nationalist weekly published in Pune, and he was significantly influenced and inspired by Tilak's famous saying 'Swaraj is my birth right and I shall have it.'

Doctor Ji lost both his parents when he was very young; during the years 1902-1904, Sh. Bali ram Panth Hedgewar, his father & Smt. Revathi his mother died on the same day due to the devastating plague which had hit the city of Nagpur. After this devastating incident in his life, he was taken aback. Still, even after such difficult circumstances, he built an organization as great as the Sangh. After the demise of his parents, Dr. Hedgewar was supported by Sh. Balkrishna Shivram Moonje, who had a significant influence in his life.

The year 1897 marked the 16th anniversary of Queen Victoria's coronation. The British celebrated the event on 22 June that year, sweets were distributed in the schools to mark the occasion, and seeing this eight year old young Dr. Hedgewar got repulsive. He refused to eat the sweets and threw it in the dustbin; for a young child such as Keshav, participation in such a celebration was a matter of utter shame. He was a born patriot, once in his childhood he formulated a plan with his school friends of digging a tunnel to the Sita Buldi fort in Nagpur; the fort was a British garrison, and the English flag, union jack, was hoisted on it; he wanted the national flag to be placed instead of the union jack.[1]

Dr. Moonje had sent Hedgewar Ji in 1910 to study medicine at the Calcutta medical college because he wanted Hedgewar to establish contacts with the revolutionaries in Bengal and give more effort towards India's independence struggle. During his six years in Calcutta, Hedgewar joined the Anushilan Samiti, which was founded by Sh. Satish Chandra Basu, the Anushilan was a revolutionary society based in Bengal and Dr. Hedgewar rose to its highest membership level.

After returning to Nagpur in 1916, he decided not to marry or practice medicine. He purely focused his energy towards founding the Sangh. During his years in Calcutta, Dr. Hedgewar worked for the Ramakrishna mission, he also helped people with disease and used his medical education for social service.

---

1   RSS Ideology: | Timespek. https://timespek.com/indian-rss-ideology-pakistan-bangladesh-akkhand-bharat/

The Idea of RSS: The Background Perspective

After returning from Calcutta, Dr. Hedgewar was briefly associated with the congress during the freedom struggle. Still, he wanted more from the methods of the congress to achieve freedom from British rule.

One of the early reasons for the formation of the Sangh was that Dr.Hedgewar could feel and get an idea from the bitter experience of the Morley Minto reforms of 1909, the Khilafat movement, the 1919 Montague Chelmsford reforms, later in the 1920's there was a period of communal animosity and riots across the nation. The communal riots left Dr. Hedgewar deeply dissatisfied from the methods and tactics deployed by the leaders of the freedom struggle.

In 1921 in Kerala, about 10,000 people, mostly Hindus died in a riot which was the Mophla rebellion (Anti Hindu Riots). In 1923 the Nagpur riots took place which further facilitated the process of the formation of the Sangh. The Sangh thus emerged during a wave of communal riots that swept the nation in the early 1920s; Dr. Hedgewar viewed the riots as a symptom of weakness and divisions within the Hindu community; he could foresee the future of Hindus if they were not united.

He saw in the riots a fundamental sociological problem of the Hindu nation, even though the Hindus were in the majority, the revivalists considered them a suppressed majority, a thousand years of foreign domination were the testimony to that weakness; the Sangh thus was an organization which powered the sense of Hindutva among the people and Hindus. He realized that the congress, a political organization, could not be relied upon to protect or fight for the demands of Hindus. The Sangh was founded four years after the 1921 riots.

During the early 1920s, Dr. Hedgewar began to develop the intellectual foundation of the Sangh, a major influence on his thinking was a handwritten manuscript of V.D Savarkar's Hindutva, which advanced the point that Hindus were a nation. It was the farsightedness of Dr. Hedgewar that he saw the Sangh as a strong force that would unite and safeguard Hindus.

Dr. Hedgewar's experience during the years of Mahatma Gandhi's non-violent national struggle and of armed revolutionary struggle taken up by freedom fighters like Bhagat Singh and Rajguru, made him realise that until a disciplined cadre based and well-trained nationalistic organisation address the issue of building strong nationalist character, India might not be able to sustain its freedom even if it is able to attain it. He respected Gandhi Ji; however, he believed that non-violence as the sole method to challenge the British would be counterproductive in the long run. Dr. Hedgewar was also profoundly influenced when Pt. Madan Mohan Malviya, the founder of the Hindu Mahasabha in 1917, stated that there is a need to arrest the deterioration of the Hindus, and there is a need to improve the socio-economic structure of the Hindus.

Many Hindu revivalists believed the divisions in the Hindu society rendered the Hindus incapable of overcoming foreign and cultural domination. Many Hindutva philosophers and thinkers observed that Hindus were separated by traditional commitments to specific occupations and religious observances, by rules of endogamy and commensality, and by linguistic and regional loyalties. Hence the Sangh was very necessary to unite the Hindus under the larger term of Hindutva. Dr. Hedgewar realised that the nation's revitalisation could be achieved only when a fundamental transformation is done with the sense of national consciousness and social cohesion, which could lead to complete national freedom and national reconstruction, the first task in achieving this was to formulate a disciplined organization and to train a dedicated cadre. The motivation behind the establishment of the Sangh was Dr. Hedgewar Ji's vision and belief that the nation does not have an evolved Hindu leadership; and thus, the Sangh men were to populate all walks of life, shaping future institutions, political, cultural, religious, social, and industrial.

Being a serious student of history, Dr. Hedgewar realised that Hindu society was deeply divided on various counts like caste, region, and language. He saw a lack of self-discipline, social commitment, and self-confidence, and found that Hindus were driven by self-interest and not by the love of the motherland. He realised that unless the people are organized into a well-knit and disciplined patriotic society with selfless members ready to do anything for the nation, the freedom that was imminent would be useless. His goal was Hindu unity and the creation of a self-confident Hindu society. Thus, the Sangh was born.

In the dark days of British rule when calling oneself a Hindu was an embarrassment Dr. Hedgewar stood up in 1925 and said, 'yes, I, Dr. Keshav Baliram Hedgewar, I am a Hindu, and this is a Hindu nation.' He placed his faith in the common people, his contribution to the creation of the Sangh has been invaluable.

Development and Formation

On 27 September, 1925, Dr. Hedgewar began the new movement of Hindu revitalization in the form of the Sangh, on the eve of the Hindu festival of Vijaya Dashami (Dussehra). He announced to a few close friends gathered at his house, "He said we are starting the Sangh today." Dr. Hedgewar was thirty-six then; he chose to remain unmarried and wanted to dedicate his life to the nation's freedom and for its unity and development.

Dr. Hedgewar founded the Sangh with a group of only 15-20 young men and teenagers. Those present included Bhauji Kawre, Anna Sohni, Vishwnathrao Kelkar, Balaji Huddar, and Bapurao Bhedi, who played a significant role in shaping the organization in the initial years. Doctor

Ji became the first Sarsanghchalak of the Sangh in 1929. The emphasis of the Sangh in the early years was on initiating unity, discipline, and culture consciousness among Hindus, by the late 1930's the Sangh was a well organized and trained group with a strong base.

At the time of establishing the Sangh, Dr.Hedgewar laid down specific objectives that were that the Sangh would focus on: – Developing the philosophy of Hindutva, harnessing unity, and the spirit of brotherhood among Hindus, and developing physical, military and political capabilities in its volunteers. In the formative times of its establishment, the Sangh believed that the nation would not become strong and independent until there is a cultural revolution.

Dr. Hedgewar ensured that Sangh does not become another organization in the society. He developed the Sangh as an organization of the entire society. He introduced the tradition of 'Guru Dakshina' to make the Sangh self-reliant and self-sufficient. He placed the traditional 'Bhagwa Dhwaj,' a symbol of dedication, renunciation, and selfless service, as the ideal 'Guru' He was against projecting any individual as 'Guru' because he was aware of the shortcomings of an individual.[2]

After establishing the Sangh, he decided to begin the shakha system in the Sangh. Intellectual training sessions on weekends were also introduced. The first daily shakha of the Sangh began on 28 May 1926 and had a regular schedule. The place where a daily gathering of the initial volunteers or Swayamsevaks of the Sangh took place was Mohite Wada ground in Nagpur, which was also the first Karyalaya of the Sangh. According to Dr. Hedgewar, the ideological zeal that bounds the Swayamsevaks together in a brotherhood is the goal to reshape the nation's social and political institutions, Dr. Hedgewar believed

---

2   "The Seed of Eternity": Dr Manmohan Vaidya – Vsk Kerala. https://vskkerala.com/ news/926/the-seed-of-eternity-dr-manmohan-vaidya/

'Rasoi' The Cooking Place in the House of Dr. Hedgewar.

The House of Dr. Hedgewar, The Sangh Was Established here.

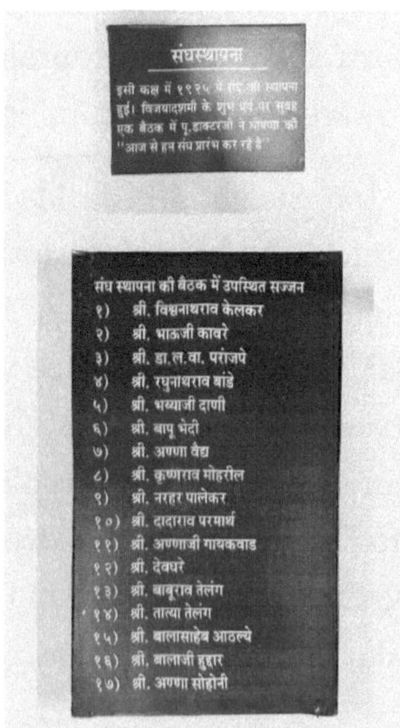

The List of People Present at the time of establishment of the Sangh at Dr. Hedgewar's House in Nagpur.

that character building was sufficient to achieve the desired social and political transformation of Bharat.

In the early days of the Sangh, Sh. Veer Savarkar had accompanied Dr. Hedgewar to hundreds of shakhas in Vidarbha to mobilize and inspire the Swayamsevaks, Ganesh Savarakar also merged his organization, Tarun Bharat Sabha in the Sangh; this helped the Sangh to increase the number of shakhas in the central provinces. In the history of Bharat, some people have been over glorified, and some have not even talked about, the Savarkar brothers; V.D and G.D Savarkar played key roles in implanting the ideology of Hindutva and strengthening the philosophy of the Sangh. Their contribution to the nation has been significant and remarkable.

Dr. Hedgewar considered Sh.Veer Savarkar as the ideological guide to the organization, and his brother Sh. Ganesh Damodar Savarkar helped in building it; the Savarkar brothers seem to have shaped the key definition of the Sangh that has been followed for years to come. It is interesting to note that the Sangh got its present name almost six months after it was founded.[3]

On 17 April 1926, Dr. Hedgewar called a meeting at his house in Nagpur, in which 26 Swayamsevaks participated. Three names were finalised after several rounds of discussion they were: Rashtriya Swayamsevak Sangh, Jari Pathaka Mandal, Bhedratoddharak Mandal, finally the name RSS was chosen. In simple language, the meaning of Rashtriya Swayamsevak Sangh is a disciplined and motivated group of people who, with their voluntary wish, want to serve the nation. None of the Swayamsevaks, including Dr. Hedgewar, were aware that the name

---

3   All That You Want to Know About RSS And Didn't Know – The Nationalist View. https://www.thenationalistview.com/research-and-reference/all-that-you-want-to-know-about-rss-and-didnt-know/

decided at the meeting would one day find such huge resonance and respect across the nation and the world in the years to come.

Sh. Hedgewar's search for a nationalist programme of action arose from a deeply felt need to restore among Hindus a sense of self-respect rooted in the Bharatiya culture. In a newspaper article titled *"The Unknown Commander of The Freedom Struggle – Dr. Hedgewar," mentioned that the post-independence government deliberately suppressed the RSS founder's contribution for the society and the nation.*

Doctor Ji's Vision & Mission - The True Nationalist

Dr. Hedgewar envisioned the vision and mission of the Sangh as "The Hindu culture is the life & breath of Hindustan. It is, therefore, clear that if Hindustan is to be protected, we should first nourish the Hindu culture. If the Hindu culture perishes in Hindustan itself, and if the Hindu society ceases to exist, it will hardly be appropriate to refer to the mere geographical entity that remains as Hindustan.

He devoted his life to the construction of a programme that would bring about the reorientation of men who would lead the movement for a new and more integrated society.

He incorporated into the Sangh a training process which came to be called character building, stressing discipline, and commitment, the process of the Sangh is based on the Hindu conception that disciplined training under an enlightened teacher (Guru) results in an introspective recognition of truth.[4] The training process of the Sangh emphasizes discipline and a desire of Hindutva. The Sangh, during its early days, believed that those men who had gone through the training would, on their own, take a leading role in reshaping the Bharatiya society.

---

4   A Book On RSS: Inherently Western but Honest. https://swarajyamag.com/books/a-book-on-rss-inherently-western-but-honest

Dr. Hedgewar chose to take a harder path to social mobilization; he chose a novel and innovative instrument of daily shakha for creating the Sangh. He understood well that it was a long-drawn and tough path. He strongly believed that it was preparedness and discipline that would make the Sangh highly effective and motivated in times to come. He also believed that an organisation like the Sangh and its unique efforts are going to be required for the safety and security of the nation.

He also felt that there was a need for a strong cadre-based organization which could take command of the independence movement and force the British government to give freedom to Bharat; he strongly felt that till 1940 the Sangh should use its setup and strengthen itself to yield a final blow to the British rule. Dr. Hedgewar argued that independence could be achieved only when the Hindu community is united.

According to him, mere geographical lumps would not make a nation, the entire society should be in such a vigilant and organized condition that no one would dare to cast an evil eye on any of our points of honour. It should be remembered that strength comes only through organization.[5] every Hindu, therefore, must do his best to consolidate the Hindu society.

Dr.Hedgewar had responded to a question what will the Sangh do in the future just by building up its organization?". He replied 'Sangh will not do anything, but Swayamsevak will do everything'. As the Sangh work spread and grew beyond the mandatory shakhas, the nature of work and methodology of such work also changed or evolved. New organizations inspired by the Sangh philosophy of unity, discipline, nation-building, and service to the society came into being as activists branched out into new areas and activities.

---

5   RSS: Vision and Mission – VSK Kerala. https://vskkerala.com/rss-vision-and-mission/

*Param **Pujaniye Sh. Keshav Baliram Hedgewar** (Doctor Ji)*
The Founder of the Rashtriya Swayamsevak Sangh.

Pathsanchalan: The RSS Route March taking Place at Pune, Maharashtra.

Abaji Hedgewar, uncle of Dr. Hedgewar, in his Book, 'Hindu Rashtra Past, Present and Future,' wrote, *"An organization such as the Sangh cannot remain satisfied with mere numbers of disciplined individuals. The Sangh should gradually find occasions to test its strength. It should create experts in every field and aspect, so that freedom may be won and maintained."*

As an organization, the Sangh is unique; no other body or forum has shown such an enormous contribution to voluntary service as the Sangh. For decades and generation after generation, the Sangh has instinctively shown austerity and devoted itself to the national cause of service.

Organizational Growth & Contributions of Dr. Hedgewar.

In the period from 1925-1939, the Sangh continued to expand; the expansion was majorly in the state of Maharashtra till 1930; in the decade 1930-1940, the Sangh grew in states such as Karnataka, Delhi, Uttar Pradesh & Madhya Pradesh.

In the 1930s, the Sangh also expanded in Punjab, Sindh, and parts of Rajasthan. Also, between 1931 and 1939, the Sangh shakhas increased enormously in number, and the cadre strength was assessed to be nearly 35,000 spread among various age groups nationwide. Within the short period of 15 years, Dr. Hedgewar had already laid the foundation for the Sangh across many states of the nation. In addition, a women's affiliate organization known as the Rashtriya Sevika Samithi was also established in October 1936 by Smt. Laxmi Bai Kelkar with the goal of Hindu revivalism and training women in martial arts.

Great national personalities like Mahatma Gandhi and Netaji Subash Chandra Bose visited the camps of Sangh and its shakhas, Gandhi Ji visited the Sangh camp in Wardha Maharashtra in 1934, and he was very praise worthy of the organization and deeply appreciated Dr. Hedgewar's efforts in building the Sangh.

Param Pujaniye Sh.Hedgewar Smruti Mandir at Reshim Bagh,
The Rashtriya Swayamsevak Sangh Headquarters, Nagpur, Maharashtra.

The Dr.Hedgewar Memorial Office Builidng,
Situated in the Sangh Headquaters at Nagpur, Maharashtra.

Later Dr. B.R Ambedkar visited the Sangh shiksha varg in Pune in 1935; he was surprised and happy to see the Swayamsevaks working tirelessly for the nation while forgetting all caste identities. In building and nurturing the Sangh, Dr. Hedgewar made every effort to ring fence the organization from any conflict, mainly legal. It is a cardinal rule in the organization that it should be protected at all costs. It is perhaps for this legal insolation that Dr. Hedgewar laid down the principle that the Sangh would not under its own banner, participate in any activity that could draw the attention of law enforcement.

Dr. Hedgewar worked so hard that his wonderful physique and health burned out within years, he passed away because of extreme exhaustion at a comparable young age of 51. He passed away on the morning of 21 June 1940 in Nagpur. His last rites were performed in the locality of Reshim Bagh in Nagpur, which was later developed as Sh. Hedgewar Smruti Mandir.

In his last address in 1940 at the Sangh shiksha varg at Nagpur, Dr. Hedgewar had said, "Sangh work and values should not be confined to the shakha but must be extended and established in the entire society."[6] To invest your time in actively working towards social change and social awakening is the complete definition of a Sangh worker.

He said with a sense of satisfaction, 'I see before me a miniature picture of Bharat today. Dr. Hedgewar will always have a tremendous influence on every Swayamsevak of the Sangh, and various incidents of his life provide extraordinary inspiration.

Former Prime minister Sh. Atal Bihari Vajpayee described Dr. Hegdewar Ji as a great patriot, freedom fighter, and nationalist during his commemoration on a postal stamp in 1999. He was described

---

6   RSS, nearly hundred – The Punjab Pulse. https://thepunjabpulse.com/rss-nearly-hundred/

as "a great son of Bharat Mata" by the former President of India Pranab Mukherjee during his visit to Dr. Hedgewar's birthplace in Nagpur.

Future generations will always be deeply indebted to him for creating an organization so powerful and vibrant as the Sangh. The young generation of Swayamsevaks and society will always see him as the greatest ever patriot and unifier that Bharat has ever seen. He was a legend, and his contribution will be remembered for generations to come.

CHAPTER – 2

Fundamentals of the Sangh
"Guruji Golwalkar" ~ Growth & Expansion

Introduction

The Sangh has been making determined efforts to inculcate in our people the devotion for Bharat and its national ethos; kindle in them the spirit of dedication, sterling qualities and character; rouse social consciousness, mutual good-will, love and cooperation among them all; to make them realize that caste, creed, and language are secondary and that service to the nation is the supreme end and to mold their behaviour accordingly; instil in them a sense of true humility and discipline and train them to be strong and robust to shoulder any social responsibility; and thus to create all-around Anushasana (Discipline) in all walks of life and build together all our people into a unified, harmonious national whole, extending from Himalayas to Kanyakumari.[7]

– Sh. Guruji Golwalkar

Sh. Madhavrao Sadashivrao Golwalkar, affectionately known as Sh. Guruji, was the second Sarsanghachalak of the Rashtriya Swayamsevak Sangh from 1940-1973.[8] Param Pujaniye Dr. Hedgewar Ji, the founder of Sangh, passed away in June 1940; he had designated Guruji Golwarkar as his successor; Guruji was a simple man with

---

7   Glorious 87: Rashtriya Swayamsevak Sangh (RSS) turns 87 today on Vijayadashami – Vishwa Samvada Kendra.https://vskkarnataka.org/glorious-87-rashtriya-swayamsevak-sangh-rss-turns-87-on-today-on-vijayadashami/

8   http://www.golwalkarguruji.org.

immense capabilities of spirituality and had a deep interest in the Hindu religion & Hinduvta.

Sh. Guruji nurtured the Sangh and helped it attain an eminent position in Bharat's national life. A seer and visionary, he articulated the fundamental guiding principles of the Sangh. He was and remains a constant source of inspiration to Sangh Swayamsevaks and several individuals and organizations from different walks of life. He enrolled in Hislop college, a missionary-run educational institute in Nagpur. There he was reportedly incensed at the "open advocacy" of Christianity and the false criticism of Hindutva; much of his concern for the defence of Hinduvta is traceable to this experience. He left Hislop college for Banaras Hindu University (BHU) in Varanasi in 1924, receiving a bachelor of science degree in 1927 in Zoology and a master›s degree in Biology in 1929. He was influenced by Madan Mohan Malaviya, a nationalist leader and founder of the university who prodded young Golwalkar to work for the Hindu cause.

Guruji was initiated into the Sangh when he was a lecturer at BHU by Sh. Prabhakar Balwant Dani, who was one of the senior leaders of the Sangh and was sent to BHU as a pracharak by Dr. Hedgewar in the 1930s, later he also served as the Sarkarvyah (General secretary of the Sangh)

Guruji first met Dr. Hedgewar in Banaras in 1931, Dr. Hedgewar began nurturing Guruji by inviting him to Nagpur for the Vijayadashmi program and sending him around to see Sangh work more closely. Guruji visited Nagpur in the summer of 1932; while speaking of his own experience of meeting Dr. Hedgewar, Guruji said, "I was humbled before the great man. His transparent passion and struggle for the nation, his brilliance of intellectualism, and his total surrender to the nation made me bow before him."

Guruji finally returned to Nagpur in 1933 and decided to pursue law at the law college of Nagpur; in 1934, he was appointed Karyavaha of the Sangh›s main shakha at Tulsibaug near Pune. He was also sent to Bombay by Dr. Hedgewar to spread the organization's work there. In 1935, Sh. Golwalkar was appointed as the Sarvadhikari of the Sangh training camp at Akola in Maharashtra.

In 1936, Guruji went to Sargachi in Bengal in search of spirituality and served Swami Akhandananda of Ramakrishna Math for two years. He returned to Nagpur in 1938, and in 1939 at the Guru Dakshina Utsav, Dr. Hedgewar announced that Guruji Golwalkar would be the Sarkarvyah (General secretary), the second most important position in the Sangh.

A day before Dr. Hedgewar's death on 21 June 1940, he gave Guruji Golwalkar a sheet of paper, asking him to be the Sangh Sarsanghchalak. On 3 July, the five state-level Sanghchalaks in Nagpur announced Dr. Hedgewar's decision. Guruji was only thirty-four years old when he was made the Sarsanghchalak.

Guruji Golwalkar held the position of Sarsanghchalak for the longest period of 33 years, a period that saw important events such as the independence movement, the partition of India, and the first ban on the Sangh in 1948. Thus, the two leaders of the Sangh during the pre-independence period were its founder, Dr. Keshav Baliram Hedgewar Ji (1925-1940) and Sh. Madhav Sadashiv Golwalkar (Guru Ji) (1940-1973), he laid a firm foundation supervising the training of full-time workers of the Sangh who would spread the organization across the nation, from its original base in Maharashtra.

Guruji as Sarsanghchalak

Guruji was the longest serving Sarsanghchalak and the youngest to be nominated for this post. He saw the Sangh through the most turbulent periods. He took charge in 1940 when the Sangh comprised of very young Swayamsevaks, Karyakartas, and leaders.

In 1941 the all-India strength of the Sangh was 37,362, which rose to 88,265 in 1944, in 1946, it stood at 100,402, and in 1950, it increased to 350,912. Under Guruji Golwalkar's leadership, 1942 was a year of comprehensive transformation in the history of the Sangh; a large number of Swayamsevaks became pracharaks. There were 48 new pracharaks from Lahore alone, 52 pracharaks from Amritsar, while Nagpur had 22 new pracharaks that year.

Guruji Golwalkar's role in the accession and integration of Kashmir is also a fact that very few know; when the Maharaja of Kashmir was unwilling to join the Indian union, all efforts to persuade him failed the then home minister of India, Sh. Sardar Patel sent an urgent message to Guruji asking for his help to persuade the Maharaja of Kashmir, Hari Singh. Guruji left for Srinagar on 17 October 1947, immediately cancelling all his other engagements. It is Guruji who then convinced Hari Singh to accede to India. Following this meeting, Hari Singh sent the accession proposal to Delhi, and Kashmir acceded to the Indian union on 26 October 1947.

Guruji was faced with multiple challenges after becoming the Sarsanghchalak, such as the partition of India and the ban on the Sangh in 1948; under his leadership from 1946 to 1947, Sangh volunteers were completely involved in protecting Hindus and Sikhs against rampant violence and their rehabilitation during the years following partition as well as protecting Jammu & Kashmir from Pakistani invasion.

During partition, the organization faced oppression, violence, and losses. This happened at a high cost to the life and property of Swayamsevaks. Guruji led the organization from the front. During partition, Guruji, Sh.Babasaheb Deoras, along with Punjab pracharak Sh. Madhavrao Muley, toured the violence-hit areas; apart from securing the lives of thousands of Hindus and Sikhs, the Sangh also organized a large number of relief camps in nearly all districts of Punjab, parts of Jammu, and also in the East of Bengal.

It was the organizational set-up built by Dr. Hedgewar and Guruji's persistent efforts that saw the Sangh through these turbulent times. Guruji had an unshakeable faith. That 'Bharat is one, and unbreakable and all her citizens are children of this unified nation'.

On 30 January 1948, the unfortunate assassination of Mahatma Gandhi Ji happened, and the Sangh was banned on 4 February. Guruji Golwalkar, along with thousands of Swayamsevaks, were illegally arrested; the ban of 1948 was a very critical and crucial time for the Sangh, but it was under Guruji's patient leadership that the Sangh survived the highly atrocious and oppressive ban, no other organization could have probably survived. After the ban on the Sangh was lifted in July 1949, there were two different streams of thought in the Sangh. One that wished to move away from the present working methodology of the Sangh and work for the reformation of society in a non-political creative way. The second view point was to enter politics and work towards rebuilding the nation.

In those intense debates about the utility of Sangh, someone asked, what if Karyakartas leave and Sangh's work crumbles, Guruji said, "Well if everything crumbles down, I will begin from the beginning'. Common Swayamsevaks believed in Guruji's intellect and strategic thinking. Slowly, they turned to the idea propounded by Guruji that a shakha-based system of the Sangh was the best way to move forward.

His ability to keep himself above political attacks and keep the good of the nation as the goal led the organization out of its worst phase. He could inculcate this habit of not carrying any animosity in his heart despite routine persecution; he motivated the Swayamsevaks and volunteers to conserve their energy for positive work.

Sh. Madhav Sadashivrao Golwalkar 'Guruji'
The Second Sarsanghchalak of the Rashtriya Swayamsevak Sangh.

Sh. Keshav Baliram Hedgewar Ji with Guruji Golwalkar in Nagpur.

In these trying times, Guruji created a superstructure built on the foundational principles of Dr. Hedgewar's view of life. He successfully oversaw the withdrawal of the ban and restored the Sangh back on track, putting it on the path of phenomenal growth, no other organization could have survived such persecution and government pressure as the Sangh did in 1948. However, Guruji's silent yet innovative approach took it forward and ensured that it reached every corner of Bharat. Guruji believed that the significant work of the Sangh was to create patriotic people with character. Getting into other fields might be counterproductive unless this work reaches a particular stage.

Guruji was instrumental in seeing the growth of a small plant that had blossomed under Dr. Hedgewar's guidance into a massive banyan tree; his term saw the expansion of the Sangh into new areas of national life. The organization took dynamic changes in its stride. The Sangh with time, was spread across every nook and corner of Bharat under the able leadership of Guruji.

Guruji institutionalized & instilled a formal structure in the shakhas and the organization; regular weekly, monthly, and quarterly meetings of the Sangh began to take place from the local level to state and regional levels. A work review system was established to discuss any problems faced by workers and local issues. Sangh shiksha vargas also became regular during Guruji's tenure. He stabilized and articulated the working of the pracharak system. The institution of pracharak, which is the backbone of the Sangh, has a spiritual and simple lifestyle, probably due to the personality of Guruji.

He systematically grew the organization through his methodology and human building potential; he was one of the most well-read people in the nation at that time with wide-ranging interest from arts to science and from technology to spiritualism, his divine spirituality created an impact on the organization far beyond physical growth and consolidation.

Expanding the Sangh's Horizon

Guruji travelled across the nation sixty times in thirty-three years continuously and untiringly, from the Himalayas to the Indian ocean, to expand the reach of the Sangh to every corner of the nation. He travelled across Bharat three to four times after becoming the Sarsanghchalak in 1940, in a short spell to get to know Sangh workers better and establish warm relations with them.

Guruji had once said. 'Train is my home: during his unending travels, he used to stay in one of these four places: first, the train bogey as he had said; second, at Sangh camps with Swayamsevaks; third, with Sangh workers or office-bearers while on tour; and fourth, at Sh. Hedgewar Bhavan, the Nagpur central office of the Sangh. This culture of staying with families began with Dr. Hedgewar, Guruji converted this into an arrangement and a part of Sangh's working system. This arrangement is still prevalent.

Understanding the situation by the end of the partition, Guruji found it necessary. He felt the need to reach out to people and explain Sangh's point of view about the nation, its people, and its goals. Thus, the print media publication of the Sangh began through the newspaper "Organiser," which started its publication in July 1947. Also, the weekly magazine "Panchjanya" was launched in 1948 by Sh. Deen Dayal Upadhyay in Lucknow, it had Atal Bihari Vajpayee as its first editor. Both of them were pracharaks. Nearly all states had their own regional periodicals over time. Dailies such as Swadesh from Lucknow and Bharatvarsh from Delhi were also established.

Guruji also took the first step towards building an organization outside the Sangh as with the establishment of the Akhil Bharatiya Vidyarthi Parishad (ABVP). It was founded in 1948 and formally registered in July 1949. During the ban, Swayamsevaks could not attend daily shakhas. To keep them engaged, the first get-together happened at Delhi university. Punjab university and more colleges followed it. Sh. Dattopant Thengadi and Sh. Dattaji Didolkar played vital roles in ABVP's growth. Prof. Yashwantrao Kelkar from Bombay later took full responsibility for the organization and took it to great heights.

In 1952, Guruji Golwalkar urged Swayamsevaks to work in the field of education. He discussed the issue with Prof. Rajendra Singh, Sh.Nanaji Deshmukh, Pt. Deendayal Upadhyay, and Sh. Bhaurao Deoras. As a result, the first Saraswati Shishu Mandir came into existence under the leadership of Nanaji Deshmukh at Gorakhpur. Guruji laid the foundation stone for the building. Today, the movement has over 20,000 schools in the country that educate over 3.5 million students.

In the same year, the Sangh also launched a cow protection movement. The Akhil Bharatiya Pratinidhi Sabha passed a resolution in Nagpur in September 1952 calling for a ban on cow slaughter across the nation. Sangh volunteers collected signatures from 94,459 villages and towns, amassing 1,79,89,332 signatures. On 8 December 1952, Guruji Golwalkar met the President of India, Sh. Rajendra Prasad and handed over the signatures. One of the key impacts of the cow protection campaign was that it galvanized the Sangh at an organizational level and increased its reach significantly.

During 1952-1953 the Sangh was also getting increasingly involved in relief and rehabilitation efforts wherever a disaster or calamity struck in the country. It resulted in the setting up of the Seva Vibhag (a wing for social services).

Later the establishment of Bhartiya Mazdoor Sangh (BMS) is also an absorbing story of the intelligence of Guruji Golwalkar, Dattopanth Thengadi, and Balasaheb Deoras; Guruji felt the need for labour reforms and protection of labour in the nation, thus on 23 July 1955 the BMS was formed in Bhopal. In 1960, Guruji warned the government about possible foreign aggression, and in 1962 China attacked India. The

Sangh came out in full force and helped the government in the war; the Sangh also organized relief camps, and the then Prime minister Pt. Nehru recognized the value of the Sangh's efforts. He invited the Sangh contingent to participate in the Republic Day parade on 26 January 1963; more than 3,000 Sangh Swayamsevaks had participated in the march.

Guruji is also credited for consolidating and bringing together Hindu societies and heads of various Hindu sects, religions, and traditions on one common platform, which was the Vishwa Hindu Parishad; it was founded on 29 August 1964. Guruji, S.S Apte, and Swami Chinmayanand were the founders of the VHP. It is one of the most influential organizations that brought different sects and sampradayas on a single platform and set the pace for reforming the Hindu society.

The construction of the Vivekananda rock memorial is also a significant achievement under the tenure of Guruji Golwalkar as Sarsanghchalak. The work for the memorial began during Swami Vivekananda's birth centenary in 1962. Guruji deputed one of the most senior pracharaks and Sarkaryavah of the Sangh, Sh. Eknath Ranade, for this task. Considering its importance, he was freed from the Sangh work. Sangh decided and made the historic decision to involve millions of citizens in the noble memory of Swami Vivekananda, who led the renaissance of Hinduism in the difficult times of our nation's history.

Thus, it was resolved that the memorial would be built with small donations from common citizens of the nation, one-rupee coupons were printed, and twenty-three lakh rupees were collected this way. This collection was done entirely by the Sangh volunteers moving door to door without any big hoardings or newspaper advertisements. The historic Vivekananda rock memorial was inaugurated in 1970 and dedicated to the nation; later, in January 1972, the Vivekananda Kendra was also established.

Guruji Golwalkar truly made the Sangh one of the strongest organizations in Bharat; by expanding the base and establishing organizations, the Sangh branched out into the political, social, religious, educational, and labour fields through multiple organizations which came to be known as the Sangh Parivar, he was a guardian to the Sangh Parivar organizations, even as he nurtured the work of Sangh and its shakhas, during his tenure the Sangh membership also expanded from 100,000 to over one million, the Sangh extended to foreign countries, where Hindus were recruited into organizations such as the Bharatiya Swayamsevak Sangh and the Hindu Swayamsevak Sangh.

Thus, he inspired and guided different Sangh-affiliated organizations to bloom in almost every field including education, empowering tribal people, socio–religious, and also the beginning of Hindu consolidation even outside Bharat.

He created a stable organizational structure that was so flexible yet so strong that it could absorb varying personalities, run organizations in different fields and maintain the philosophy and goal of the Sangh.

Guruji & The Bharatiya Jan Sangh

The Akhil Bharatiya Jan Sangh was a Hindutva driven political party that existed from 1951 to 1977, the founder of the Bharatiya Jan Sangh was Sh. Syama Prasad Mukherjee, the Bharatiya Jan Sangh was started by Dr.Mukherjee on 21 October 1951 in Delhi, as a nationalist alternative to the congress, the ideology of the BJS was Hindutva. The process that led to the birth of Bharatiya Jan Sangh began in 1950 when Dr. Syama Prasad Mukherjee resigned from the union cabinet government in 1950 due to strong differences with Nehru.

The RSS Uniform Band Contingent Performing in the Republic Day Parade of 1963, Rajpath, New Delhi.

The Swami Vivekananda Memorial, Kanyakumari
It was an initiative of Sh.Eknath Ranade Ji and was constructed during the Tenure of Guruji Golwalkar as Sarsanghchalak.

Sh. Mukherjee had been thinking of setting up a political party and had met Guruji Golwalkar, Sh.Balasaheb Deoras, and Sh.Bhaurao Deoras in early 1951 at the home of Nagpur Sanghchalak Sh.Babasaheb Ghatate. Guruji Golwalkar inspired Mukherjee, but the Sangh strictly prohibited political activity. The problem was resolved by the decision to send few pracharaks who were thoroughly socialized in the Sangh discipline to the Jan Sangh.

Guruji was clear that Sangh Swayamsevaks must refrain from getting favours from their political colleagues in Jan Sangh. He drew a sharp line between the Sangh and Jan Sangh, between social obligations and politics. Guruji had two points in mind that he felt must be addressed. One was the issue of Hindu nationalism, and the other was that the Sangh would not get involved in politics.

Guruji deputed some of the best pracharaks to Jan Sangh. They included Sh.Nanaji Deshmukh, Sh.Balraj Madhok, Sh.Sunder Singh Bhandari, Sh. Jagannathrao Joshi, and Sh.L.K. Advani. Sh. Atal Bihari Vajpayee was appointed secretary to Dr Mukherjee. Guruji chose Sh.Deendayal Upadhyaya to take on the important responsibility of organizing the party, and he was made the party's general secretary. All pracharaks whom Guruji had sent went on to become brilliant ideologs of the BJS and Sangh Parivar; Sh.Upadhyaya was the proponent of integral humanism and was also the main editor of the monthly publication Rashtra Dharma; Upadhyaya Ji is also known for drafting Jan Sangh's official political doctrine which focused on Sarvodaya meaning progress of all and Swadeshi meaning self-sufficiency.

Guruji - Thoughts & Philosophy

Guruji Golwalkar believed that it was very important to establish Bharat as a land of Hindus; he said to establish in this land that, Hindu means nation, and nation means Hindu, that is why the Sangh was called the Rashtriya Swayamsevak Sangh.

Sh. Atal Bihari Vajpayee & Sh. Deendayal Upadhyaya.

On Hindutva, Guruji Golwalkar said, "This is our dharma, our culture, our society; and built from all this is our nation, that is all. Our birth is only to build a powerful, capable, grand, radiant sovereign life for it. Therefore, we must motivate people for this mission. There is no need to be embarrassed or be afraid in declaring this belief." "We will create our own way of life from the philosophy of Hinduvta, a system that symbolises our sense of pride that would also be built around Bhartiyata that flows perennial to the Bharatiya tradition, that is a system of national way of life". Guruji Golwalkar had said in his speech at the Vijayadashami festival in 1947.

Guruji Golwalkar clarified and commented about the Sangh and its views on the national flag. He said that Sangh has its own flag that symbolises an epitome to create unity amongst the Hindus, being a part of the nation, the Sangh has complete faith and respect for the national flag and each member of the Sangh will readily sacrifice his life to defend the national flag.

His faith in the cultural unity of Bharat came from his actual experience across the nation during his travels. Witnessing diversity radiating out of the same unity, he said, "our next goal is to achieve peace in the world. Spreading the spiritual message and creating the feeling of brotherhood is our real work". On untouchability and casteism, he declared that the Sangh's objective is to remove the feeling of untouchability and weave together all sections of Hindu society in a single unifying thread.

According to Guruji, "the Sangh is not merely a place for teaching ideas and ideals. It is a school for practical education in character building; the Swayamsevaks are trained in the Sangh shiksha vargas and participate in Baudhik discussions and physical exercises. Thus, the habits and motives for service of the motherland are built into the character. He nurtured that sapling left behind by Dr. Hedgewar into a massive banyan tree consisting of small and big organizations that reached every nook and corner of the nation and touched nearly every aspect of social life.

Guruji Golwalkar worked tirelessly for the Sangh and devoted his life to the organization until his last breath to lay the groundwork and restore glory to our nation among the entire world. His energy, dedication, and perseverance were never-ending; he was a true inspiration. Guruji is regarded as one of the most influential Sarsanghchalaks of all time and has influenced many generations of Swayamsevaks; his ideas, leadership, and excellent management skills were unparalleled.

Guruji's health started deteriorating by the early 1970's he passed away for heavenly abode on 5 June 1973 after him Sh. Balasaheb Deoras became the third Sarsanghchalak of the Sangh.

Guruji nurtured the Sangh and helped it attain an essential and eminent position in the nation. He established the foundational principles of the Sangh, which reaped results for decades to come; he was a seer and visionary par excellence, and he articulated the fundamental guiding ideals of the Sangh. He was and remains a constant source of inspiration to Swayamsevaks and several individuals and organizations from different walks of life.[8] His thoughts on various issues concerning Hindutva and society are relevant even today. Indeed, he was a Rashtra Rishi.

---

8   http://www.golwalkarguruji.org.

CHAPTER – 3

The Organizational Structure of the Sangh & Constituents Units

Introduction

The Sangh is a finely structured organization established on the basic building blocks of strong interpersonal relationships and team spirit. If one considers the Sangh as a living organic entity, then the 'Shakha' is the most fundamental aspect of it, to that with the Akhil Bharatiya Pratinidhi Sabha (ABPS), which is the highest decision-making body with finely designed operational units at various levels.

The symbiotic links in the Sangh are maintained by the recruitment of voluntary Swayamsevaks in the Sangh; the Swayamsevaks are physically and mentally tested in games, running competitions, different sports and academic simulations conducted across Bharat; this has resulted in a high degree of loyalty and dedication to the organization on part of the cadre.

This chapter focuses on the organizational structure of the Sangh, such as the shaka, the pracharak, the Sarsanghchalak, Sarkarvyah, Sah Sarkarvyahs, the Sangh training process, which is the Sangh shiksha varg. Through this chapter, the organizational process of the Sangh can be understood in a better way.

The Sangh Shakha

The shakha is the most effective instrument of the Sangh; the shakha showcases the most powerful yet simplest form of coming together of Swayamsevaks every day; shakha has its essence of establishing personal contacts; this is the main reason for the success and growth of the Sangh across the nation. The daily shakha is undoubtedly the most visible symbol of the Sangh; after nearly ten decades since the inception of the Sangh, people continue to be surprised that how such a simple gathering as shakha has produced patriots and leaders of such sterling worth, herein where lies the extraordinary vision, skill, and foresight of Dr. Hedgewar.[9]

The beginning of man making (Vyakti Nirman) begins at the Sangh shakha, Dr. Hedgewar had designed it to mould men of a certain character. The Sangh's daily routine was to build and unify volunteers who would create 'Nitya Siddha Shakti' or innate capability in the Hindu society.

The pledge of a Swayamsevak is important as he signs up to the oath to work for "Hindu Rashtra ki Unnati" (the progress of the Hindu nation). The shakha is the smallest but the most crucial unit of the Sangh. Shakha is a daily gathering of Swayamsevaks, and it is the primary entry point for getting into the Sangh. The first daily shakha of the Sangh was held on 28 May 1926.

Dr. Hedgewar conceived the concept of shakha; the shakha is a concept in which a saffron flag called the Bhagwa Dhwaj flutters in an open playground, young men and boys of all ages engage in different types of games and exercises; all such activities in the shakha are disciplined, these programmes and games are followed by singing of patriotic songs also.

---

9   RSS Vision and Mission – VSK Kerala. https://vskkerala.com/rss-vision-and-mission

Swayamsevaks attending the evening Sangh Shaka.

The Sangh Shrung Ghosh Vaadaks (Brass Band).

Shakhas are conducted on an open ground, the shaka begins with the Swayamsevaks arranging themselves in rows before the Bhagwa Dhwaj. The rows are of Shishu, Bal, Tarun, and Praud; at the front is the leader, usually the Ghatnayak; at the back is the Shikshak. When the rows are assembled, the Bhagwa Dhwaj is raised. The Dhwaj is one of the most important perspectives in the Sangh and is honoured as a symbol of the nation's god.

At the end of the shakha, the Swayamsevaks again assemble in rows before the Bhagwa Dhwaj. They sing the Sangh Prarthana, which is the most pious prayer, it is recited by the whole group of Swayamsevaks – *'Namaste Sada Vatsale Matrabhume'*. The prayer concludes with a heartfelt utterance of the slogan 'Bharat Mata Ki Jai'.

Each Shakha is Divided Into 4 Age Groups -

1. Shishu Swayamsevaks 6-10 years in age.

2. Bal Swayamsevaks 10-14 years in age

3. Tarun Swayamsevak 14-28 years in age

4. Praud Swayamsevaks 28 or older.

The Shikshaks teach games and yogic exercises to Swayamsevaks in the shakha. Apart from physical exercises, Baudhik sessions are conducted within the shakha which consists of mental exercises and discussions; the themes of these discussions typically relate to attributes of a good character which is focused upon honesty, commitment to the nation, and personal discipline.

Many kinds of games are played in the shakha to inculcate a spirit of nationalism, such as Kabaddi, Kho-Kho, Bajrang Daud, and Sitolia, among many others. The spirit of competitiveness in these games is very high, and these games also attract youth towards the Sangh in a large number, there are around 50 games listed in the 'Shakha Surbhi', one of the important publications of the Sangh.

In terms of the shakha discipline, absence from the shakha without prior information by any Swayamsevak, is considered as indiscipline, indiscipline during shakha often brings immediate forms of punishments. The shakha in the Sangh is the most important aspect in the hierarchy; it is the root and the core of the organization; the Sangh conceives the shakha as the chief instrument for organizing the Hindu community.

Important Segments of the Shaka Structure

The age groups in the shakas are divided into Gata's (groups); Gata rarely exceeds 20 participants. A Gata is composed of a common age group, and the participants tend to live in a particular locality. Attached to each Gata is Gatnayak and a Shikshak (teacher), both appointed by the shakha Mukhya Shikshak. These two functionaries are the first level in the Sangh hierarchy and are the initial testing ground for leadership.

The captain of the shakha is called as the Mukhya Shikshak while travelling across the country, national and regional office bearers conduct reviews with the Mukhya Shikshak and discuss the ways to improve the shakha system. The Shikshak teaches games and exercises which the Swayamsevaks are expected to master; apart from games and exercises, the Sangh also conducts Baudhiks in the shakha. The authority of every shakha is the Karavyah, an older and respected member of the locality. The ability of the Sangh to sustain a high level of commitment and be motivated always suggest that it has successfully recruited the best of men in the nation. Above the shakha in the pyramid of authority which is the Mandal committee (composed of representatives from 3 or 4 shakahas in a given locality), representatives from 10 to 12 Mandals form a Nagar (city committee).

Above the city committee, there may be a Zila (district and regional committees). Most of the day-to-day work in the structure takes place at the city level, the city committee consists of a Sanghchalak, and heads the local Sangh department. Representatives from each shakha are represented in the Mandal committee, and the Mukhya Shiikshak or the local pracharak passes information to the lowest level of the communication circuit.

At the bottom of the organization pyramid is a shakha, a number of shakha could range from 3 to 10, put together they are known as Mandal, a number of Mandals generally 5-10 are clubbed together and known as Nagar, a number of Nagars form a group called as Zilla. A number of Zilla's put together are known as Vibhaag, 5-15 Vibhaags put together are known as Sambhag, a number of Sambhags when put together known as Prant.

A number of Prants are clubbed together under the title of Kshetra, the whole country has been divided into eleven Kshetra's by the Sangh for its organisational structure. It is important to remember that the organisation structure of the Sangh does not adhere to the demarcation of states proposed. With the emergence of several new states in the country, the Sangh is also making adjustments to ensure smooth organizational functioning.

Shakha – Inspiration & Contribution

In all the shakhas, the most important lesson taught is that Bharat is a Hindu Rashtra, Hindutva is the essence, and the unity and integrity of Bharat is the utmost important task. Emphasis is also laid on the principle of Akhand Bharat; the Sangh also believes that prejudices and differences based on caste, region, and religion should not exist in society.

Almost 50.000 people per month are becoming part of the shakha system today in the nation; the swayamsevaks contacts the new entrants and holds an introductory meeting called Sangh Parichay Varg. The

Sangh also hosts the IT shakhas and IT Milans in big cities like Bombay, Bengaluru, Pune, Hyderabad, and Delhi. This has been a unique experience where professionals have built shakha networks using technology through e-shakhas for debate and discussions.

The shakha is the core organisational strength of the Sangh; it is the powerhouse that energises and powers ordinary people to carry out extraordinary feats and create a pan nation organisation. It is through the shakha that the Sangh has gathered hundreds and thousands of dedicated volunteers called Swayamsevaks, who form the backbone of the organization. The process of induction is the shakha is so simple that even before one realises, he is adopted into the saffron brotherhood. No social organization can match the vast network and discipline of the Sangh shakhas; every minute of the lives of Swayamsevaks and the pracharaks is dedicated to serving society and strengthening the Sangh.

People often wonder how a small group of ten – twenty people who come together for an hour for playing games, doing some physical drills, singing patriotic songs, discussing social issues, and praying together can build such a significant organization with more than 72,000 shakhas all over the nation with a daily collective attendance of more than half a million.

Gandhi Ji visited the Sangh training camp in December 1934 at Wardha; he appreciated the manner in, which the welcome salutation was expressed, along with the uniformity, equality, and cleanliness in the camp; Gandhi Ji asked Swayamsevaks how they interacted. To which he got a response in Hindi ***"Hum Sab Hindu Hai Aur Hum Sab Bandhu Hain,"*** meaning we are all Hindu, and we are all brothers. Thus, the message of the daily shakha is the restoration of a sense of brotherhood among Hindus.

The thought behind, this unique set of tools or working style of the Sangh through daily shakha, is that a person dedicates at least one hour in a day for the nation. Once, this thought becomes a part of his personality. One willingly, increases his participation ultimately, he reaches a state of mind reflected in the Sangh song that says, *'Tan Samarpit, Man Samarpit, Aur Yah Jeevan Samarpit, Chaahata Hoon Main, Tujhe Kuchh Aur Bhi Doon'* (I have dedicated my body, soul, and life to you, motherland, I long to give you something more).[10]

The Core Organizational Structure

There are two main bodies of the Sangh which form the core of the organizational structure and takes all important decisions. The Akhil Bhartiya Karyakarni, broadly known as the central RSS executive council, and the Akhil Bharatiya Pratinidhi Sabha (ABPS) is known as the all-India representative council. The constitution and the roles of the ABPS are outlined in article 15 of the constitution of the Sangh.

The elected members of the ABPS elect the Sarkaryavaha (equivalent to the general secretary, executive head), as per the constitution, the ABPS "shall meet at least once a year" and shall review the work and lay down the policy and program of the Sangh. The Pratinidhi Sabha is considered as the highest decision-making body of the organization, and has representatives from various Sangh Parivar organizations, the Sangh functionaries at the Prant level and above participate in the ABPS, it is held for a duration of three to four days.

---

10 Circles: Starting the Indian Revolution – Rajesh Jain. https://rajeshjain.com/circles-starting-the-indian-revolution/

RSS is working directly at 71,355 places across the country

68,651 Shakhas are being organised at 42,613 places

Saptahik Milan takes place at 26,877 places

Maasik Mandali takes place at 10,412 places

121,137 youth received Prathmik Shikshan in last one year

RSS received a whopping 7,25,000 applications to join the organisation between 2017 and 2022

The Data of the Sangh Activities Presented in the Akhil Bhartiya Pratinidhi Sabha, 2022.

A Bal Swayamsevak Addressing Sangh Commands to Swayamsevaks.

Swayamsevaks 'Ghosh Tarang' (Band Members).

The Akhil Bhartiya Karyakarni comprises the Sangh Sarsanghchalak, (Sarkaryvyah) (Sah Sahkarvyahs) and heads & deputy heads of various wings such as physical (Sharirik), intellectual (Baudhik), media (Prachaar), public relations (Sampark), social services (Sewa) and logistics (Vyavastha). The Akhil Bhartiya Pratinidhi Sabha and similar sabhas at the state level meet once a year, and it includes delegates chosen by the state assemblies, Sanghchalaks, pracharaks, and members of the central executives, like the state assemblies participate. The Sangh structure gives it a supervisory power over the whole organization. The administrative power is exercised by the Kendriya Karyakarni Mandal (Central working committee) and Sarkaryavah (The General secretary).

"Pracharak"
The Major Linking Position in the Sangh

A full-time volunteer in the Sangh is known as a pracharak; the Swayamsevaks who are committed and devoted to the activities of the Sangh, and are capable, trained, and wish to dedicate their full time to the Sangh are known as pracharaks.[11] The life of a pracharak is based on commitment, dedication, and discipline. Generally, the Swayamsevak who completes all the three training camps of the Sangh, known as Sangh shiksha varg, are deputed as pracharaks. The pracharak system is a critical institution within the Sangh. A pracharak is a full-time volunteer of the Sangh; he stays in the Sangh offices known as Karyalaya in the Sangh terminology.

Currently, there are more than seven thousand pracharaks who work in the Sangh, and in several Sangh parivar organizations; a pracharak remains a bachelor till the time he wants to serve as a pracharak and

---

11 Know About RSS – Prabhat Paperbacks, Arun Anand – Chapter 6 (The Pracharak), (1 January 2019). pg.61

does not marry. The pracharak, forms a communicative network outside the formal system of the Sangh, they are the links between the various level of the Sangh; they have the commitment, expertise, and time to manage the Sangh activities.

While the pracharak binds the Sangh structure together, they are recruited through a very tough process by a state level pracharak in consultation with local Sangh functionaries who know the applicant. The pracharaks are on probation for one or two years, and during this period, they are referred to as vistaraks. The pracharaks retain a close working relationship with the organization in whatever area they are assigned.[12] The typical pracharak is recruited in his early 20's. He is very well educated and usually is a college graduate; many a times, even doctors, lawyers, architects, engineers are pracharaks. This showcases the well-educated base inside the organizational structure of the Sangh.

The pracharak is fluent in Hindi and English, besides the language of the area in which he works; an ideal pracharak has been associated with the Sangh activities since adolescent age. The lifestyle is very simple and is often connected with the ideals and philosophy of Hindutva. He is a pure vegetarian, his apparel is also traditional, like pyjama kurta and ethnic clothes.

He lives with very simple and bare necessities of life and leads the life of a Brahmachari. Though he lives amongst families and in society as a normal worldly being but he is a Sanyasi (monk) for all practical purposes. The pracharak is the soul of the organization. He is respected by every Swayamsevak. The traits of a Sangh pracharak are his utter simplicity and humility. An interaction with a pracharak is a humbling and learning experience in itself.

---

12   A Book On RSS: Inherently Western but Honest. https://swarajyamag.com/books/a-book-on-rss-inherently-western-but-honest

The pracharak system is the bedrock on which the Sangh stands, a high sense of dedication and sacrifice, strict discipline and self-denial is necessary to become a pracharak, the pracharak system is one of the greatest & significant developments of the Sangh.[13]

Development of the Concept of Pracharak

The concept of pracharak has its roots in the early years of the Sangh. After it was established, initially Dr. Hedgewar who was the only full-time volunteer; he used to travel extensively to expand the activities of the Sangh by establishing and starting new shakhas.

Till 1932, the word pracharak was not officially used in the Sangh; with time, there arose an increasing need for Swayamsevaks, who would spend a few days in the places where new shakhas were set up. Dr Hedgewar used to travel extensively and personally guided the work at most of these places, but with the rapid expansion of the Sangh, it was becoming difficult for him to reach every place. Dr Hedgewar often used to get letters from villages, towns, and cities where several individuals requested him to start a shakha at their native places. They needed someone experienced to come there and establish shakhas.

By 1933, senior Sangh workers Sh.Dadarao Parmarth, Sh.Babasaheb Apte, Sh.Rambhau Jamgade, and Sh. Gopalrao Yerkuntwar, became full time pracharaks and were sent to different parts of Maharashtra; they comprised the first batch of Sangh pracharaks. Dr. Hedgewar delivered an emotional address at a small function organized formally to start the tradition of becoming a Sangh pracharak, the robust tradition of becoming a pracharak inspired and attracted many young and talented men in years to come.

---

13 Andersen and Damle, RSS: A View to the Inside (Penguin Viking, August 2018) pg.64

In 1937, regular shakhas were established by pracharaks in several parts of Maharashtra, Madhya Pradesh, and Uttar Pradesh. In the late 1930's Sh. Bhaurao Deoras, went to Lucknow, Uttar Pradesh; Sh. Digamber Praular went to Lahore (pre-independent India); Sh. Morehswar Munje to Rawalpindi; Sh. Vasantorao Oak went to Delhi and Sh. Naryana Tarte to Gwalior, to expand the Sangh footprint.

Sh. Atal Bihari Vajpayee, joined the Sangh as a young swayamsevak in 1939 and was deeply influenced by the Sangh pracharaks in his formative years. He gave up his studies in 1947 to become a pracharak. He had been writing poetry since his pracharak days; he wrote the famous poem **"Hindu Tan Man, Hindu Jeevan, Rag Rag Hindu Hindu Meraa Parichay"** (Hindu body and soul, Hindu life, Hindu, this is my identity).

The pracharak, or full-time worker system, was formally started in 1942. The divisions of pranth (province), kshetra (region), came into existence in 1950; the structure of the ABPS was also created during this period. It is the highest decision-making body of the Sangh regarding policies and priorities.

Importance & Work in the Sangh Hierarchy

The work of a pracharak is to start new shakas, improve the existing ones and bring new people to the shakhas, and spread the Sangh's ideology of Hindutva. A sense of community is maintained among the pracharak, they inspire the young Swayamsevaks and introduce them to the Sangh's worldview; the training and ideology pays special attention to the importance of group solidarity. Those Swayamsevaks who become pracharaks have demonstrated the greatest commitment to each other and to the ideology.

The life of pracharak is full of sacrifices, they live under austere physical conditions. Many have also severed virtually all their ties with their own families. The importance of the pracharaks can be gauged from the fact that two Prime ministers produced by the Bhartiya Janata Party – Sh. Atal Bihari Vajpayee Ji and Sh. Narendra Modi Ji have formerly been Sangh pracharaks.

The number of pracharaks, who have had significant influence on the socio-economic and political discourse of the nation is almost endless. To name a few as, Pandit Deendayal Upadhyay who established the theory of integral humanism; Sh. Dattopant Thengadi, stalwart Sangh leader, founded various Sangh Parivar organizations as Bharatiya Mazdoor Sangh, Akhil Bhartiya Adhivakta Parishad, Sh. Nanaji Deshmukh, founded the first Saraswati Shishu Mandir, he also played a pivotal role during emergency in coordinating with J.P Narayan and was one of the key architects of the Janata party government in 1977.

The Sangh has produced a galaxy of stalwarts and leaders who have contributed to every sphere of the society and nation; the top Karyakarni mandal functionaries of the Sangh and heads of the many Sangh Parivar organizations are pracharaks. A pracharak cannot choose his place of work or field of work. He may be deputed to any area across the nation. He may even be assigned to another affiliated organization of the Sangh. Pt. Deendayal Upadhyay, Sh. Nanaji Deshmukh, Sh. Sunder Singh Bhandari, Sh. Atal Bihari Vajpayee, Sh. L.K. Advani, were deputed to the then Jan Sangh on request of Dr. Syama Prasad Mukherjee, founder of the Jan Sangh. Eknath Ranade was relieved of his very important duties as Sarkaryavah of the Sangh to take up the work of the Vivekananda rock memorial at Kanyakumari.

The institution of pracharak has also been adopted by the other Sangh affiliated organizations like the Rashtra Sevika Samiti, ABVP, VHP, BMS, among others. The Sangh is generally requested to loan a pracharak by a Sangh-inspired organization that starts or expands its work in a new field.

Thus, there are thousands of pracharaks all over Bharat spreading the good word about Hindu heritage, national unity, equality, social amity, dedication to society, upliftment, and citizen duty in nation-building. In general, they are helping the nation become a better place for all its citizens.

Sarsanghchalak – The RSS Chief

At the apex of the Sangh is the Sarsanghchalak, who is generally chosen by his predecessor; he is described in Sangh as the guide and philosopher of the organization. The Sarsanghchalak holds the position generally till life. Sarsanghchalak is one of the top most person in the organization. By virtue, each Sarsanghchalak commands respect and impacts the Sangh's work. He is the public face of the Sangh; he becomes synonymous with the organization and personifies the organization. His views are taken as the most important, his word is considered as the final word for the organization, he shapes the organization.

The previous Sarsanghchalak nominates him. However, this nomination, too, goes through a process of discussions with senior karyakartas. He chooses within the shortlisted names, so it is not purely a personal choice. The post of the Sarsanghchalak has no fixed tenure, organizations affiliated with the Sangh also look up to him to advise them and provide the necessary moral support. He can also start the process of forming new policies by giving specific guidelines. This is where his role becomes critical in the way the organization moves ahead in a particular direction.

All the Sarsanghchalaks have a very high intelligence quotient. They are academically brilliant. They are at the top in their field, yet, they forsake the fruits of their success for service to the society. Beginning from Dr. Hedgewar to all Sarsanghchalaks down the line, all of them have had a brilliant character and memory. While some maybe are naturally gifted, others may have trained themselves to remember people, names, and places. This quality is essential to connect with people.

The Six Sarsanghchalaks of the RSS Since 1925 till Present. Sh. Keshav Baliram Hedgewar Ji, Sh. Guruji Golwalkar, Sh. Balasaheb Deoras Ji, Sh. Rajendra Singh Ji, Sh. K.S Sudarshan Ji, Sh. Mohan Rao Bhagwat Ji.

Param Pujaniye Sarsanghchalak Sh. Mohan Bhagwat Ji & Sangh Sarkaryvah Sh. Dattareya Hosbale Ji Addressing the Akhil Bhartiya Pratinidhi Sabha, 2023.

Sarkaryavah & Sah Sarkaryavahs

The next person in the Sangh hierarchy after the Sarsanghchalak is the general secretary or the Sarkarayavah, who is the number two person in the organization and is responsible for the daily functioning of the Sangh. The general secretary is responsible mainly for the outreach activities related to the Sangh across the nation.

As the Sangh expanded and more and more affiliate organizations grew, it was difficult for a Sarkayarvah to manage the organization. After the emergency and the second ban on the Sangh were lifted, there was a policy change, and a post of Sah Sarkayavah (Joint general secretary) was created. Sah Sarkayavahs are given the responsibility of specific verticals within the organization and the task of coordinating with affiliate organizations and guiding them whenever needed. The Sah Sarkaryavah of the Sangh has his work differentiated. For example, one Sah Sarkaryavah is responsible for keeping in touch with Sangh Parivar organizations such as the Vishwa Hindu Parishad, the Akhil Bhartiya Vidhyarthi Parishad etc. While the others take care of media relations and social media communications of the Sangh, others are related to physical and intellectual activities division.

Sah Sarkayavahs regularly meet with the leaders of other teams. The number of Sah Sarkayavahs was four initially, and it has recently been increased to six; they, along with other all India office bearers, are stationed in different parts of the nation.

The Institutional Core Training of the Sangh

The Sangh organizes many camps to train the Swayamsevaks; this training is the formal sangh training and is done through the Sangh shiksha vargas, primarily instructions regarding the teaching of Sanskars and Vyakti Nirman within the Swayamsevaks is done through them. The first Sangh training camp was held at Nagpur in 1929.

Through the institutional training, a sense of solidarity is developed among the swayamsevaks and volunteers. The institutional training of the Sangh is considered to be of utmost importance in the organization. Initially, the Sangh shikha vargas were called summer camps as they were organized during the summer months; the name Sangh shiksha varg was used after 1950.

Dr. Hedgewar said that these camps are organized to prepare Swayamsevaks in a formal way for the Sangh, who can give the maximum amount of time to the organization, so it should be called officer's training camp; Guruji Golwalkar, the second Sarsanghchalak of the Sangh, renamed these camps as 'Sangh shiksha varg' if one wants to understand why and how Sangh cadres have such a high level of commitment and dedication to work selflessly for the nation, how thousands of full-timers (pracharaks) left highly paid jobs and very prosperous looking careers at a very young age to live, work tirelessly for the organization. In that case, it is essential to understand the philosophy, evolution, and functioning of the Sangh training camps.

The RSS Camps (Sangh Shiksha Varg)

The RSS camps fall roughly into 4 major categories which are: –

Sangh Shiksha Varg (Prathimki)

The first camp is the instructor's training camp which, which is also known as the Prathmiki; the local Sangh committee usually manages it; these camps last about seven days, usually during the winter months, like other camps. These camps are isolated from the outside world and are conducted within some specified schools and colleges. The duration of Prathmiki is one week, it is well organized, there are kitchens, medical clinics and laundry besides residential and infrastructure facilities, each Swayamsevak is identically dressed and wears the Ganvesh; as the Sangh Ganvesh must be worn by everyone attending the camp, even the Shikshaks, do not wear any additional insignia to indicate their position, Swayamsevaks pay a very nominal fees for attending the camp.

The Sangh funds are used for participant Swayamsevaks who cannot afford the fees of the camp, the camp is intended primarily to induct new Swayamsevaks in the Sangh, and emphasis is laid on both intellectual and physical growth.

In synchronization with seven-day camp, which is the Prathmiki. Numerous three-day camps of the Sangh are also conducted throughout the year; these are designed for specific groups such as high school students, college students, traders, and people from all walks of life; these three-day camps are very important as they are a preliminary basis of moulding a simple person into a Swayamsevak, these camps are also highly attractive for the students, lakhs of young students and professionals participate in these three days camps held in a year across the nation.

Sangh Shiksha Varg (Pratham Varsh)

After completing the Prathmiki, Swayamsevaks, who wish to devote their time to the Sangh activities, participate in the Pratham varsh. The Pratham varsh is important as it prepares the Swayamsevaks in a better way; it is a twenty-day camp for which the selection process begins several months before the camps are held; the Pratham varsh is presided by the core committee members who are part of the national central executive of the Sangh. The Prathimiki, Pratham varsh camps are organized at the state and sometimes at the district levels.

Swayamsevaks Participating in the Baudhik Session at the Tritya Sangh Shiksha Varsh in Nagpur.

Swayamsevaks Performing Physical Exercises During the Sangh Pratham Shishka Varg.

Sangh Shiksha Varg (Dwitiya Varsh)

The Sangh shiksha varg (Dwitiya varsh), is the twenty-day camp which is conducted for Swayamsevaks who have completed the Prathmiki and the Pratham varsh; in the Dwitiya varsh, senior Sangh members such as Sarkarayavah and sometimes Parampujaniye Sarsanghchalak Ji also preside over intellectual and physical sessions. The participants of the Dwitiya varsh are assigned to Ganas as a group of 15-20 Swayamsevaks. The Gana Pramukh is responsible for maintaining the group and teaching exercises and conducting Baudhik sessions, which form the most important part of the curriculum of the Sangh.

One more interesting aspect of the Sangh is that in the training camps Swayamsevaks from different states and regions are also intermingled to create a sense of brotherhood and commonality. Swayamsevaks serve food to each other, they help each other in important task in the shakha. A day at the camp begins early morning and ends at night, the morning and evening hours are used for physical games and exercises in the afternoons and evening hours are used for Baudhik sessions.

Sangh Shiksha Varg (Tritiya Varsh)

The Sangh shiksha varg (Tritiya varsh) is conducted at the Nagpur headquarters of the Sangh and held during the summer months of May and June, only selected few of the Swayamsevaks across the nation who are considered best in physical and mental exercises are considered for selection in the Tritiya varsh at Nagpur, for this proper lists are approved by the Mukhya Shikshak at the local level, then at the pranth level and ultimately at the state level, the Kshetra pracharak also approves the list at the apex level of the state.

Senior Sangh Functionaries Addressing Swayamsevaks During the Tritya Sangh Shiksha Varg.

Param Pujaniye Sh. Kadsidheshwar Swami Ji along with Param Pujaniye Sarsanghchalak Sh.Mohan Rao Bhagwat Ji at the 2023 Sangh Tritya Varsh 'Samapan Samaroh' in Nagpur.

The Tritiya varsh is a 25-day camp, after completing the Swayamsevaks then go on to become pracharaks in the Sangh. Parampujaniye Sarsanghchalak Ji presides over valedictory function (Samapan Samaroh) of the Tritiya varsh; the Tritiya varsh is considered to be one of the most important camps of the whole training structure in the Sangh curriculum. The varsh is attended by those Swayamsevaks who have completed the Prathmiki, Pratham, and the Dwitiya Sangh shiksha varg.

The Aim & Purpose of Sangh Shiksha Varg

The aim and purpose of the Sangh shiksha varg is to build men of character who have the physical power and the mental strength to face any adversity, also senior Sangh ideologues deliver lectures to Swayamsevaks coming from different states, parts of the nation. This is one of the most effective ways for the senior Sangh functionaries to connect with the Swayamsevaks.

The camps provide an opportunity for Sangh Shikshaks and seniors to observe closely the progress of the Swayamsevaks which gives them a comprehensive pool of Swayamsevaks which could lead the Sangh in the future in different positions across the nation, many Swayamsevaks after the completion of the camps are associated on the full-time basis with the Sangh, while some go back to their lives and profession and spread the Sangh ideals at their work places; sometimes trainings are also followed by a kind of probationary assignment at the local level of the organization.

Param Pujaniye Sarsanghchalak Sh. Mohan Bhagwat Ji Addressing the Sangh Tritiya Varsh 'Samapan Samaroh' in Nagpur, 2019.

Param Pujaniye Sarsanghchalak Mohan Bhagwat Ji performing Darshan and Pujan at Shri Kashi Vishwanath Dham Mandir, Varanasi, 21ˢᵗ July 2023.

Dr Bhimrao Ambedkar visited a Sangh shiksha varga in Pune in 1939. When Dr. Ambedkar asked Dr. Hedgewar whether there were any untouchables in the camp, Dr.Hedgewar replied that there were neither touchable nor untouchables, but only Hindus.[14] Dr. Ambedkar said, "I am surprised to find the Swayamsevaks working in absolute equality and brotherhood without even caring to know the caste of the others."[14] The most appreciable part about the Sangh shiksha varg camps is that every Swayamsevak is considered equal, and there is no racism or casteism. The Sangh is inclusive in nature and has never been an organization of any person or any community; it is the organization for the nation and stands with the ideals, philosophy of Hindutva.

The Sangh shiksha varg is hence one of the most important aspects which forms the part of the core curriculum of the Sangh and it is a life changing experience for a Swayamsevak to participate and attend the vargs.

---

14   Because India Comes First by Ram Madhav – Indic Today https://www.indica.today/reviews/because-india-comes-first-ram-madhav/

CHAPTER – 4

Beliefs, Notions & Philosophy of the Sangh

Introduction

The Sangh follows the ideal of protecting "Jati Dharma Sanskriti" and works to make this pledge meaningful and to serve the society. The Sangh maintains spiritual brotherhood with all the communities; this is primarily because the Sangh's definition of Hindu is not linked to any religion but to a national identity of Bharat. It is an all-inclusive term that encompasses all communities and faith of the nation.

This is the reason that the Sangh has become an organization of the ordinary people and has expanded over the years; it is related to the ordinariness and common simplicity of the people, it gives them confidence that they can bring about changes in the society and in the nation. Dr. Hedgewar had said to Sh. Guru Golwalkar, "that the Sangh should cultivate experts in economics, education, armed forces, politics, linguistics, intelligence, and other fields and the work of the Sangh should positively impact all spheres and segments of the society." Sangh believes that Bharat is a Hindu Rashtra and belongs to followers of Hindutva; it believes that the idea of Hindu Rashtra is drawn from the ideals of Swami Vivekananda & Sh. Veer Savarkar. The preservation of culture and pride is the dominant theme in the Sangh's narrative; the Swayamsevaks often chant "Vande Mataram" and say "Bharat Mata ki Jai."

The Sangh has also taken parts of its ideology from the central proposition of Veer Savarkar's manuscript on Hindutva, that Hindus are the indigenous people of the subcontinent and they form a single national group. Sangh is the consolidator and protector of Hindus and the Hindu nation. Sangh believes that those who belong to Bharat, are descendants of Bharatiya ancestors, and the ones who are working for the ultimate glory of the nation & joining hands in enhancing peace, respecting, and welcoming all diversities, all those Bharatiyas are Hindus.

Sh. Balasaheb Deoras, the third Sarsanghchalak, said the "Sangh has only one principle that Hindustan is a Hindu Rashtra, and it belongs to Hindus; everything else can change." The Sangh is away from publicity campaigns and glittering statements. It works quietly and diligently for social harmony in the society at all levels. The efforts are very sincere in nature; the Sangh has grown immensely even though certain sections of people have tried to campaign negatively against it.[15] As time passes, there will be a multiplicity of Sangh's involvement in different fields in society; the Sangh has always been an organization which has remained ahead in time; Swayamsevaks are laborious, disciplined in nature, and with the correct mental aptitude; the outcome of the Sangh hard work will always be seen in the society. The saying **Sangh Samaj Banega** is, was, and always will be true.

Principles on Which the Sangh is Shaped

1. According to Dr. Hedgewar's experience, for the purpose of longevity and stability, movements needed to have a life of their own, and they should survive for permanence beyond the lifespan of great personalities. Therefore, he formed the Sangh, an organization which was much bigger than a person or a group of people.

2. Hindu society for centuries was disorganised and was in a state of attack; it was therefore required to work consistently for several

decades and become assertive for nationhood; for this goal, the Sangh was established.

3. The comprehensive awakening of national character was not possible based on the qualities of a great leader alone, it requires many individuals to work tirelessly for the goal of a nation. Thus, the Sangh ensures the collective working for a philosophy.

Dr. Hedgewar saw many loop holes, in the ways and methods of functioning of political parties as they were only driven by politics; they lacked the dedication for the all-round national development of the nation. Therefore Dr. Hedgewar created the Sangh, the phrase Bharat Mata ki Jai, and the Bhagwa Dhwaj, have been the twin inspirations for the Swayamsevaks. The Sangh is Bharat's biggest assimilated and integrative force. The activities of the Sangh are planned and directed by experience, conviction, and pragmatic imagination; the philosophy of the Sangh is the eternal spirit of Bharat.

The aims and objects of the Sangh are to weld together the various diverse groups within the Hindu Samaj and to revitalise and rejuvenate the same based on its Dharma and Sanskriti,[15] that it achieves an all-round development of Bharatvarsh. The Sangh believes in the orderly evolution of society and adheres to peaceful and legitimate means of realisation of its ideals.

---

15 What is Hindu Rashtra? Frontline. https://frontline.thehindu.com/cover-story/what-is-hindu-rashtra/article23595906.ece

Dr. Hedgewar's thoughts on Sangh & Hindutva.

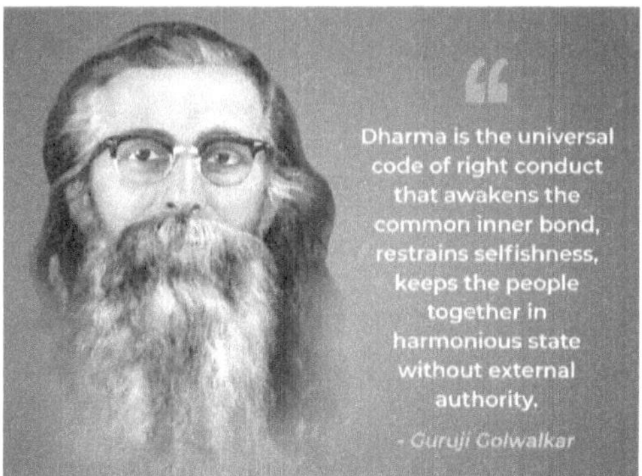

Guruji Golwalkar's Thoughts on Dharma.

Dr. Hedgewar Ji & Guruji Golwalkar had a profound influence on the ideals and principles that shaped the Sangh.

Core Ideas & The Philosophy of Sangh

The constitution of the Sangh which was written in 1949 lays down the basic philosophy of the organization, the preamble states – 'To eradicate the fissiparous tendencies arising from diversities of sect, faith, caste, creed, economic and linguistic differences amongst Hindus' this was the aim which Dr. Hedgewar has propagated, to make Hindus realize the greatness of their past and to inculcate in them a spirit of service, sacrifice, and selfless devotion to the Hindu samaj and the society as a whole; to build up an organized and well-disciplined life and to bring about an all-round regeneration of the Hindu society on the basis of Dharma and Sanskriti.[16]

Dr.Hedgewar believed that due to foreign rule, the nation had lost its cultural unity and identity. Thus, the restoration of that identity, unity of people, and connecting the nation's past to the future became important; from this idea, the core postulates of the Sangh's philosophy emerged, which were Rashtriyata (cultural nation), (Ekatmata) spiritual unity and (Samuhikta) oneness.

1. Rashtriyata (Cultural Nation)

The Sangh considers cultural unity as the most important in the nation; it considers language as a medium of carrier of culture thus, the Sangh believes it is necessary to promote all Bharatiya languages and different cultures existing in the nation.

2. Ekatmata (Spiritual Unity)

Sangh believes that Bharat is a cultural nation, and its foundation is in Ekatmata; it believes that spiritual unity and mutual understanding

---

16 Walter K. Anderson and Shridhar D. Damle, The Rss: A view to the inside, Penguin Viking, 2018 Appendix IX pg, 273-4

between different groups of people is most important for guiding the entire society.[17]

3. Samuhikta (Oneness)

Sangh's fundamental philosophy believes in creating harmony, trust, and mutual respect in the society, Sangh also considers the idea of collective spirit as important. Hence the, Sangh's temperament is scientific, and its decisions are logically derived.[17] The doctrine of Samuhikta believes that only when society irons out its internal differences only then a nation can progress.

According to the Sangh, its practise of Hindutva has three basic values: loyalty to the nation, respect for ancestors, and a common culture. The Sangh works to promote fraternity, and that is only possible through unity and diversity; Sangh emphasises that Hindutva comprises within itself the moral values in personal and public life, a deep sense of patriotism, and respect for all religions.

Equality and Samajik Samrasta

The Sangh works for uniting all classes, castes and establishing a strong Hindu society; at the individual level; the Sangh's training in personal qualities like diligence, moral imperatives, productive works, reflecting oneness with society, and carrying the message of Hindutva is of utmost importance. The idea of the Sangh for the alleviation of caste injustices is Samajik Samratsa, or social harmony, where equality is envisaged based on fraternity.

The Sangh shakha, which is the core philosophy of the Sangh, offers a unifying experience for the participants providing them with a similarity in speech and outlook. It also creates an aura of uniqueness

---

17   ABPS Resolution: Need to Protect and Promote Bharatiya Languages.; http//rss.org//
     Encyc/2018/3/10/aabps-resolution-2108.html, Access date July 12, 2019.

among those who successfully complete the training and induces them to respect each other to what they have become; members of all castes are welcomed into the Sangh and are treated as equals if they conform to the behavioural standards and discipline of the Sangh.

Dr. Hedgewar said caste discrimination has no place in the Hindu society, he was a believer in social equality. Untouchability, and the caste taboo have been kept out of the Sangh; he started the Sangh based on equal relations among all castes, no member is asked about caste identity in the organization, and no special arrangement is made for anyone in the shaka or in the daily activities of the Sangh.

The Sangh's faith lies in the Hindu nation, everyone belongs to Bharat Mata and are sons and daughters of Bharat Mata. All are Hindus, so there cannot be discrimination in relationships with each other. Swayamsevaks come from all castes, and all are equal. Thus, equality among them is an established principle.

The Sangh's work is constructive, and its people centric activities in all fields are related to progress and unity. It works to rebuild the Hindu society on the principles of equality; this is what distinguishes the Sangh from other organizations. Thus, for Sangh, there is no place for discrimination; Samajik Samrsata (social harmony) is a Sangh Samskara; the Sangh wants to see the inculcation of this Samajik Samrasata Samskara in society. For the past 98 years, Samrasta has been a ritual in the Sangh's daily conduct and in all events and programmes.

Sangh's focus is on Hindu Utthan, which means the upliftment of each and every section of the society. Away from publicity campaigns, the Sangh works quietly and diligently for social harmony in the society at all levels. The Sangh is firmed in its belief that the road to Samajik Samrasta lies in treating the Hindu faith and traditions with respect because only those parts of the Bharatiya subcontinent have survived as a multicultural, multifaith, open society where Hindus are a majority, and the Bharatiya world view is a vibrant force.

In consonance with the cultural heritage of the Hindu Samaj, the Sangh has abiding faith in the fundamental principle of respect towards all faiths. Bharat is recognised and respected for its non-aggressive way of life. It has spread its influence far and wide within philosophies, whether vedic or buddhist, but never did it resort to violence and conquest to spread its religions or faith.

"Om sarvey bhavantu sukhinaha
Sarvey santu niramaya
Sarvey bhadrani pashantu
Maa kashchit dukh bhag bhave
Om shanti shanti shanti."

Notions & Beliefs

Hindutva has an innate inclusive nature that flows from its philosophy ***"Ekam Sat, Vipra Bahudha Vadanti"***. The Hindu civilisation represents the true 'republic of faith' where every faith can have its say and be respected. The primary goal and the divine object of the Hindu nation inspired by the Sangh cadre is the concept of a nation that rests on the assumption that the cultural heritage of Bharat is derived from a common source. The Sangh is focussed on Vyakti Nirman (development of individual character) and Samajik Samrasta (social harmony).

The only thread that binds people together from Kashmir to Kanyakumari and from Gujarat to Guwahati is the ancient Hindu civilisation and its belief system. Sangh says that Bharat is a Hindu nation; it is only stating the obvious without malice towards anybody or any sense of negativity. We should, instead, celebrate this as a unique country in the world and the historical fact that the Hindus do not fight wars or impose their faith or way of life on others. From the time of the Cholas, Pallavas, and Pandyans, and prince Bodhidharma, the message of Dharma and religious faith has been spread with love and not the sword.

The Sangh believes that you elevate others only if you are elevated. Therefore, the Sangh has a mission of man making (Vyakti Nirman); this is the reason which has led the Swayamsevaks to be great and historic legends in every field of the society; Hindu upliftment is one of the important aspects of the Sangh.

Dharma, as per the Hindu tradition, is the 'rule of law' and the ethical conduct. The Sangh has only affirmed that Bharat cannot be an irreligious state in the name of secularism. The term 'Sarva Panth Samabhav' (equal respect for all faiths) is closer to the Hindu ethos, and should ideally be the conceptual framework for the country. Hindu connotes the national identity of Bharat as not merely religious faith but identification with the national mainstream. It indicates policies and practices based on this spirit of Hindutva.

It must be noted that Sangh does not have a closed-door policy towards christians and muslims; it welcomes them into the shakha and the organization. The Sangh is neither against the freedom of religion nor does it want christians and muslims to be banished from the nation. The Sangh rightly sees christianity and islamism as non-indic religions that were imposed on Bharat through military conquest and political domination. However, it does not insist that christians and muslims should abandon their faith.

The Sangh believes Bharat is a Hindu Rashtra, but that does not mean that it will not include muslims or other communities. The Sangh believes that muslims of the nation form an integral part of the nation and they should be taken along in the nation building process.

Importance of Mission

The mission of the Sangh is to unite and rejuvenate the nation on the sound foundation of Dharma. This mission can be achieved by a strong and united Hindu society. Therefore, the Sangh has undertaken the task of uniting the Hindus.

Guruji Golwalkar described the mission of the Sangh as the revitalization of the Bharatiya value system based on universalism, peace, and prosperity to all, which is *"Vasudhaiva Kutumbakam,"* the worldview that the whole world is one family, propounded by the ancient thinkers of Bharat, is considered as one of the ideologies of the organization.[18] The rejuvenation of the Hindu nation is in the interest of the whole humanity. From Dr. Hedgewar's time till today, Hindu unity has been an essential perspective of the Sangh.

The Sangh is Built on Human Relations

A Swayamsevak learns to overcome his own personal likes and dislikes, and even modify his basic personality traits to have better relations with people. He learns to work with people from diverse backgrounds. As he moves up the ladder of hierarchy, he learns to coordinate between different teams and work without bias and prejudice with different kinds of people.

Personality Development

One learns to recognise his own inherent skills and of his colleagues and nurtures them, as a Swayamsevak becomes a Karyakarta (a more active volunteer), giving more time and energy to organizational work, he hones his skills further. From being a member of a local shakha, he graduates to being a senior worker who handles the coordination of various activities of the Sangh. A Swayamsevak, thus, gradually gets

---

18   Rashtriya Swayamsevak Sangh – https://www.rss.org/

involved in management, managing as well as building teams. He learns how to motivate his team members and get tasks done with a sense of joy. He is trained to identify a problem, study it and resolve it. He learns how to manage things by taking people together, this leads to personality development and building of character.

The Intellectual Discourses & Learnings
(Baudhik Sessions)

In the Sangh shiksha varg camps, Swayamsevaks are taught moral and civic lessons which are very close to the core Sangh philosophy; the Baudhik sessions are such discussions in which the Swayamsevaks learn about the core ideology and philosophy of the Sangh, also many issues of national and international importance are discussed and debated in the Baudhik sessions.

The Baudhik session constitutes one of the most important parts of the Sangh shiksha vargs and the training methodology. A Swayamsevak learns and records certain aspects of their learning during the Baudhik sessions Such as: –

- A Swayamsevak should behave like an ideal person in the society; he should never indulge and commit any anti-social activity or action which could harm the society and bring disrepute to the Sangh.
- The main philosophy of the Sangh was always to prevent the disintegration of the Hindu society and to stop the dilution of Hindutva.
- The Sangh emphasises that proper Sanskar creation and inculcation in a Swayamsevak is the main philosophy of the Sangh.
- The objectives of the shakha is to develop and create leadership qualities in the Swayamsevaks and to affirm their devotion towards the Hindu Rashtra.

- In the Sangh, each and every one is equal, and everyone shares a common brotherhood, without any discrimination.
- At the end of the Sangh shiksha varg, the Swayamsevaks write about their experiences in the camp on topics such as;
- What are the main ideals and philosophy of the Sangh, what is the Sangh's perspective about Hindutva.

New topics are regularly introduced and discussed in Baudhik sessions and workshops. Even guest speakers are invited for specialised topics. Topics like comparative religious studies, study and analysis of different ideologies and challenges to the nation have also been introduced.

Through the Baudhik sessions, personality development and character building happen effortlessly and unknowingly. One learns to think, give speeches, discuss issues, work together and relate to people belonging to different ages, social status or educational backgrounds. In a few years, he becomes a better person emerging from this system that hones his personality.

The Bhagwa Dhwaj (Saffron Flag)

The Bhagwa Dhwaj is hoisted in Sangh shakhas and functions of the Sangh; the shakha begins with the salutation to the Dhwaj, this tradition has been followed since the Sangh was established. At the beginning and at the end of every shakha, a salutation is given by the Swayamsevaks to the Dhwaj. The Sangh shakha begins daily with a ceremonial hosting of the Dhwaj and ends with the lowering down of the Dhwaj in a prescribed manner; it is hoisted in almost all programmes and functions of the Sangh.

A unique feature of the Sangh is that the Guru, the supreme teacher of the Sangh, is not a person. It is the Bhagwa Dhwaj, Dr.Hedgewar realised through his long social career that no person can be perfect.

A Guru has to be as perfect as possible; the Guru must also reflect all the qualities that the organization. Considering all these factors, Dr.Hedgewar decided that Bhagwa Dhwaj should be the supreme teacher (Guru) of the Sangh.

Every year on the day of Vyas Poornima, the Bhagwa Dhwaj is worshipped formally, this is known as Guru Pooja and is one of the main festivals of the Sangh. The first Guru Pooja was organised in 1928; since then, there has been no break in this tradition, and the Bhagwa Dhwaj continues to occupy the highest position in the Sangh hierarchy.

The Bhagwa Dhwaj is a symbol of the national culture and tradition of Bharat since ages, the Bhagwa and similar coloured flags have been adopted by several organizations like the Bhartiya Mazdoor Sangh, ABVP, Bhartiya Kisan Sangh and the Vishwa Hindu Parishad. The Bhagwa Dhwaj has always been respected in Hindu social life; it finds its mention in vedic literature, as Arun Ketu, the Bhagwa Dhwaj has been a source of inspiration for Hindus.

The Bhagwa colour is also related to the spiritual tradition of Bharat and also with the Bhakti movement, which was connected to the revival of Hinduism; the Dhwaj reflects inspiring qualities like passion, renunciation, sacrifice, and patriotism.

Why Bhagwa Dhwaj is the Guru in the Sangh: -

1. First, to make an organization stand unitedly, and for this, a flag remains historically one of the most influential means.

2. Cultural nationalism, one of Sangh's key building blocks, finds its most comprehensive reflection in the Bhagwa Dhwaj.

Sangh wanted to ensure that it does not become a person centric organization. Therefore, the Bhagwa Dhwaj is considered a symbol of the highest position in the Sangh.

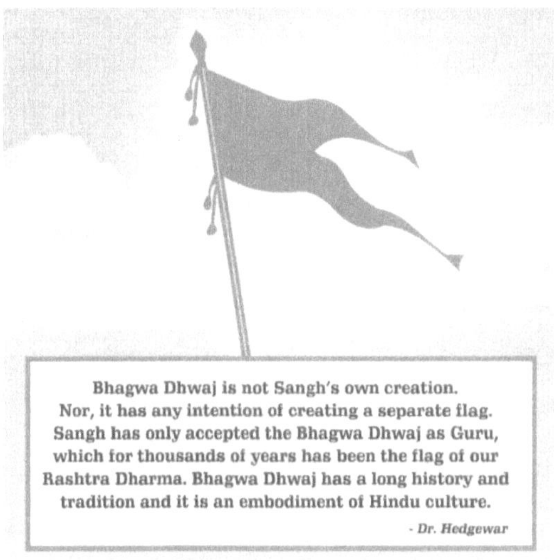

The Bhagwa Dhwaj which is Considered as the 'Guru' in the Sangh.

Swayamsevaks Preform the Sangh Prayer (Prarthana)
Infront of the Bhagwa Dhwaj.

The Prayer

Everyday all the Sangh shakas end with a prayer (Prarthana) recited by the Swayamsevaks present at the shaka. The Swayamsevaks stand in columns and rows in attention at the venue where the shaka is taking place, one person recites the prayer and the rest of the Swayamsevaks repeat the lines and bow their head to the Bhagwa Dhwaj. In addition to the daily shaka, all the major programmes of the Sangh wind up formally with the recital of the Sangh prayer. The prayer is in Sanskrit and is considered to be very sacred by the Swayamsevaks as it is an explicit tribute to the motherland; the objective of the prayer is to strengthen the feeling of nationalism among the Swayamsevaks.

To bring uniformity in the shakas, the idea of a prayer came forward, and the issues of developing a Sangh prayer in 1930s was discussed within the organization, initially the prayer was penned in Marathi, and then the Karvayah of the Mohite shaka at Nagpur, Sh. Naraynrao Bhide was entrusted to convert the Marathi prose into the Sanskrit prayer.

The Sangh Prarthana in Sanskrit – *'Namaste Sada Vatsale Matrbhume'*, was first publicly sung by Sangh pracharak Sh. Yadav Rao Joshi on May 18, 1940 in Sangh shiksha varg held at Nagpur. During the same period, in another Sangh shiksha varg held in Pune, the Sangh Prarthana was sung by pracharak Sh. Anant Rao Kale. The prayer is inspiring, humbling, and arouses the most noble and selfless thoughts to serve the motherland and dharma. In every Sangh shiksha varg, special Baudhik sessions are earmarked for explaining the prayer in depth and detail.

प्रार्थना

नमस्ते सदा वत्सले मातृभूमे
त्वया हिन्दभूमे सुखं वर्धितोऽहम्।
महामङ्गले पुण्यभूमे त्वदर्थे
पतत्वेष कायो नमस्ते नमस्ते॥1॥
प्रभो शक्तिमन् हिन्दराष्ट्राङ्गभूता
इमे सादरं त्वां नमामो वयम्
त्वदीयाय कार्याय बद्धा कटीयम्
शुभामाशिषं देहि तत्पूर्तये।
अजय्यां च विश्वस्य देहीश शक्तिम्
सुशीलं जगद्येन नम्रं भवेत्
श्रुतं चैव यत्कण्टकाकीर्णमार्गम्
स्वयं स्वीकृतं नः सुगं कारयेत्॥2॥
समुत्कर्ष निःश्रेयसस्यैकमुग्रम्
परं साधनं नाम वीरव्रतम्
तदन्तः स्फुरत्वक्षया ध्येयनिष्ठा
हृदन्तः प्रजागर्तु तीव्राऽनिशम्।
विजेत्री च नः संहता कार्यशक्तिर्
विधायास्य धर्मस्य संरक्षणम्
परं वैभवं नेतुमेतत् स्वराष्ट्रम्
समर्था भवत्वाशिषा ते भृशम्॥3॥
॥भारत माता की जय॥

Festivals of The Rashtriya Swayamsevak Sangh

Each year the Rashtriya Swayamsevak Sangh celebrates six festivals which are known as Utsav; these festivals not only articulate the experience of those taking parts in the shaka but also cultivate the ideology and spirit of the Swayamsevaks.

The Sangh has chosen these festivals as they synergise the organization with happiness and joy, one must understand that the Sangh has not created any festival, but these festivals are of national importance. The Hindu society has been celebrating them since time immemorial.

The Sangh celebrates six festivals through a Hindu calendar year.

- **Varsha Pratipadh.** – The festivals begin with the Hindu new year, which generally is in the month of April; it is also known as Gudi Padwa in Maharashtra and with other names such as Bihu, Polia, Baishakh, and Cheti Chand in different parts of the nation.

  This festival provides the shaka leadership with an opportunity to evaluate the previous year's progress. The date also coincides with the birthday of Dr. Hedgewar Ji and is also celebrated as Founder's Day. The Sangh celebrates this festival as the Hindu new year; many important events are associated with this day as king Vikramaditya defeated the shakha invaders, so a new Hindu calendar began on this day called Vikramsamvat. Lord Rama's coronation as the king of Ayodhya happened on this day, Maharishi Dayananda established the Arya samaj on this day. The Swayamsevaks wear full Ganvesh (uniform) on this day and a salute is given to the founder of the Sangh, which is called as 'Aadya Sarsanghchalak Pranam', senior Sangh functionaries also deliver intellectual lectures on this day, several Sangh shakhas and sports competitions are also held.

- **Hindu Samrajya Divotsava** – The second festival is the coronation ceremony of Sh. Shivaji Maharaj, which is known and celebrated to honour the Hindu victory over Mughal rule. The Baudhiks at this festival frequently emphasise the virtue of strength, bravery and courage. Shivaji Maharaj was the first Hindu to declare a kingdom based on Hindutva. His act of setting up the Hindu empire boosted the morale of the Hindus immensely. The Sangh chose this date to awaken the spirit of bravery and self-confidence.

- **Guru Dakshina** – This is the third festival; on this occasion, an annual function named Guru Poojan and Guru Dakshina (worshipping the guru), takes place on the auspicious occasion of Guru Purnima. Worshipping and expressing one's gratitude to teachers is done and celebrated all over Bharat since time immemorial.

On this occasion, the Swayamsevaks make contributions to their Guru, which is the Bhagwa Dhwaj; most of the funds of the organization are raised in this Utsav; each Swayamsevak goes before the Bhagwa Dhwaj and offers pranam and flowers to the Dhwaj, near the Bhagwa Dhwaj are photographs of Hindu warriors and respected men such as Sh. Guru Gobind Singh Ji, Sh.Shivaji Maharaj and Rana Pratap Maharaj. The Swayamsevaks, on the occasion, wear white clothes, such as kurta pyjama and the Guru Purnima Mahotsav, forms the most important festivals of the Sangh. This day is also called Vyas Pooja in the memory of ancient Guru Ved Vyas. In this programme, all members bow before the Guru (Bhagwa Dhwaj), offer flowers and dedicate their contribution in an unmarked envelope. This contribution is deposited with the local branch and is used for various Sangh activities thus, the Sangh is a fully self-financed organisation. It is a self-propelled

The Gurudakshina Festival of the Sangh.

Swayamsevaks Perform During the Vijayadashmi Festival (Utsav) in Nagpur.

movement, powered by selfless citizens. It is a powerhouse for all the activities of nation-building.

- **Raksha Bandhan** – It is the fourth festival which celebrates the pious relationship between brother and sister; this festival provides an opportunity for a sister to reaffirm her brother's obligation of continued safety and protection; she does this by tying a silk thread around her brother's wrist. In the Sangh's adaption of this festival, the Mukhya Shikshak or Karavyah gives each Swayamsevak rakhis to tie around the wrist of the fellow Swayamsevaks; the Baudhik sessions emphasises that this festival creates brotherhood and fraternity. On this festival, the Swayamsevaks also tie rakhi to the members of the society.

- **Vijayadashmi (Dusshera)** – The fifth festival, is the festival which celebrates the victory of truth over deceit and malice, the victory of good over evil; it is a victory of light over darkness; it is considered to be one the biggest festival across Bharat and the world.

This festival commemorates the victory of Prabhu Sh. Ram over Ravana; before this formal function, the Sangh band march (Path Sanchalan) is organized throughout the city in which uniformed Swayamsevaks participate in full Ganvesh. The band plays martial music, and Swayamsevaks sings patriotic songs. There is another vital significance of this day: the Sangh was founded on the (Vijaydashmi Day) on September 27, 1925
Also, on this day in central and north states of the nation, the ceremony called Shastra Pujan is held, which symbolises the qualities of bravery and valour among the Swayamsevaks; on this day, the Param Pujaniye Sarsanghchalak delivers a speech at Nagpur, the headquarters of the Sangh.

- **Makarsankarnti Mahostava** – Concluding the festival year is the celebration which is personal renunciation and service to the nation. It is one of the most important festivals of Hindus and is celebrated in the month of Magh (January), this festival is also known as Uttrayan, and this festival marks the commencement of the sun's journey to the Makar Rashi. The festival celebrates the revival of activity in every aspect as it demarcates a change of season. It is the last festival in the calendar year of the Sangh when peer review begins informally, resulting in new responsibilities and reorganization of activities.

The Sangh has given new meaning to the traditional festivals; the festivals are celebrated with immense enthusiasm among the Swayamsevaks and are also a means to project a social message among people and inspire the society.

Women's Perspective in the RSS

"Woman is the inspiring force for the family and the nation. So long as this force is not awakened, society cannot progress" – **Laxmibai Kelkar, Founder of Rashtra Sevika Samiti.**

"If we want to build a Vishwa Guru Bharat, then just men's participation is not enough. Equal participation of women is also required; Parampujaniye Sarsanghchalak Mohan Bhagwat Ji had said this at the Vijaydashmi festival a few years back.[19] He emphasised the value of women in achieving the goal of Bharat regaining its position as a 'Vishwa Guru', in the nation women are revered as the 'Mother of The Universe' or 'Jagat Janani', and the Sangh considers women as a quintessential part of the nation's development and growth.

---

19 Organiser – https://organiser.org/2022/08/22/91956/bharat/rss-working-to-make-india-a-model-society-for-the-entire-world-mohan-bhagwat/

Smt.Laxmibai Kelkar (Mausiji)
Founder of the Rashtra Sevika Samiti.

**Sevikas Participating in the March
Past in Rajkot, Gujarat.**

The Insignia of the Rashtra Sevika Samiti.

Women in the Sangh are associated with the Rashtra Sevika Samiti founded by Smt. Laxmibai Kelkar in 1936; she wished to fight the marginalisation of women in society. She was convinced that the woman of the house was the one who initiated and nurtured the value system or Sanskar in the society. She needs to, be made aware of her responsibility & role in the outside world.

A woman is more than only a wife, mother, or sister. With this in mind, Laxmibai Kelkar had met Dr. Hedgewar in the mid 1930's and had an idea for an organisation on the lines of the Sangh. He conveyed his inability to organise such an organisation for women, however he assured full cooperation to her if she were to start such a parallel organisation for women. Thus, Rashtra Sevika Samiti was born.

The Sevika Samiti is a mirror image of the Sangh, in terms of its programme, priorities, and departments; many women of the Sevika Samithi have contributed to many important events, such as the relief works of the Sangh during partition, during emergencies and many disaster relief operations of the Sangh also. The Sevika Samiti also has a uniform (Ganvesh) like the Sangh, the training programme of the Sevika Samithi too resembles the Sangh as it has first year, second year and third year training camps for fifteen days in May and June each year, every year more than ten thousand women attend these camps.

All positions in the Sevika Samithi are controlled by women, and they carry out all responsibilities. Each state has a Pracharika; approximately there are 4,900 Shakhas of the Sevika Samithi across the nation. The Sevika Samithi runs 15 education projects and has nearly 385 service initiatives. Globally it has its network in 22 countries across the world. It has established overseas branches in 10 countries, which use the name *Hindu Sevika Samiti.*

The Samiti operates in 5215 centers, and 875 centers conduct the Shakhas daily. The estimates of active membership range from six lakhs to one million. The samiti also runs numerous service projects all over the nation for the underprivileged and weaker sections, these include goshalas, libraries, computer training centres, and orphanages. The Samiti is headquartered in Dhantoli Nagpur, commonly known as Ahilya Mandir; it has a well-developed intellectual training material and methodology, though it borrows physical training process from the Sangh. The Samiti is focused on women's issues, it has a presence across the nation; the organisation is doing a great service by defining women's important role in society.

The Samiti has a "three-point ideal" of 'Matrutva' (Motherhood), 'Kartrutva' (Performance and Efficiency) and 'Netrutva' (Leadership). Three personalities who stand for the above ideals are Jijabai Bhonsle, Ahilya Bai Holkar & Rani Laxmibai of Jhansi, respectively; they are the role model for every Sevika. The organization believes that all women can positively change their community and society. The Samiti is actively contributing to the development and growth of the nation, and the Sangh appreciates its efforts; the Sangh sees women as playing a very pivotal role in imparting the right value systems in the family and providing moral and physical support to the development of society in every sphere today and for times to come.

CHAPTER – 5

Leadership & Impact ~ Sarsanghchalaks of the RSS

Introduction

The Sarsanghchalak is the head of the Sangh, it is the topmost position in the Sangh's organizational hierarchy. He plays an important role when it comes to the structure, scope, and direction of the Sangh. He is not just the face of the organization but takes on the role of its guide and philosopher.

The Sarsanghchalak is the head of the organization to whom every person within and outside looks up to, because he is the person whose conduct mirrors the Sangh itself. This puts an enormous responsibility on him as he is supposed to personify the best traditions of the Sangh. The personality of the Sarsanghchalak, their humility and transparency in behaviour is another significant quality. They are always balanced in their approach, they radiate happiness, their lives are an inspiration for millions of Swayamsevaks and Sangh volunteers. The Sangh has been very fortunate in terms of its leadership bank.

All those who have become Sarsanghchalaks have been stalwarts amongst men; this is a rare achievement to have. This chapter gives an insight in the lives, tenures, and contributions of the six Sarsanghchalaks of the Sangh, since its formation in 1925, till today

Sh. Keshav Baliram Hedgewar (Doctor Ji)
First Sarsanghchalak (Founder of The Sangh)

Param Pujaniye Doctor Ji, is the founder of the Rashtriya Swayamsevak Sangh, he founded the Sangh in Nagpur in September 1925. On the day of Vijayadashami, to organize the Hindu community for its cultural and spiritual regeneration and for achieving complete independence for a united Bharat. He oversaw it as an organization based on the ideology of Hindutva and Hindu Rashtra.[20]

Sh. Hedgewar was born in Nagpur in a Telegu-speaking family in 1889; his parents, unfortunately, died in the plague epidemic when he was only 13 years old. Sh. Balakrishna Shivram Moonje, who was the national president of the Hindu Mahasabha, became the guardian and father figure to him. After completing his education at the Rashtriya Vidyalaya in Yavatmal, Pune, he was sent to Calcutta by Sh. B.S Moonje, to study medicine, in Calcutta he had joined the Anushilan Samithi, which was the underground movement of the revolutionaries.

In his initial years, he was a member of the congress, but later became deloused by their politics and policies; he was deeply influenced by the writings of Sh. Bal Gangadhar Tilak, and Sh. Madan Mohan Malviya.

He considered that the cultural and religious heritage of Hindus should be the basis of Bharatiya brotherhood and nationhood. He was deeply influenced by V.D Savarkar's treatise on Hindutva. Dr. Hedgewar designed the Sangh as a distinct organisation of selfless workers called Swayamsevaks; through this, he also strengthened and reignited the spirit of Hindutva. He also supported the setting up of the Rashtra Sevika Samiti in 1936.

---

20   We Must Always Be Proud to Serve – Balagokulam. https://balagokulam.hssus.org/course/we-must-always-be-proud/

During his tenure as Sarsanghchalak, national personalities like Mahatma Gandhi, Netaji Subash Chandra Bose and Dr. B.R Ambedkar visited the camps of Sangh and its shakhas, Gandhi Ji visited the Sangh camp in Wardha Maharashtra in 1934, and he was very praise worthy of the organisation and deeply appreciated Dr. Hedgewar's efforts, Dr. B.R Ambedkar was surprised to see the Swayamsevak's working tirelessly for the nation while forgetting all caste identities.

There are not many individuals like Dr. Hedgewar who cast such a long spell on the nation's history and its political destiny; he established the Sangh as an organisation which, arguably is the largest and the most enduring voluntary organisation in the world; he was such a great personality who let his creation speak rather than pushing himself to the front. He was a nation builder, a visionary, and a thinker; he was a unique person, and a strategist par excellence; he was a motivator for millions of people to forget personal gains and comfort for the national cause. One could have imagined Doctor Ji's vision of creating an organisation so huge and multifarious in all aspects of society.

In times when political parties were busy with personal gains, Doctor Ji envisioned creating an organisation for the Hindus and for Bharat Mata. Dr. Hedgewar's contribution to the Hindu nation through the creation of the Sangh is incomparable; he will always inspire the future generations.

Sh. Laxman Vasudev Paranjape Ji
(Interim Sarsanghchalak)

Sh. Laxman Vasudev Paranjape was one of the founding members of the Sangh along with Dr. Keshav Baliram Hedgewar Ji. He founded a volunteer organisation called as Bharat Swayamsevak Mandal, what is more interesting to know is that all the volunteers of the Bharat

Swayamsevak Mandal were asked to wear a uniform which was interestingly later on adopted by the Sangh as its official uniform (Ganvesh) from 1925 to 1940.

Sh. L.V Paranjape was also instrumental in setting up and expanding Sangh's base and shakhas in Maharashtra. He became the Sarsanghchalak for a year. When Dr. Hedgewar was arrested and jailed for participating and leading the forest satyagraha, he relinquished the post of Sarsanghchalak, on July 12, 1930. Sh. Paranjape took over the leadership of the Sangh. The short stint of Sh. Paranjape was continued till February 14, 1931.

Sh. Madhav Sadashivrao Golwalkar Ji (Guruji)
Second Sarsanghchalak

Madhav Sadashivrao Golwalkar was the second Sarsanghchalak of the Sangh; he is fondly known as Guruji, a name initially used by his students at Banaras Hindu University, where he used to teach. He was born in a Marathi family in Ramtek near Nagpur in Maharashtra. He is considered the most influential and prominent figures among the Sangh; he was the first person to put forward the concept of a cultural nation called a Hindu Rashtra, which is believed to have evolved into the concept of the Akhanda Bharat theory.

He initially enrolled at Hislop college, a missionary run institute in Nagpur; he revolted against the open advocacy of christianity and the anti-Hindu sentiment in the college; he refused to abide by anti-Hindu views and left for the Banaras Hindu University in Varanasi, there he received the bachelor of science degree in 1927 and a masters in biology degree in 1929. Madan Mohan Malviya, the founder of Banaras Hindu University, greatly influenced him. Guruji Golwalkar started teaching at the BHU in August 1931 and taught zoology for three years.

In 1931 Dr. Hedgewar Ji visited Banaras, and he met Guruji Golwalkar; after returning to Nagpur, Hedgewar Ji exerted greater influence on Guruji; according to Sangh sources, Sh. Hedgewar encouraged Guru Golwalkar to pursue law as it would give him the reputation required as a Sangh leader. In 1934 Dr.Hedgewar made Sh. Golwalkar the Sarvardhikari of the Sangh shiksha varg in Akola, Maharashtra. In October 1936, Sh. Golwalkar, for a brief period, became a Sanyasi and a disciple of Swami Akhanananda, who was a disciple of Guru Ram Krishna Paramhans.

After a short period in West Bengal, he returned to Nagpur, and Dr. Hedgewar made him realize that his services and obligation to society could best be utilized by working for the Sangh. Dr. Hedgewar personally groomed Sh. Golwalkar, and from 1937 to 1939, he was in charge of the all-India officers training camp. In 1939 at the Guru Dakshina Utsav of the Sangh Sh. Hedgewar announced that Guru Golwalkar would be the Sarkaryavaha (General Secretary) of the Sangh.

A day before his death on June 21, 1940, Dr. Hedgewar gave Sh. Golwalkar a sheet of paper asking him to be the Sangh leader. On July 3, the five state-level Sanghchalak in Nagpur announced Dr. Hedgewar's decision, and Guru Golwalkar was made the Sarsanghchalak. Guru Golwalkar was an ordained Sanyasi. He was deeply impressed by Dr. Hedgewar's selfless patriotism and immense hard work; he was elevated as the Sarsanghchalak at the young age of 34.

The task at hand for Sh. Guruji was huge when he took over as Sarsanghchalak in 1940, firstly he had to make the Sangh a cadre-based organization which had a pan nation spread, and secondly, he had to train himself mentally to lead such a huge organization.

Dr. Keshav Baliram Hedgewar Ji
The Founder & First Sarsanghchalak of the Sangh.

Sh. Guru Golwalkar Ji
The Second Sarsanghchalak of the Sangh.

Sh. Laxman Vasudev Paranjappe Ji
(Interim Sarsanghchalak).

He remained the Sangh Sarsanghchalak for 33 years, from 1940 to 1973. Sh Golwalkar is regarded as one of the most influential figures in modern Indian history. As the Sangh Sarsanghchalak, he made the Sangh as one of the strongest social service and volunteer organization in the nation, the membership of the Sangh expanded from 35,000 Swayamsevaks to nearly over one million, under his leadership. Sh. Golwalkar is regarded as a builder and organiser of the Sangh; when he passed away in 1973, there were nearly 10,000 active shakhas across the nation. Many organizations affiliated with the Sangh Parivar and the Sangh were established under his tenure.

The Sangh was initially banned in 1948, under his tenure, but despite many challenges and censures by the government, he took the Sangh to great institutional strength. The Swayamsevaks of today are greatly indebted to Guruji Golwalkar as he ensured that Sangh gets over the ban and emerges as an organization with greater ideological clarity and stronger organizational structure.

The Sangh began the system of having full-time pracharaks; under his tenure, pracharaks were sent across the country for the propagation and expansion of the Sangh work. He will always be remembered as a leader under whom the Sangh grew considerably as an organization, and will always be regarded as a person of highest integrity and an organizational genius.

Jagadguru Shankaracharya of Puri said, "He was a saint in white robes," he inspired the qualities of patriotism, dedication, and service in thousands of youths of the country. Sh. Guruji will always be an inspiration to Swayamsevaks, he was a person blessed with exceptional intellectual capability, and there is no doubt that he was truly a Rashtra Rishi.

Sh. Madhukar Dattatreya Deoras Ji
(Balasaheb Deoras) | Third Sarsanghchalak

Sh. Balasaheb Deoras was the third Sarsanghchalak of the Sangh; he was born in Nagpur and raised in Andhra Pradesh, his younger brother Sh. Bhaurao Deoras was also a senior leader and a pracharak of the Sangh. Dr. Hedgewar inspired him, and he decided to dedicate his life at a very young age to the Sangh. He was a quint essential man of the organizational process setup by Dr.Hedgewar; he joined the Sangh in 1926-1927. He was one of the few Swayamsevaks who attended the first batch of shakha, which was initiated and started by Dr. Hedgewar at Mohite Wada in Nagpur.

During his tenure as in charge of Nagpur, Balasaheb displayed exemplary organizational skills, he is known to have started 15 new shakas simultaneously, and he ensured a steady flow of full-time workers to take the Sangh's work to other states, this helped Dr.Hedegwar to focus on the expansion of the organization.

The concept of morning shakhas was started in 1938, by the effort of Balasaheb; the first morning shakha of Sangh was started at Mohite Wada in Nagpur.[21] He obtained his law degree from the Nagpur university in 1938, and though being trained as a lawyer, he dedicated his life to the Sangh. He worked as a pracharak in north India, and spent a major part of his life in Uttar Pradesh. He nurtured many wonderful leaders such as Sh. Deendayal Upadhyay, Sh. Atal Bihari Vajpayee, Sh. Ashok Singhal, Prof. Rajendra Singh, Sh. Murli Manohar Joshi, Sh. Baleshwar Agrawal, and Sh. Laxmanrao Bhide.

He played an influential role in the publication of Tarun Bharat, which is currently the 7th largest daily selling newspaper in the country. Under Sh. Deoras the Sangh took a turn towards activism. He said that

---

21   https://organiser.org/2022/11/28/16070/bharat/harbinger-of-samajik-samarasata-remembering-balasaheb-deoras-on-his-birth-anniversary/

the Sangh believes in one culture and one nation, that is Hindu Rasthra, but the definition of Hindu is not limited to any faith.

A brainchild of Sh. Deoras was the Swadeshi Jagran Manch; he also wrote many books in both English and Hindi language, he was a crusader against untouchability in society, and he said that we should accept that untouchability is a grave error and we must do away with it completely. Sh. Deoras instilled the idea that the only guiding principle of Hindustan is a Hindu Rashtra. He pioneered the strategy of the Sangh, not limiting itself to shakhas but expanding into all walks of life. He was responsible for training and sending pracharaks across the nation. He was one of the important leaders in the struggle to oversee the Sangh work in 1948, during the ban, he took guidance from Guruji for managing the underground activities of the Sangh.

After the ban on the Sangh was lifted in July 1949, he wrote an article titled '***Sangh Ka Agla Kadam***', in the Hindi weekly Yugadharma, which outlined the Sangh's future course of action; in the article, he elaborated on how the Sangh would expand in all walks of life. In 1963, Balasaheb was appointed as 'Sah Sarkaryavah' (Joint general secretary) when Sh. Bhaiyyaji Daani was 'Sarkaryavah' (General secretary) of the Sangh. In 1965, Balasaheb was appointed as Sarkaryavah. In 1973, he became Sarsanghchalak of the Sangh. He was an organizer par excellence, he was the Sarsanghchalak during the emergency, and he led a spectacular fight against the emergency imposed by the congress government in 1975.

Sh. Balasaheb contributed immensely to the social service aspect of the Sangh; what started as a plan to set up one thousand social service projects during Dr. Hedgewar's birth centenary celebrations in 1989 has grown today to over 175,000 service projects across the nation. He was also at the helm of affairs during the historic Ekatmata Yatra and Ram Janambhoomi Andolan. The movements that changed the perspective of Hindus about their national identity and unity. He also played a crucial role in expanding Sangh's work in Assam, Bihar, and Bengal.

Balasaheb was an organizational scientist trained in Dr Hedgewar's school of thought. His initiative of starting the Samarasta Manch to propagate harmony and equity within Hindu society was a major initiative to defeat casteism in the society. He supported inter-caste marriages. In his presence, a new platform, Sarva Panth Samadar Manch (Equal respect to all faiths), was created by Sh.Dattopant Thengadi. It was an effort to have honest interfaith dialogue.

He pursued the idea of Sewa (service), Samarasta (social harmony), And Sangharsh (struggle) and infused a new consciousness into the organization. He guided the Sangh cadre to the mainstream issues of society as corruption, environmental conservation & propagation of Hindutva. Balasaheb Deoras's tenure as Sarsanghchalak was very successful, and the changes he brought in the Sangh have been instrumental in helping the organization spread its base across the nation.

Sh. Rajendra Singh Ji

(Rajju Bhaiya) Fourth Sarsanghchalak

Prof. Sh. Rajendra Singh, popularly known as Rajju Bhaiya, was the fourth Sarsanghchalak of the Sangh between 1994 and 2000; he was born in Bulandshar district of Uttar Pradesh, he obtained his education from the University of Allahabad and completed his B.Sc, M.Sc & Ph.D. Doctorate.

He worked as a professor and head of the department of physics at the University of Allahabad, but to devote his life to the Sangh and the organisation, he left his job in 1965, in 1966 he became a pracharak. He was acknowledged as an exceptionally brilliant student by Dr. C.V Raman; he was an expert in nuclear physics, which was very rare in the nation in those days.[22]

---

22   Rajju Bhayya – Nuclear Physics Professor who became Sarsanghchalak | Arise Bharat. https://arisebharat.com/2019/01/29/rajju-bhayya-nuclear-physics-professor-who-became-sarsanghchalak/

He came in active contact with the Sangh during the Quit India movement in 1942; he began his journey in the Sangh from Uttar Pradesh and progressed up to the level of Sarkaryavah (General secretary) in the 1980s. Sh. Rajju Bhaiya was appointed the Sarsanghchalak of the Sangh in march 1994, after Sh. Balasaheb Deoras retired from the position of Sarsanghchalak due to health grounds.

His passion for education encouraged the Sangh affiliate organizations to contribute to education across Bharat. Interestingly he along with Sh. Nanaji Deshmukh and Sh. Bhaorao Deoras, with the support of Guruji Golwalkar initiated the education movement of the Sangh, which was the Saraswati Shishu Mandir, in 1948-1950. The Saraswati Shishu Mandir is one of the nation's largest chain of schools, with nearly 27,000 schools; the first Shishu Mandir was founded in 1952 in Uttar Pradesh.

Sh. Rajju Bhaiya, for twenty-five years, was a teacher as well as a pracharak, a rare combination. He was moulded by first-generation pracharaks like Sh. Bapurao Moghe, Sh. Bhaurao Deoras, Sh. Nanaji Deshmukh and Sh. Madhavrao Deshmukh, among others. He also explained how to make a shakha stronger and more impactful. He used a simple formula for this. He called it the Sangh five formula.

S1: Sankhya (Good attendance in large numbers that can make the shakha experience better)

S2: Sanch (Structured teams that can conduct programmes in a shakha)

S3: Samskara (Programmes that impart values)

S4: Sampark (Regular contact with swayamsevaks and people in the locality)

S5: Sneh (Warm relations and programmes that enhance brotherly bonds).[23]

---

23 Ratan Sharda – RSS, Evolution from an Organization to a Movement (Chapter – 5 Rajju Bhaiya.), Rupa Publications India (10 October 2020). Pg-251.

Sh. Rajju Bhaiya's scientific temper, keenness about numbers, and eye for detail were seen in his reporting style as the Sarkaryavah. He was the first Sarkaryavah who asked for written reports from the state units of the Sangh and presented statistical details of the Sangh's work in the Pratinidhi Sabha.

He was the Sarkaryavah during the Ram Mandir movement and played a crucial role as the interface between the movement and the government. It was a period when there was a gain in the strength of the Sangh and its affiliates like the VHP. His scholarly scientific study of Hindutva gave a direction to Sangh Karyakartas about how an intellectual approach could be used to present the Sangh philosophy to people at large in a simple way.

He donated his paternal house to Saraswati Shishu Mandir in Allahabad, the prime qualities of Sh. Rajju Bhaiya were to love all, treat all as his own, tell what is the truth and adapt a simple lifestyle in a tribute to Rajju Bhaiya, the Allahabad state university was named as Professor Rajendra Singh university Prayagraj; he was a Swayamsevak par excellence and groomed a nursery of Swayamsevaks who went on to became leaders in the society.

Sh. K.S Sudharshan Ji
Fifth Sarsanghchalak

Sh. K.S Sudarshan Ji was a telecommunication engineer by profession. He became Sarsanghchalak of the Sangh on March 10, 2000; he was the fifth Sarsanghchalak of the Sangh from 2000 to 2009. He was known for his sharp intellect, wisdom, and deep knowledge of a wide range of subjects ranging from Hindutva to foreign policy. He became a Swayamsevak when he was only nine years old.

Sh. Madhukar Dattatreya Deoras Ji
(Balasaheb Deoras) | Third Sarsanghchalak.

Sh. Rajendra Singh Ji
(Rajju Bhaiya) Fourth Sarsanghchalak.

Sh. K.S Sudharshan Ji
Fifth Sarsanghchalak.

In 1954 he became a pracharak of the Sangh, he was appointed Prant pracharak of Madhya Pradesh in 1964. Sh. Eknath Ranade was the inspiration behind Sudarshan Ji's decision to become a pracharak; after lifting of the ban post-emergency, he was posted in the sensitive northeast region in 1977 as a kshetra (regional pracharak), he worked with local tribes, reviving their indigenous faiths, promoting education and health among them.

He was appointed as the all-India head of physical training and later head of intellectual training; he is the only Sangh leader to hold both posts. In 1979 he took over as the head of the Sangh Baudhik cell (Akhil Bhartiya Baudhik Pramukh); in 1990, he was appointed as Sah Sarkarvyah (Joint general secretary of the Sangh).

He was regarded as a strong supporter of Swadeshi, Bharatiya culture and traditions; he was a scholastic person who always spoke words of wisdom on issues of importance concerning the nation, such as science, meta physics, environmental issues and issues of foreign policy. He was an ardent devotee of Sh. Aurobindo and always said, 'A new Bharat will rise again under the Hindu leadership'. He wanted to create a happy, wealthy, and successful Bharatvarsh; he was an ideal Swayamsevak and a person of utmost unparallel knowledge.

He was a polyglot with knowledge of six languages and was very analytical with his approach; his main focus was on self-sustainable rural economy, sustainable consumption, and the scientific Hindu ways of personal and social life. He was passionate about rural development; subjects of his interest were organic farming, non-conventional resources of energy, water management, and cow protection.

He considered muslims and christians to be a part of the Hindu Rashtra. He instilled the belief in muslims that they are neither minority nor foreigners, but Indian muslims are Bharatiya Hindus. He believed that we can be believers of different ways of worship, but all of us are the children of the one supreme being. Our forefathers are common. We are all sons of Bharat Mata. He was of the perspective that the glory of Hindus be restored, and he would often say, "the time is very near" when Hindu society will unshackle the colonial mindset; no one can keep Hindus subjugated for long.[24]

He believed that the Arth-Kaam-driven (economic & pleasure-driven desires) consumerist lifestyle is the root cause of ills that society is facing. He said we have to go back to the 'Dharma, Arth, Kaam, Moksha' paradigm and create models of economic development based on it. Only consumption and enjoyment has led to a life of only non-human, animal-like enjoyment, leading to a consumerist world.

He also studied martial arts and designed 'Niyuddha' – the martial art based on ancient Kalaripayattu from Kerala that became part of physical training in the Sangh syllabus. He also introduced many small but significant exercises in the training of the Sangh cadre in shakhas and various camps. His fine tuning of intellectual inputs in daily shakha improved the training methodologies of shakhas.

He introduced a Shloka called 'Ekatmata Mantra,' which explains the underlying unity of Hindu thought about the supreme being. This Shloka is the unifying philosophy of Hindu culture that manifests itself in different forms. Sudarshan Ji will be remembered for creating a new training methodology in the Sangh and also for his intellectual push towards a 'Swadeshi rural based self-sustainable economy that cared for conservation and ecology.

---

24   KS Sudarshan – A leader who broke barriers: writes Tarun Vijay – Vishwa Samvada Kendra. https://vskkarnataka.org/ks-sudarshan-a-leader-who-broke-barriers-writes-tarun-vijay/

Sh. Mohan Madhukar Rao Bhagwat Ji
(Param Pujaniye Sarsanghchalak) 2009 Till Date

Sh. Mohan Rao Bhagwat Ji is currently serving as the sixth Sarsanghchalak of the Sangh; he was chosen as a successor to Sh. K.S. Sudarshan Ji in March 2009. Sh. Mohan bhagwat was born in a Maharashtrian family in Chandrapur, Bombay state; his father, Sh. Madhukar Rao Bhagwat Ji was the Karyavaha of the Chandrapur zone and later a Prant pracharak for the Sangh in Gujarat.

His grandfather, Sh.Narayan Nana Bhagwat Ji was a school mate of Dr. Hedgewar Ji, Sh. Bhagwat graduated in veterinary sciences and animal husbandry from the government veterinary college Nagpur. He became a full time pracharak of the Sangh in 1975; with time, he rose within the organization and became a pracharak in the areas of Nagpur and Vidharbha. In 1975 when the emergency was imposed in the nation Sh. Bhagwat worked underground, and his contribution was immense in organising the Sangh cadres and Swayamsevaks.

He became the Akhil Bhartiya Sharirik Pramukh (in charge of physical training) from 1991 to 1999; he was further promoted as the Akhil Bhartiya Pracharak Pramukh (In charge of Sangh volunteers working full time). Sh. Bhagwat became the Sahkaryavah (General secretary) of the Sangh in 2000; he was chosen as the Sarsanghchalak on March 21, 2009.

In the tenure of Sh. Bhagwat, the Sangh has very drastically progressed with the change in circumstances and times; the Sangh has become more proactive in its social media communication, Sh. Bhagwat has also spoken on important issues concerning the nation, such as population, economic growth, and developing cohesiveness, and a sense of brotherhood in the nation. He has brought immense flexibility to the organization by making the Sangh shakha timing more flexible, making it very comfortable for working professionals to attend shakhas and remain connected with the Sangh, under Sh. Bhagwat, the Sangh uniform (Ganvesh), has also been changed, earlier it was the khakee shorts, and now the full pant trousers are inducted into the Ganvesh.

He is always open to new ideas, this attracts Swayamsevaks and workers to him for any discussion, he is an organization man who has given top priority to the Sangh above anything else; his lectures are precise and to the point, which shows his clarity of thought.

Like all Sarsanghchalaks, he too believes that shakha is the life breath of the Sangh. It is the powerhouse; his vision is to reach the last village of Bharat with a shakha before 2025. The Sangh will achieve this ambitious target given the steady increase in shakhas and the rising number of Swayamsevaks joining the Sangh. Dr Bhagwat's significant contribution has been to reach out to those segments of society that had previously remained outside the purview of the Sangh. This includes leaders of various sects and religions as well as industry, commerce, and sports.

Dr Bhagwat's famous three-day conclave called 'Future of Bharat' was held on 17-19 September 2018 in Delhi. It was path – breaking in many ways, it was for the first time that the senior-most Sangh functionary had spoken to a global audience about the Sangh, its basic principles, its work, and its views on Bharat's socioeconomic and political issues.[25] According to him, the Sangh, as an organization, strives to create selfless people of character and discipline, because it wishes to bring in changes to create a more harmonious society.

Dr. Bhagwat's readiness to experiment with new ideas with a positive frame of mind has created a very pleasant atmosphere for young Karyakartas and Swayamsevaks to experiment with social outreach programmes.[25] His tenure as Sarsanghchalak has seen appreciable expansion in the Sangh shakha network as well as huge improvements in coordination between different affiliated organizations. Sh. Bhagwat's contributions to the Sangh have been very praiseworthy. He is a very brilliant and inspirational example of proactive leadership; the Sangh has progressed as an organization under his leadership.

(Param Pujaniye Sarsanghchalak)
Sh. Mohan Madhukar Rao Bhagwat Ji
2009 Till Date

---

25 Ratan Sharda – RSS, Evolution from an Organization to a Movement (Chapter – 7 Dr. Mohan Bhagwat.) Rupa Publications India (10 October 2020) pg. – 308

CHAPTER – 6

RSS & The Hindutva Paradigm

Introduction

Hindutva is a way of life. It is 'Sanatan' in nature, Sanatan refers to the "eternal" truth and teachings of Hindutva; it is a word used to explain certain values and life principles that are eternal, an accretion of wisdom that has held way beyond time and historical events.

Hindutva is primarily a cultural framework rooted in the civilizational values of Bharat. The core of these values is *'Vasudhaiv Kutumbakam'* (The whole world is one family).[26] It is a force of goodness and an idea of welfare for life and the methods by which life is ought to be lived; the fundamental principle is oneness. Hindu dharma, the Hindu way of life, which is self-evolutionary and known as Hindutva, is the purest form of national consciousness and is seen in the personification of Bharat as Bharat Mata.

The modern definition of Hindutva was presented before the world by Swami Vivekananda at the Chicago world parliament of religions on September 11, 1893. According to Swami Vivekananda, a Hindu believes in the authority of the vedas, god's cyclical order of creation, preservation, and dissolution, the immortality of the Atman and its innate purity, perfection, reincarnation, and religion as realization.[27]

---

26   The new book throws light on Hindutva and calls it 'Sanatan' in nature. https://www.mynation.com/india-news/new-book-throws-light-on-hindutva-calls-it-sanatan-in-nature-pz7ltg

Swami Ji learnt about the Bharatiya religious and spiritual practices from his master, Sh. Ramakrishna Paramhansa, who had mastered his ego and had realized the ultimate truth, that the purpose of life was the realization of god. Revered as an extraordinary saint, he possessed childlike simplicity. The land of Bharat had special sacred significance for Swami Vivekananda; he referred to Bharat as a 'Punyabhumi' He used the term, however, in a more descriptive manner to describe 'Bharat as a land of spirituality and as the place of origin for several of the world's religions.[27]

A better understanding was also laid by Swami Dayanand Saraswati, a reformist leader, he founded the Arya Samaj that sought to re-establish the vedas as the earliest Hindu scriptures and helped to free the society from the prevailing dogmas that enhanced the scientific and pragmatic elements of Hindu faith. Similarly, Swami Shradhanand Saraswati promoted the movement for the education of girls. He started vedic schools for the masses and began the 'Shuddhi' movement for the reconversion of Hindus who had converted to other faiths.

According to Sh.Vinayak Damodar Savarkar (Veer Savarkar) the tenets of Hindutva in the nation's context are common nation (Rashtra), a common race (Jati), and a common civilization (Sanskriti). The unique, natural, and organic combination that exists in our land goes by the name of Hindu.

Sh. Veer Savarkar's Hindutva became the source of the principles that shaped the ideology of Hindu nationalism in the 1920s, and the term is widely employed today to describe various expressions of the Hindu nationalist movement.[27] He asserted that Hindus are bound together by ties of blood, birth, and culture. Veer Savarkar wished to see the consolidation of the Hindu society.

Hindus worship the same gods with different regional variations from south to north. For example, Vishnu, Shiva, Krishna, Ram, Ganesh, Durga, Laxmi, and Saraswati are worshipped in all the regions of Bharat, though some form of supreme being may be more popular than the other in different areas. There are same festivals all over the nation with different names and minor variations. Bihu, Baisakhi, Vishu, Cheti Chand, Yugadi, and Baishakh all signify the beginning of the Hindu new year based on similar Hindu calendars and the harvest time.

Adi Shankaracharya had set up four Mathas 1,800 years back – Sringeri (south), Dwarka (west), Joshimath, Badrinath (north), and Jagannathpuri (east), to stress the geographical spread a unity of Bharat.[27] These are examples to underline some unique features of our national life which are common to all citizens living in Bharat, whatever their faith or religion. Such traditional practices all over this land define the Hindu culture that has evolved in what is called 'Bharatvarsh.'

In its judgement, the Supreme court bench led by Justice J.S Verma analysed Hindutva, as a way of life, it also said that words could not confine the narrow limits of religion alone and Hindutva is a broadening concept.

Hindutva in Culture

Hindutva is the Bharatiya culture, it refers to an understanding of the network of relationships among people with different traditions, cultures, and countries, and with nature, as an extension of the common soul. This commonality and unity in an expansive form is the idea of 'Vasudhaiva Kutumbakam', or 'the world is one family'. Hindutva is immersed in this philosophy; it encompasses the relationships between human beings and nature, between man and rivers, the mountains, the plains and valleys, the desert & the trees. Hindu ethics have led to the development of sciences like yoga, ayurveda, material sciences, mathematics, astronomy, architectural marvels, and fine arts like classical music and dance.

---

27 Hinduism, Hindutva and the Contest for the Meaning of Hindu Identity: Swami Vivekananda and V.D. Savarkar – Irénées. https://irenees.net/bdf_fiche-analyse-878_en.html

The Hindu way of life was developed through the austere practice, study, and efforts spanning thousands of years that have nourished Bharat since time immemorial. Examples of kings and Maharajas like Maharana Pratap, Shivaji, and Sayaji Gaekwad, Rudrapratap's rule in Warangal and Krishnadevaraya's reign over the kingdom of Hampi at its zenith are representative of this ethical standard. The Hindu way of life raised universities like Nalanda and Takshashila so that these ideas could flourish and be studied by students in Bharat and from overseas to benefit all of humanity.

In the modern context, Hindutva and Hindu Rashtra are the two most expressive terms of this way of life. Sangh believes that Hindutva's great reserves of knowledge are the source code of solutions for many socio-political, economic, and environmental problems engulfing the world today and the cure for many of the ills plaguing the nation. Driven by an essentially sattvic propensity, many saints and scholars have nurtured Hindutva, and in modern times this idea of Hindutva was incorporated and sculpted into the form, and working of the Sangh started by Dr. Hedgewar Ji. The Hindutva of the Sangh is thus for the well-being of all humanity.

We can see logically that Hindu nation is a result of thousands of years of experiential living and history. It is not an idea propelled by any political or economic motivation. It is a comprehensive conception of civilization developed through the observance of certain values and cultural ways of life.

To be born an Bharatiya means to be a descendant of Bharatiya culture; it is not just the physical act of being born; it is being mindful of cultural ethos laid down by our progenitors. That is why Guruji Golwalkar said that culture counts.[28]

---

28   Ratan Sharda – RSS 360* Demystifying Rashtriya Swayamsevak Sangh – Chapter III – What Defines India. Bloomsbury India (18 June 2018) pg – 51

Tenets of Hindutva

When Dr. Hedgewar began the Sangh, he outlined the project of Bharatiya greatness to be achieved through the ideal of Hindutva. Hindutva, as revealed in his work, and instructions, is the material and spiritual aspect of the Hindu way of life, organizing the work and life of an individual and that of the nation according to its cultural values.

Hindutva is the underlying unity that runs through the diverse, regional, linguistic, and geographical forms of the Bharatiya landmass and even beyond, to the shores touched by Hindu cultural impacts, of which Angkor Wat complex in Cambodia and the Prambanan Shiva temple in Indonesia are impressive examples.

For Dr. Hedgewar, the first condition was that Hindus should be united and awakened for the renaissance of Bharat as a nation because the major cause of the downfall of Bharat was disunity, internal fights on language, caste, and region between Hindus. Guruji Golwalkar gave an even broader definition of Hindus, saying that Bharat, as the motherland of people with common ancestors and familiar traditions, has provided a unique identity to the people living in Bharatvarsha for centuries.

The Tenets of Hindutva can be laid as follows:

    i.   Belief in the theory of Karma,

    ii.   Belief in Rebirth,

    iii.   Concept of Mukti (nirvana) or Shunya,

    iv.   Worshipping and showing respect to nature.

    v.   Sharing of the most important philosophy, that is, Ekam Sat, Vipra Bahudha Vadanti.

Hindutva is the Sangh's vision of Bharat of the future. It is opposed to discriminations. It emphasizes the brotherhood and sisterhood of all Hindus. In fact, Guruji Golwalkar formed the Vishwa Hindu Parishad

(VHP), to carry forth this message across the nation, and to bring various sects and orders (Sampradyas) under one umbrella.

No one is high, or low, all are equal, every Swayamsevak bears this as an immutable fact and carries onward the task of the regeneration of Hindu society. Guruji Golwalkar felt that the unity and integrity of the nation could not be fully secured unless Hindutva became the collective consciousness of our society, and this work is being done by the Sangh. This is the essence of the 'Vyakti Nirman' mission of the Sangh. It is about the development of body, mind, intellect, and spirit. Hindutva is always modern, flexible, and adaptable for every generation.

The Essence of Hindu Rashtra

Hindu Rashtra is a derivative of Hindutva. It is the imagination of a contemporary, non-violent nation where peace and prosperity prevail, which promotes freedom of worship and equality for all. The Sangh works towards making the all-encompassing dimensions of Hindutva widely known and is determined in its resolve for the establishment of Hindu Rashtra. The relation between Hindutva and Hindu Rashtra is the relation between ideas and action; both are inseparable. Hindutva represents our constitutional values of equality, liberty, and justice; it is the combination of three sutras – coordination, consent, and coexistence. It is the twenty first century meaning of peace, democracy, a fulfilling life, and a conflict-free world. Hindutva believes in the coexistence of all forms of worship.

Hindutva is not a means for acquiring political power. If it had been so, Dr. Hedgewar would have formed a political party and would not have created the Sangh, a social organization. For the Sangh, Hindutva is a comprehensive theory and a range of life practices. Based on it, the Sangh envisages all around reform and regeneration of the country with the full participation of society. The propagation of Hindutva is a foremost national service that all Swayamsevaks engage in throughout their lives.

The Sangh considers Hindutva to be the natural destination of the world. It is Bharat's greatest cultural export to the world, just as the Ramayana and Mahabharata epics, which travelled to Southeast Asia in the age of antiquity and shaped the culture there.[29]

Sangh and the Akhand Bharat

The Akhand Bharat theory is one of the most important perspectives in the Hindutva ideal of the Sangh. Since its formation, Akhanda Bharat implies undivided Bharat, whose geographical expanse was from the present-day Afghanistan in the west to the parts of present-day Indonesia & Thailand in the east. It implies a concept of a unified greater Bharat.

The idea of Akhanda Bharat is as old as the Sanatan Bharatiya civilisation and culture, and it is in very detailed mentioned in old historical sculptures, the great strategist Chanakya also articulated the idea of an Akhanda Bharat, which means all states in the region being under one authority, rule, and administration. The idea of Bharat as Bharatvarsh appears to have existed for thousands of years, even before the existence of America or Great Britain; from the ancient scriptures and Hindu text, there is evidence of the land of Aryavarta stretching from the Himalayas and Vindhya, all the way to the eastern and western oceans.

The story of Mahabharat in the Hindu significance shows a remarkable degree of pan Bharatiya context and interrelationships from places such as Gandhara, Khandhar (present day Afghanistan), extending to Manipur in the east to Dwarka in the west, these all places have been in detailed mentioned in the Mahabharata which has historical significance in the Bharatiya scriptures and traditions.

---

29 Hindutva to be our greatest cultural export: ABVP leader | Latest News India – Hindustan Times. https://www.hindustantimes.com/india-news/hindutva-to-be-our-greatest-cultural-export-abvp-leader/story-LIDA87wDeCOXiMnGmB9pOL.html

Sh. Veer Savarkar, at the 19th annual session of the Hindu Mahasabha in 1937 in Ahmedabad, propounded the notion of Akhand Bharat that must remain indivisible from Kashmir to Rameswaram and from Sindh to Assam; he emphasized the cultural, religious, and political unity of Hindus. Thus, he emphasized that that mythologically and historically, the Akhand Bharat existed. He said, 'the entire land from Cuttack to Kutch and Kashmir to Kanyakumari is not only sacred to is but is a part of the whole philosophy of the Hindutva' The people who have been born in this area of the world since times immemorial and who still live in it may have all the difference superficially brought about by place and time. Still, the basic unity of their entire life can be seen in every devotee of the Akhand Bharat.

He defined a Hindu nation consisting of the Aryans and the non-Aryans of the subcontinent, he defines a Hindu as a person who is united by blood ties with all those whose ancestry can be traced to Hindu antiquity and who accepts Bharat from the Indus River in the north to the Indian ocean in the south as his Mathrubhumi (Motherland). According to the Sangh, the idea of Akhand Bharat is not a geopolitical conquest but a geo cultural concept proven historically.

Sangh pracharak, the founder of the integral humanism theory, Pt. Deendayal Upadhyaya Ji defined the idea of Akhand Bharat, he said that Akhanda Bharat (Undivided Bharat) includes all the basic values of nationalism and integral culture. The map of Akhand Bharat that the Sangh endorses shows the entities of present-day Afghanistan, Pakistan, Bangladesh, Sri Lanka, Myanmar, Tibet, Bhutan, Nepal, and Aksai Chin. The whole idea of Akhand Bharat is historically and mythologically known as Bharatvarsh. Thus, Sangh's perspective of Akhand Bharat has existed for thousands of years and is not a new concept; it has been historically and scientifically proven.

*The Reimagination of the Akhand Bharat
with Bharat Mata*

WHO IS A HINDU?

आसिंधु सिंधु-पर्यन्ता यस्य भारत-भूमिका ।
पितृभूः पुण्यभूश्चैव स वै हिंदुरिति स्मृतः ॥

A HINDU means a person who regards this land of
BHARATVARSHA, from the Indus to the
Seas as his Father-Land as well
as his Holy-Land that is
the cradle land of his religion. "

The Hindutva Ideology Transcript of Sh. Veer Savarkar

Ram Mandir & The RSS

The Ram mandir & the Ayodhya issue has been an important political, historical, and socio-religious issue in the nation after independence which was centered on the Sh.Ram Janmbhoomi in Ayodhya, Uttar Pradesh. The issue basically revolved around the control of the land, which the Hindus proved and regarded as the birthplace of Prabhu Sh.Ram. According to the facts, ancient scriptures, and documents, the Sh.Ram Janmabhoomi site was initially demolished to construct a mosque known as Babri Masjid. However, Muslims claimed that the land was titled to them. People in 1949 saw an idol of Bhagwan Sh.Ram inside what was then a mosque, both Hindu and Muslim sides had claimed ownership of the site, which led to an eventual lockdown of the area by the government.

The Timeline of the Issue

On December 17, 1959, Nirmohi Akhara (a party to the dispute, a group of Hindu Sadhus and Godsman) filed a suit seeking possession of the site. It claimed to be the custodians of the disputed land. Following this, the Sunni central waqf board filed a lawsuit claiming ownership of the site on December 18, 1961.

B.B Lal, a renowned archaeologist along with K.K Muhammed, a historian and archaeologist, and three others, had for the first time excavated the Ram Janmabhoomi site in 1976-77, and the team corroborated that they found a temple structure below the Babri Masjid. K.K Muhammed stated in his report that twelve pillars with Hindu ritualistic scriptures were found beneath the mosque structure; these archaeological finds were conclusive proofs that the Ram Mandir in Ayodhya stood at the place where the invading armies of Mughals had built the Babri Majid after destroying the Mandir.

Professor B.B Lal, who led the excavation team, in his book (***Rama, Historicity, Mandir, And Setu,*** *published in 2008)*, said there is a temple-like structure beneath the demolished Babri Masjid. He mentioned, "attached to the piers of the Babri Masjid, there were twelve stone pillars, which carried not only typical Hindu motifs and moldings but also figures of Hindu deities. It was self-evident that these pillars were not an integral part of the masjid but were foreign to it".[30] Despite all the research which came out in the open, many left dominated historians consistently neglected these important findings and reports of ASI, headed by Prof. Lal & K.K Muhammed.

Decades later, the incident took place when the Karsevaks, on December 6, 1992, demolished the Babri Masjid. In 2003, by order of the Allahabad high court, where the matter was initially contested, the court ordered that the Archaeological Survey of India (ASI) would conduct an in-depth study and excavate to ascertain whether the type of structure that was beneath the rubble indicated a definite proof of a temple or a mosque.[30] A fifty-member team of the Archaeological survey did the excavation. They found over sixty pillars, hinting that below the mosque stood a Hindu temple that could be dated back to the 12th century A.D.[30] Thus, the ASI led research under the supervision of the Allahabad high court resulted in a report that pointed to a large number of properly laid out pillars bearing Hindu designs discovered under the mound that proved the existence of a temple.

The ASI Report Cited Three Points Specifically: –

1. There is archaeological evidence of a massive temple like structure beneath the mosque.

2. The structure has distinctive features associated with ancient temples of North India.

3. There is specific evidence of building and construction work from early as the 10th century.

In the words of ASI researchers, they had discovered "distinctive features associated with temples of North India." The excavations by the ASI were used as evidence by the court that the predating structure was a massive Hindu religious building and not a mosque.[30] The ASI team unearthed several remains of a temple's 'Shikhara' (tower) from the mosque's premises, adding to the evidences of a Hindu structure underneath;[30] ASI team had also found another architectural artefact known as 'Amalka.' below the 'Amalka,' there was also the 'Grivah' and the 'Shikhara,' which are the constituent parts of temples found in North India.

These reports were quietly hidden, till it was resurrected by the Allahabad high court when it delivered its judgement on September 30, 2010, in the matter; the court said "there were efforts to discredit the ASI reports". The court ruled that the disputed 2.77-acre land in Ayodhya would be divided into three parts: the Hindus, Muslims, and the Nirmohi akhara. The petitioners later moved the Supreme court, and the apex court stayed the High court's order.

In 2016, the court had started a fresh hearing of the matter. In 2017, the Supreme court had said that the matter was sensitive and suggested that the case be settled out of court. It asked all the stakeholders to hold talks and find an amicable solution. However, no solution was achieved. In 2018, the Supreme court had set up a five-judge constitution bench to hear the matter.

RSS & its Role in The Ram Janmabhoomi Movement

The Sangh's resolution of 1959 on the issue of temples turned into mosques was the first step towards the Ram Mandir issue. It laments how tyrannical foreign aggressors destroyed numerous Hindu temples and built mosques to smite the sentiments of the Hindus across the nation.

---

30 *B. B. Lal (2008)*. Rāma, His Historicity, Mandir, and Setu: Evidence of Literature, Archaeology, and Other Sciences. *Aryan Books.* ISBN 978-81-7305-345-01

The 1959 resolution stated, "There is an intense desire to resurrect the places of worship of Hindus; it is a matter of great regret that even after the end of British rule, the government has remained totally callous to the legitimate rights of Hindus over the temples, out of all temples the Ram Janmabhoomi, Ayodhya, the Kashi Vishwanath, Varanasi, and the Krishna Janmabhoomi, Mathura occupies a special place because of their unique position as the centre of devotion and faith of Hindus throughout the nation. The resolution also stated, "the present conditions of the temple is such at the present time that it severely wounds the feeling of the devotees. The Sabha urges the government of Uttar Pradesh to take steps to return these temples to the Hindus."

The Ayodhya movement was the brainchild of Sh. Moropant Pingle, Sh. Nanaji Deshmukh, and Sh. Bhaurao Deoras, who had been preparing the ground for it since the early 1980s, Sangh had supported various Hindu organizations such as the VHP and others who organized Bhajans at the Ram Janmabhoomi site. After the Meenakshipuram mass Hindu conversion in Tamil Nadu in 1981, the Sangh decided to mobilize Hindus, and the Ram Janmabhoomi issue was the utmost important aspect which took the centre stage.

In the mid-1980s, the Sangh and the Vishwa Hindu Parishad meticulously planned agitations to mobilise Hindus for the main goal of the Ram Mandir in Ayodhya, building a temple at the birth place of Prabhu Sh.Ram was one of the main goals of the Sangh. In 1983, the VHP also organized the month long Ekatmata Yatra (unification march); the main aim was to raise funds for temple reconstructions across the nation. Sh. Moropant Pingle, was appointed the convenor of the Ekatmata Yatra. During the yatra, there were multiple processions across the nation, with the image of Bharat Mata, the response was outstanding, and people from across the nation participated in it; there was a powerful wave of Hindutva across the nation during that time. Many slogans were also coined during the yatra such as:*"**Ram Lalla Hum Aayenge; Mandir Wahi Banayenge."***

An Artistic Creation of Prabhu Shri Ram.

The Structural Model of the Shri Ram Mandir.

A Caricature Creation of The Shri Ram Mandir.

The Ram Janmabhoomi issue has figured many times in deliberations of apex decision-making bodies of the Sangh like the Pratinidhi Sabha as well as in Karyakari Mandal. Several resolutions expressing the wishes of the people for constructing a grand Ram mandir at the birthplace of Prabhu Ram have been passed.

In March 1986, the Sangh passed a resolution titled 'Ram Janambhoomi Locks'; this was again a reminder of Sangh's priority for the Ram Mandir at Ayodhya. The Pratinidhi Sabha resolution started engaging new stakeholders in the struggle for the Mandir by thanking the "Sadhus" steered by the VHP for "pushing the demand for a Ram Mandir at Ayodhya."

The Sangh urged the government "to hand over the Janmabhoomi site and adjacent land for development to the newly minted Ram Janmabhoomi Nyas." By 1987, the Ram Mandir at Ayodhya had become the mainstay of the Sangh. In that year came another resolution by the Pratinidhi Sabha titled 'Rama Janmabhoomi.'

For the Ram Janmabhoomi agitation, the BJP organized a rath yatra, across the country to Ayodhya in 1990. The Yatra was led by then-BJP President Sh. LK. Advani Ji. The Yatra also contributed immensely to building support and momentum for the Ram Janmbhoomi Movement. Many leaders of the Sangh, VHP, BJP played commendable and instrumental role in the movement of the Ram Mandir, such as Sh. Balasaheb Deoras, the third Sarsanghchalak of the Sangh, Mahant Sh.Nirtya Gopal Das Maharaj, Sh. Lal Krishna Advani, Sh. Ashok Singhal, Sadhvi Ritmabhara, Sadhvi Uma Bharti among many others.

Sh.Balasaheb Deoras, the third Sarsanghchalak of the Sangh, had said, "if you take out Hindutva & Prabhu Sh. Ram from the historical scholarship of Bharat, you not only harm the nation, you harm humanity." He also said, "whenever we think of lofty ideals and virtues, the image of Prabhu Ram emerges; he is all that is good and noble in this world. Bharat's identity is linked with Prabhu Ram. 'Bharat, Ram ki Bhoomi' (India, the land of lord Ram) is a repeated sentence among the masses. He emphasized that archaeology proves the presence of the Ram Mandir; hence, a magnificent Ram temple at the Janmasthan, his birthplace in Ayodhya, is of paramount importance.

In many historical scriptures and books, Prabhu Ram has been praised as the one with unparalleled valour; his defence of Dharma and his model conduct as a king, student, brother, son, husband, and friend is a bedrock of inspirational and motivational values. Prabhu Ram is the pre-eminent and most magnificent symbol of Hindutva.

On November 9, 2019, the Supreme court bench led by Chief Justice Ranjan Gogoi unanimously ruled that the disputed area would be given to Ram Janmabhoomi Nyas to construct a temple. The court also asked the government to frame a plan within three months and set up a trust for building a temple in Ayodhya.[31]

The trust was constituted following the 2019 Supreme Court verdict that backed the construction of a temple at the Ram Janmabhoomi.[32] In January 2020, Prime Minister Sh, Narendra Modi Ji announced in the Lok Sabha that the government had given its approval to the "Shri Ram Janmabhoomi Tirtha Kshetra" proposal to take care of the construction of the grand Ram Mandir in Ayodhya.

---

31 A New Twist in the 20-year-old Babri Masjid verdict: Will the case step into the International Court? – Lex Insider. https://lexinsider.com/a-new-twist-in-the-babri-masjid-verdict/

32 https://www.indiatoday.in/news-analysis/story/rss-ram-mandir-campaign-1708330-2020-08-06

Prof. B.B Lal, Former Director General of the Archaeological Survey of India

Sh. KK Muhammed

Sh. L.K Advani along with Supporters Leading the Ram – Rath Yatra from Somnath, Gujarat to Ayodhya, Uttar Pradesh, October 1990.

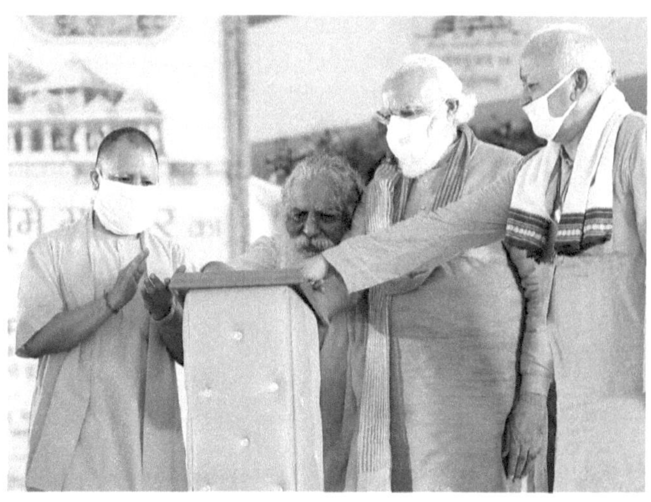

Hon'ble Prime Minister Sh. Narendra Modi Ji, Param Pujnaiye Sarsanghchalak Mohan Bhagwat Ji, Hon'ble Chief Minister of Uttar Pradesh Sh. Yogi Adityanath Ji & Mahant Sh. Nrityagopal Ji Maharaj laying the Foundation Stone (Shilanyas) of the Shri Ram Mandir, Ayodhya, August 2020.

Hon'ble Prime Minister Sh. Narendra Modi Ji, Param Pujnaiye Sarsanghchalak Mohan Bhagwat Ji During the (Foundation Ceremony) Shilanyas of the Shri Ram Mandir, Ayodhya, August 2020.

Prime Minister Sh, Narendra Modi Ji receiving the invitation for the Sh. Ram Mandir 'Prana Pratishtha' Ceremony to be held on 22nd January 2024, from Sh. Champat Rai Ji (Vice President of Vishva Hindu Parishad, and the General Secretary of Shri Ram Janmabhoomi Teerth Kshetra, along with Sh. Nripendra Misra, Chairman of Shri Ram Janmabhoomi Teerth Kshetra, and other dignitaries.

Param Pujaniye Sarsanghchalak Sh. Mohan Bhagwat Ji & Sangh Sarkaryvah Sh. Dattareya Hosbale Ji, along with Renowned Singer Sh. Shankar Mahadevan Ji at the Sangh Vijayadashmi Utsava in Nagpur, Sh. Mahadevan was invited as the Chief Guest for the Utsav, 24th October 2023.

On February 19, 2020, the first meeting of trust was held, it elected Ram Janmbhoomi Nyas chief, Mahant Sh. Nrityagopal Das Ji Maharaj, as the chairman and VHP vice-president, Sh. Champat Rai Ji as the general secretary. Both were elected unanimously to the trust. Former IAS officer Nripendra Mishra was nominated as the chairman of the construction committee.

In August 2020, the Prime Minister visited Ayodhya to lay the foundation stone (Shilanyas) to construct the Ram Mandir at the Ram Janmbhoomi site, Parampujaniye Sarsanghchalak, Sh. Mohan Bhagwat Ji, the Chief Minister of Uttar Pradesh Sh.Yogi Adityanath Ji, were present in the Shilanyas of the Ram Mandir.

Sarsanghchalak Sh. Mohan Bhagwat Ji mentioned Sh.LK.Advani Ji & Sh. Ashok Singhal Ji for their unparalleled and significant contributions to the Ram Janmbhoomi Movement. At the (Shilanyas) ceremony, Prime Minister Sh. Narendra Modi Ji said that Ram Mandir would become the modern symbol of our tradition. It will become a symbol of devotion and national sentiment. The temple will also symbolize the power of joint resolution of crores of people. It will keep inspiring future generations.

The reawakening of Bharat Mata and the construction of the Ram Mandir at the Janmasthan is an important milestone of the Hindutva movement as it gives expression to a national cultural requirement. The Sangh was always committed to constructing a Ram Mandir at the Janmasthan, and it wanted the Mandir to be constructed within the constitutional framework.

The Historic epitome of Hindutva, the Sh. Ram Mandir will be inaugurated in January 2024.

"जन्मभूमि है राम की श्री राम ही पूजे जायेंगे,
जन्म जहाँ पर हुआ प्रभु का मन्दिर वहीं बनायेंगे।"

Jai Shri Ram.

CHAPTER – 7

Contribution of Sangh in Nation Building & Challenges

Introduction

Since its establishment in 1925 the Sangh has come a long way to become the only ever-growing movement of Bharat. However, this epic journey has not been without its ups and downs. The Sangh has faced many challenges by silently working at the grass root level, by person-to-person contact, and heart to heart dialogue.

The initiatives of different times were different, ranging from the struggle to save democracy in the emergency period to a very strong initiative of social service projects in the last few decades.[33] The impact of Sangh's work and contribution has been cumulative; there have been multiple milestones of achievements in Sangh's journey.

The place, position, and respect that today, the Sangh has in society was not always the case. Far from being powerful and influential, the Sangh was least understood as an organization by many; it was banned thrice after independence and systematically slandered and ridiculed by the ruling dispensation. A systematic disinformation campaign was conducted against the Sangh over decades. Even those associated with it were excluded from positions of importance, whether in the government or civil society.

---

33 https://www.rss.org/

Dr. Hedgewar participated in the independence movement, he took part in the satyagraha and went to jail twice for his involvement in the freedom movement; countless Sangh workers were jailed during the freedom struggle but still braved repression to oppose the British rule. Similarly, Guruji Golwalkar lead the Sangh relief work during the tumultuous times of partition. The Sangh's defence of Hindus during partition in areas of Punjab and its refugee relief work was remarkable. Thousands of Sangh Swayamsevaks and volunteers were jailed during the emergency; the Sangh fought bravely to restore democracy during the emergency.

This chapter will give an insight into the work of the Sangh during the partition, the emergency, and the challenges it faced during the bans; this chapter also highlights the Sangh's role in disaster management and its contribution to different nation-building activities.

RSS and the Partition of India

The partition of 1947 was a significant event that marked the end of the British colonial rule in India. The partition led to the creation of two separate nations, India and Pakistan; it also led to the change of political borders and the division of other assets that accompanied the dissolution of the British Raj in the Indian subcontinent. The partition was outlined in the Indian Independence Act 1947. The British government, eager to leave India, supported the demand for Pakistan, and the partition of India was announced on August 15, 1947.

The partition was one of the most unfortunate incidents the nation saw; the Sangh played a very proactive role to protect people and defend the honour of women who were the target of abduction and violence. The Sangh became the stoutest defender of human rights during the dark phase of partition; killings took place at a mass level;

the displacement and exodus of population at a large scale made it one of the bloodiest events in the Indian history.

The partition of the nation in 1947, and the time before it let to major religious clashes and riots; this experience of bloodshed made it very clear that Hindus have to be united, and ultimately, the partition made Hindus realize that they will have to be united, the partition was a very important moment in the history of the Sangh as many people specially Hindus joined the Sangh in numerous numbers. In couple of years, the Sangh had its presence across the nation.

Sangh Sah Sahkarvyah for many years, Sh. H.V Seshadhri has written extensive accounts of how bravely the Swayamsevaks worked in the areas of Punjab, West Punjab, and Sindh to protect the Hindu community; many Swayamsevaks sacrificed their life during the partition. At the time of partition, the Sangh played a very crucial role of saving and defending Hindus in areas in which Hindus were in minority; hundreds of young men began joining the Sangh, especially in cities and villages of pre-partition Punjab, such as Rawalpindi, Lahore, Peshawar, Amritsar, Jalandhar, and Ambala, among others.

Recalling the role of the Swayamsevaks during partition, Prof. A.N Bali, in his book **Now It Can Be Told,** wrote about the role of Sangh during partition. – "Who came to the rescue in those difficult times to protect the people, except those young men known as Sangh Swayamsevaks, they arranged for safe passage of women and children in each and every mohalla, in every city of the state," "They arranged for their food, medical help, clothing and took care in every possible way. When the entire Punjab was on fire and congress leaders were sitting helplessly in Delhi, at that time, volunteers of the Sangh saved the people of Punjab with their discipline, and physical strength, risking their own lives"[34]

---

34   Professor A.N. Bali | Now it can Be Told. | Prabhat Prakashan (28 December 2020)

When people across borders were shifting sides as new nations were formed, a picture depicting a train of the northern railway.

The Hindustan Times Newspaper Frontpage on 15th August 1947.

In 1944 the British sources indicated that nearly 76,000 men participated and attended shakas; between 1945 and 1948, the Sangh membership surged, during 1945 to 1950, Shakhas rapidly increased in Punjab, Kashmir, and regions of Himachal by the growing popularity of the Sangh.

The situation during partition had deteriorated so badly that even the home minister Sh. Sardar Patel, had to admit, 'it will not be possible for the government to defend everybody. Each person will have to try to defend self.' For the Hindus, these words presented a helpless, worrying situation. The Sangh volunteers took it upon themselves to protect the society at the risk to their lives. Sangh leaders Sh. Guruji, Sh.Balasaheb Deoras, Sh.Madhavrao Muley, and Sh.Vasantrao Oak, were on the field to coordinate the relief activities of the Sangh in areas of Punjab and Sindh.

Though the Sangh succeeded in the mission of saving lives of people and helping refugees reconstruct their lives, the eternal regret of the Sangh leadership has been that it was too young and not big enough to stop the partition. At the time of partition, hundreds of Swayamsevaks lost their lives defending people, stuck in areas that were to go under Pakistan, many volunteers lost their own families and fortunes while they defended the Hindu community in the chaos of the partition.

Even though the Sangh was a nascent organization in 1947, it still did its level best to protect people during the partition; the Sangh's role and contribution was exemplary and inspirational. On September 16, 1947, Gandhi Ji himself visited a shakha, and he praised the work of Sangh for uniting and protecting people; he said: "I had visited the Sangh camp years ago at Wardha; at the time Sh. Hedegwar Ji was alive, I was very much impressed by the rigorous discipline and complete absence of untouchability and simplicity of Swayamsevaks."

RSS & The Emergency

Emergency was the 21-month period from 1975 to 1977 when Indira Gandhi, the Prime minister of India, declared a state of emergency across the nation. The emergency was declared under article 352 of the Constitution; the emergency is seen as one of the darkest periods for Indian democracy; it was seen as the beginning of autocratic rule.

The prologue to the emergency was a time in which there were multiple agitations and protest against the corruption and maladministration of the government; the first agitation was started in Gujarat as the Nav Nirman Andolan in 1974, which was led by students who wanted to displace the highly corrupt government of Chiman Bhai Patel of congress, the ABVP participated actively in the protest, ultimately the government fell down, and the first non-congress, government in Gujarat, was established, headed by Babu Bhai Patel.

A similar student's agitation also took place in Bihar, and Lok Nayak Jai Prakash Narayan became the emerging face of the agitation. He also launched the total revolution (The Sampurna Kranti) movement and mass protest to combat the rampant corruption in the system and address major issues such as unemployment & the systemic undermining of democratic institutions.

The last trigger for the imposition of emergency was the order of the Allahabad high court; on June 12, 1975, the court declared Prime minister Gandhi's 1971 election to the parliament invalid due to violation of the election law, subsequently by overriding the Constitution, on 25th June midnight, Mrs. Gandhi declared a state of emergency in the nation.

She declared the emergency, citing a grave internal security threat to the nation, imposing a draconian act, the Maintenance of the Internal Security Act (MISA), an act which allowed the government to detain a person without trial for at least two years. During the emergency, thousands of Sangh Swayamsevaks were jailed, and hundreds were sacrificed, mostly in captivity.

Role & Work of The Sangh

The emergency in the country was imposed on the night of June 25, 1975; the then Sarsanghchalak Sh. Balasaheb Deoras was taken into custody on June 30, 1975, at Nagpur railway station. The government illegally banned the Sangh on July 4, 1975, but the Sangh was prepared; it very well knew that the leadership was tyrannical; the Sangh was the first to be banned, along with 23 other organizations which were banned. Senior leaders of the Sangh were arrested, and the primary responsibility of handling the Sangh work during the emergency was done By Sh. Yadav Rao Joshi, Sh. Rajendra Singh (Rajju Bhaiya), Sh. Ram Bhau Godbole, and Sh. Eknath Ranade.

On June 25, just a day before the emergency was imposed, JP Narayan and opposition leaders met in Delhi to form the Lok Sangarsh Samithi (LSS), a coordinating body to direct the activities of the total revolution, Sh. Nanaji Deshmukh, the organizing secretary of the Jan Sangh and a senior Sangh pracharak was named its general secretary.

The Lok Sangarsh Samithi was formed, and it organized an anti-emergency struggle that included Satyagraha against the emergency rule. In July 1975, there was a secret meeting of senior Sangh members, and specific goals were established for the underground Sangh organization during the emergency period.

- To maintain the morale of Swayamsevaks by providing them opportunities to meet each other
- To establish an underground press and distribution system and solicit overseas Indian support for the Sangh in the underground activities.

- To prepare for a nationwide satyagraha, establish contact with significant nonpolitical figures nationwide.

For the Sangh, the emergency ensured a complete makeover, from an organization which was limited to running shakhas and social service projects, it extended to new areas of social life and activist role also, in fact, a major push for social service projects were made during the time of emergency as Swayamsevak's and volunteers had to find ways of working for society while the Sangh shakhas were shut down.

The Sangh did noteworthy work and stood as an organization that fought the emergency with ultimate bravery and fearless dedication. The underground movement was organized, funds for the movement were collected quietly, and arrangements were made for the free distribution of literature. During this emergency period, the Sangh's struggle for the revival of democracy led to an increased acceptability of the organization. The Sangh defied the ban, and thousands participated in Satyagraha against the ban and the curtailment of fundamental rights.[35]

The Sangh was at the forefront of the restoration of democracy; nearly 1,25,000 people were arrested during the emergency from the Sangh ranks. The ban on the Sangh was from July 4, 1975, to March 21, 1977; for a period of 21 months, the organization emerged more powerful than the first ban of 1948-1949, and it learned from the first ban that it can take up challenges of each and every nature, and can emerge victorious.

The Sangh activism reached a high point during this time, and it set the stage for a more dynamic organization in the post emergency period, numerous newspapers described the Sangh's important role in the underground movement; the organization had also mobilized its extensive support network across the world to publicize the anti-emergency effort internationally. During the emergency, the Sangh saw

---

35   Emergency. https://www.atishmathur.com/polity/emergency

a great surge in memberships; newspapers reported in 1978 that there were nearly 13,000 shakhas across the nation, a government of India report claimed that the regular attendance nationally of the Sangh was nearly one million in number and that the financial contributions at the Guru Dakshina were over fifteen million rupees.

The Sangh affiliated organizations, such as the Bharatiya Mazdoor Sangh, had nearly 2.2 million members, in 1982, making it the second largest labour union in the nation. Also, the ABVP had nearly 4,80,000 members in 1985, which made it the largest student group in the Nation.

During and after the emergency the Sangh found widespread acceptance, and following, Sangh was working underground in a very powerful method of reaching out to people across the nation, bringing awareness about their democratic and constitutional rights, which were taken away by the imposition of the emergency.

Distribution of Work During the Emergency

Sh. Balasahab Deoras was the Sarsanghchalak of the Sangh when the emergency was imposed in the nation; the Sangh led the anti-emergency movement with spectacular strength, the fifty years of continuous hard work had yielded hardworking and committed Swayamsevaks. Despite the fact that senior leaders were arrested, still, an efficient team was available on the ground, there were 1356 Sangh pracharaks, out of which 189 were in jail, and the rest were underground and working actively.[36]

Sh. Deroas said, "The Sangh will not be closed down by putting a couple of thousand Swayamsevaks in jail; in its work, the Sangh does not think whether there will be a ban on it or not. Our determination to carry on Sangh work is unflinching. We have to carry it on fearlessly

---

36   RSS, The: A View to the Inside, Walter Andersen, Shridhar D.Damle | Penguin Viking (10 August 2018) pg.184

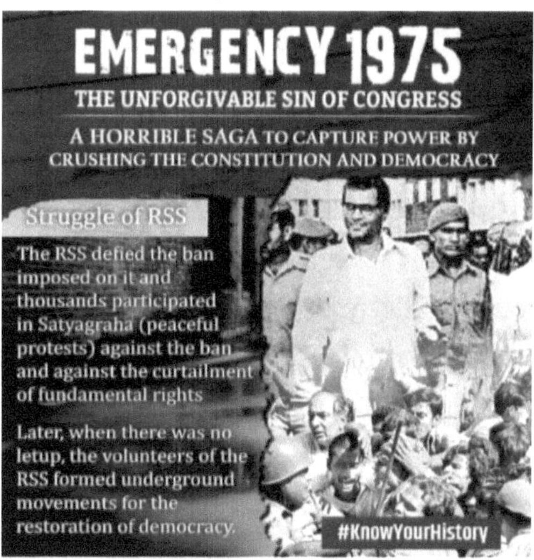

The Emergency is considered as one of the darkest periods of Indian democracy, the Sangh was illegally banned.

The Emergency Struggle was a short descriptive note on the period 1975-1977, RSS Sarsanghchalak Sh. Balasaheb Deoras Ji (Middle).

without bothering about the ban. We should rather think of utilizing a ban, to our benefit," he told volunteers in Rohtak ten days before the emergency was announced.

In August 1975 Sh.Deoras said "There is not a single instance during the past 50 years of Sangh Swayamsevaks indulging in violence and subversion. There were many riots and incidents of violence in the country but no court verdict and no report of any commission appointed by the government shows that Sangh Swayamsevaks had a hand in it." "The Sangh is engaged selflessly in the work making every Hindu an excellent citizen and a patriot of noble character. It is tragic that the government should impose ban on it."[37]

During emergency, the Sangh coordinated with the Lok Sangarash Samiti, and four zonal pracharaks were given the responsibility, Sh.Yadav Rao Joshi (south), Sh.Moropanth Pingle (west), Sh. Bhaurao Deoras (east) and Sh. Rajendra Singh (north), Moropant Pingle also handed the responsibility to coordinate with the Lok Sangarsh Samiti and to organize a nationwide Satyagraha. The grassroots structure of the Samiti included many Sangh workers, which presented the Sangh cadre with an unprecedented opportunity to gain experience and establish a working relationship with political leaders.

A Nagrik Swatantrata Morcha (citizens freedom movement) was formed, and its work was directed by the fourth Sarsanghchalak Sh. Rajendra Singh, foreign relations were looked after by Sh. Balasahab Bhede and Sh. Chamanlal, who were pracharaks in the Sangh, protest literature preparation was based out of Delhi and handled by Sh.Bhanu Pratap Shukla, who was editor of Panchjanya, relations with the religious head was maintained by Sh. Dadasaheb Apte.

---

37   The Organiser | https://organiser.org/2018/06/26/120884/bharat/Shri-Balasaheb-Deoras

No shakhas could be held anywhere in the country during the emergency; Swayamsevaks who were jailed, conducted their shakhas from jails, and jails became shakha centers, Swayamsevaks held on to each other and fought the most tyrannical regime to restore life and liberty in the Nation. The *'Apatkaleen Sangarsh Ghatha'*, a compendium on the Sangh's role in anti-emergency movement, was put together by professor K.Nagraj, Sh. Dassi Desai and Sh. Narendra Modi, the current Prime minister of India. The compendium was widely circulated across the nation.

The anti-emergency movement showed that no matter how difficult the time was, the Sangh would not veer away from its social agenda.

The End of Emergency

The emergency ended in March 1977, all political prisoners were released, and elections were announced; the emergency had officially ended on March 21, 1977. Elections to the Lok Sabha were scheduled from March 16 to March 20, 1977; Indira Gandhi lost her Lok Sabha seat, as did the majority of the congress candidates.

The congress party was so worried that Prime minister Indira Gandhi instructed a very highly placed bureaucrat and, an influential person to meet underground Sangh pracharaks two weeks before the polling to discuss an offer to lift the ban on the Sangh, if it would withdraw its support from the Janta party alliance which showcases that the Sangh was one of the most influential organization at the time of emergency in India.

Results of the elections came, and the congress was reduced to just 154 seats, 92 of which were from four southern states. The newly formed Janata party won 298 seats and its allies 47 seats, giving it a significant majority. Morarji Desai became the first non-congress Prime minister of

India. The Sangh cadre had supported the Janta party alliance but took the least credit for the defeat of Indira Gandhi; this showcased that the Sangh was never interested in politics; the Sangh remained aloof from all political activity as it was never a political outfit, a role in politics would have made the Sangh an organization dominated by politicians and Sangh never wanted to be a political outfit.

In the post 1977 era, after the emergency ended, the Sangh witnessed a surge in membership. The number of shakas had increased from 8,500 in 1975 to approximately 12,000 in 1977. The Sangh had proved itself during the emergency that when it comes to protecting the pillars of democracy, developing each other's personal and national character, and focusing on what is right and for the welfare of the nation, the Sangh has indeed stood like a pillar. The Sangh's fight against the ban and emergency was recognized nationally and internationally.

Bans on the RSS

After independence in 1947, the Sangh was on several occasions officially censured because the government feared that the Sangh had the potential to develop into a major socio-political force and the organization had the power to unite Hindus and the object of Hindutva. It was envious of the growing popularity of the Sangh and its organizational unity and strength.

The Sangh was banned thrice by the government after independence in 1948-1949, during the emergency in 1975-1977, and in 1992-1993. However, still, it emerged from the lows because of the inherent strength which Sangh has and exercises, each and every time the Sangh was banned, it emerged more stronger, millions and millions of volunteers and Swayamsevaks have contributed to nation building, this has led to the continued sustenance of the Sangh even during times of difficulty.

The First Ban (1948 - 1949)

The first ban on the Sangh was put after Sh. Mahatma Gandhi was assassinated on January 30, 1948, and the government allegedly banned the Sangh on February 4, 1948; leaders of the Sangh, including Sarsanghchalak Guruji Golwalkar, were arrested, the assassination was an opportunity for the congress to suppress the Sangh. Guruji was deeply disturbed by the tragic incident and had condemned the assassination in unequivocal terms.

It was a grand conspiracy to ban the Sangh in disguise and to dismantle the whole organizational setup; the Sangh was maliciously blamed for the assassination; there was never an iota of proof or evidence to even comment or say that the Sangh was involved in the assassination, it was completely a dictatorial decision of the government by which it illegally banned the Sangh.

All Sangh records and funds were confiscated, and the property of the Sangh was impounded; despite the report submitted by CID investigation, within days of the assassination that absolved the Sangh of any role in the plot, the ban was not lifted. The report was suppressed for a long time, and it came to light decades later. Nehru had made up his mind about crushing the Sangh. It was clear from his speech in Amritsar, about a week before the assassination, when he said the 'The Sangh should be totally uprooted from India.' this was in line with the resolutions passed by the congress committees and its chief ministers in some states demanding a ban on the Sangh.

The congress saw the Sangh as a threat to their monopoly, given the huge popularity of the Sangh based on the work that it had done for people who had suffered immensely during the partition. After the ban of 1948, the Sangh aimed to fight the illegal ban with a Satyagraha by reopening the Sangh shakhas; during the Satyagraha, the organization ensured that common man was not disturbed, there were no dharnas in front of government offices and roads, the method was that a pre-dedicated team of Swayamsevak's would reach a place and begin shakha activities with shouting slogans like 'Bharat Mata Ki Jai', 'Sangh Se Pratibandh Hatao'.[38]

There was a galaxy of talented Pracharak's such as Sh.Eknath Ranade, Sh.Vasant Rao Oak, Sh. Deendayal Upadhyaya & Sh.Bhai Mahavir, who had demonstrated exemplary managerial skills during the ban, which was later used to rebuilt the organization. Speaking in a public meeting, Sh. Sardar Patel said that it is not possible to suppress an organization like Sangh with the power of penal action; Sangh and its Swayamsevaks are not the type of people who will fight for selfish interest; they are patriots who love their country and motherland, this was in the context before the government had banned the Sangh in 1948.

Sh. Patel, in his speech in 1948 in Lucknow, also stated that the Sangh did not have any role in the assassination of Mahatma Gandhi. Despite this fact, Pt. Nehru, due to his political reasons and fear from the rise of the Sangh, banned it. Sh. Bana Hatti, in his weekly Savdhaan, wrote 'That in this period, the Sangh is the only organization which is working for uniting Bharat, the men of Sangh are disciplined, talented and a dedicated young class of high character which is organized in strength'.

The government, with time, was not able to show any involvement of the Sangh in the assassination; on July 11, 1949, the ban was finally lifted from the Sangh. The constitution of organization was then formulated, ending the ban. Later the Kapur commission, appointed by the government, released a report in 1967 that too exonerated the Sangh of any part in the assassination.

---

38 How the Ban on the RSS Was Lifted | Economic and Political Weekly Vol. 47, No. 16 (April 21, 2012), pp. 71-78 (8 pages) | Published By: Economic and Political Weekly | https://www.jstor.org/stable/23214601

The Sangh was banned for the first time on 4th February 1948 and the ban was lifted on 12th July 1949.

VHP, RSS, Bajrang Dal banned

The Times of India News Service

NEW DELHI, Dec. 10

THE Narasimha Rao government, through a gazette extraordinary issued tonight, banned five organisations under the Unlawful Activities (prevention) Act, 1967.

The organisations are the Rashtriya Swayamsevak Sangh, the Vishwa Hindu Parishad, the Bajrang Dal, the Jamaat-e-Islami Hind and the Islamic Sevak Sangh.

An official spokesman announced the ban order tonight. However, the government is not contemplating large-scale arrests of leaders and prominent members belonging to these five organisations in view of the communally surcharged atmosphere.

The government order was stated to be in fulfilment of its decision to ban communal organisations in the wake of the demolition of the Babri Masjid in Ayodhya on December 6 by kar sevaks under the command of the BJP-VHP-Bajrang Dal-RSS combine.

The Unlawful Activities (prevention) Act was used to impose a ban on the Jammu and Kashmir Liberation Front and the Liberation Tigers of Tamil Eelam. But the legal proceedings in the case of both these organisations are still continuing in court even though the act stipulates that such proceedings should be completed in six months.

Once an organisation is banned, according to the act, the government is required to refer the matter to a court within 30 days of the notification. The court then calls upon the organisation to show cause, within 30 days from the date of service of such notice, why the organisation should not be declared unlawful.

A decision in the matter has to be taken within six months to either confirm the declaration made in the notification or cancel the same. The judicial authority dealing with such matters has to be a judge of the high court.

Dilip Chaware reports from Bombay: RSS circles in Maharashtra, where the headquarters of the 67-year old organisation is located, today reacted coolly to the ban announcement while most prominent RSS functionaries have vanished since Monday anticipating such a move.

The RSS network was activated even before kar seva began in Ayodhya on Sunday. The message that no additional kar sevaks should be sent to Ayodhya was part of this strategy.

The ban is not expected to dent the organisation to any great extent, RSS sources here said. On the other hand, the organisation would emerge much stronger this time like it had done following two earlier bans, they feel.

A veteran RSS worker recalled how the first ban was imposed in 1948 in the aftermath of the assassination of Mahatma Gandhi. The situation then was much more overwhelming and very few people opposed the ban at that time. The RSS emerged almost unscathed and resumed its activities with a new vigour.

In 1975, Mrs Indira Gandhi banned the RSS with the imposition of emergency. The RSS mood continued to be defiant and a majority of swayamsevaks, whether jailed or outside, carried on their activities. Their network was almost intact and their undercover communications went on. Many RSS workers held their shakhas inside jails.

This time, the ban is expected to be even more ineffective since the government of Mr P. V. Narasimha Rao is in a tight corner already and does not possess a commanding majority of its own, they say.

According to the latest estimates, the RSS has an active membership of over 2.5 million and its swayamsevaks meet periodically at more than 25,000 shakhas and 37,000 upa-shakhas. The organisation is among the most closely-knit.

RSS circles said here tonight that they were anticipating the ban and most frontline RSS workers all over the country were asked to make themselves "not available".

P. K. Surendran reports from Nagpur: The RSS headquarters wore a gloomy look as also the VHP and Bajrang Dal headquarters. VHP and Bajrang Dal leaders have already gone underground.

Mr M. G. Vaidya, a confidant of the RSS chief, Mr M. D. Deoras, said, "We do not care although we are not happy. We were expecting such nonsense from the Congress government."

Mr Deoras, now convalescing after a surgery, is reportedly shifted to a new location, which is kept a secret.

In Nagpur, the Congress MLA, Mr Satish Chaturvedi, said he welcomed the Prime Minister's step. He refused to elaborate. Another five Congress MLAs refused to comment.

The Janata Dal leader, Mrs Mrinal Gore, said in Bombay that the ban on communal organisations must be implemented properly. However, merely a ban would not be sufficient when communal forces have already vitiated the mind of society. Large-scale

▶ See Edit: Victory For Hardliners, Page 8

efforts would be needed by secular forces to change this and the ban would be just one part of it.

The state BJP general secretary, Mr Dharamchand Chordia, said the ban was anti-democratic. The government had forgotten what happened when the RSS was banned during emergency, he said, adding the government would not be able to implement the ban.

He said the Muslim League was not banned because it was supporting the Congress.

Ban on communal organisations was not a proper solution and the problem would be compounded, according to the Shiv Sena chief, Mr Bal Thackeray.

He said the decision to ban these organisations

(Continued on Page 9)

The Times of India edition of 10 December, 1992 when the Sangh was banned for the third time.

For a young organization whose members had suffered grievously in this period, building it up was a big challenge. After the ban was lifted in 1949, Guruji received outstanding reception all over Bharat; he appealed to the volunteers to dedicate at least one year to nation-building. His emotional appeal was so great that hundreds of Sangh volunteers left their jobs and business to become pracharaks and vistaraks to rebuild the Sangh.

The Second Ban (1975 - 1977)

The second ban on the Sangh was imposed during the 21-month emergency imposed by PM Indira Gandhi in June 1975; the Sangh became the first organization to be banned in the emergency; this was the second ban on the Sangh after the first ban in 1948.

Sh. Balasahab Deoras was the Sarsanghchalak during the ban, and he led independent India's struggle for the restoration of democracy against the autocratic emergency. This time the ban was part of the overall repression of the country and was lifted once democracy was established in 1977, through the anti – emergency struggle. The illegal ban upon the Sangh by the government led to strengthening the core conviction of the Sangh, which led it to become a more dynamic organization; the illegal ban on the Sangh stumbled the organization for a bit, but the Sangh was roaring to revive.

Sh. Balasaheb Deoras, during the emergency, wrote, "I am pleased to learn that the volunteers and Swayamsevak of the Sangh as well as other Hindutva affiliated groups have openly collaborated and supported those who are opposed to the emergency and the Sangh workers and Swayamsevak's have worked with great enthusiasm and integrity against the diabolical regime that has resorted to blatant repression and a bunch of lies. He also said, "The Sangh is engaged selflessly in making every Hindu an excellent citizen and a patriot of noble character. It is unfortunate and tragic that the government has banned the Sangh".[39]

Seeing the bravery of the Sangh cadre and their great valour leading the movement in the face of police atrocities and brutality, even senior congress leaders became emotional and said "There must be some high ideal and goal which is giving them an indomitable courage for such a heroic act and sacrifice".

The Sangh led an underground movement during the ban; its communication system also worked flawlessly during the emergency and ban; the houses and homes of the Sangh workers proved to be the greatest boon to the fabric of the underground movement. The second ban ended in March 1977; it was a 21-month ban, the Sangh emerged as a far more self-confident and enormous organization which was more assertive about its role in society; the Sangh cadre had developed a great sense of mission. The detailed work distribution of the Sangh during the ban has also been mentioned in the RSS & emergency part of this chapter.

The Third Ban (1992 - 1993)

Karsevaks had removed the Babri structure on the Ram Janmabhoomi on December 6, 1992; following which the government of India allegedly banned the Sangh for the third time on December 10, 1992. Also, the Vishwa Hindu Parishad (VHP) was banned. In 1993, a tribunal was formed by the government of India to investigate the Babri Masjid dispute and demolition, and it was headed by Retd. Justice PK Bahri, the Bahri tribunal found the ban on Sangh unjustified, and the ban was lifted on June 4, but the ban on the VHP continued until it was removed in 1994.

---

39   https://indianexpress.com/article/explained/explained-politics/short-history-of-the-bans-imposed-on-rss-since-1947-8181011.

Restrictions & bans on the Sangh had been placed since independence till 1992. Still, these restrictions could not weaken the Sangh and the commitment of lakhs of Swayamsevaks; on the contrary, the Sangh as an organization has strengthened itself and become a more vibrant and powerful organization.

RSS & its Role in Disaster Relief

The selfless work of Sangh volunteers and Swayamsevaks during natural and manmade disasters has been unparalleled; what is most important is that during disaster relief, the Sangh does not practise the slightest bit of discrimination based on caste, gender, class, or religion, neither the Sangh gives any press release or publicity to the immense relief work it has done since decades. Countless disasters have seen the Sangh Swayamsevaks risk their lives for people's welfare, safety, and security.

Disasters like the famine of Bihar in 1966-1967, dam break and flooding in Morbi, Gujarat in 1979, the earthquake in Maharashtra in 1993, cyclone in Kandla port in Kutch in 1998, followed by the most devastating earthquake in Gujarat in the year 2001, the tsunami in South India in 2004, drought in Maharashtra in 2013, Uttarakhand flash floods of 2013 and floods in Bihar in 2017, the corona pandemic in 2020 are some of the incidents and disasters where the Sangh has contributed immensely to the relief and rehabilitation work. The Sangh has established relief camps in disaster-hit areas in the shortest possible time with the least resources, to which local Sangh volunteers and other members of society in that region contributed.

Many senior Sangh workers realised that disasters are a part of life, and the Swayamsevaks have worked in these situations for many years. Every time, a disaster occurs, it is a re-learning process. So, it was decided to have some structure for disaster management work and it

Sangh Volunteers and Swayamsevaks Providing Food & Ration to People During Covid-19 Lockdown.

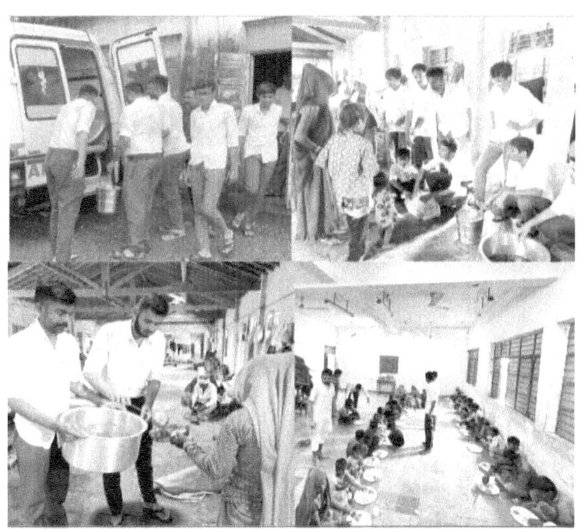

A Collage of Pictures Showcasing Sangh's Disaster Relief Activities and Aid to People in Times of Need.

should be inducted in the Sangh training, with this in mind and the learnings over the years, a management module has been introduced in the Sangh shiksha vargas.

The Sangh has stood in the forefront whenever there has been any need by the society and the nation, from Sangh's inception till now, as the organization completes hundred years, its role in partition, restoring democracy during the emergency, sustaining the multiple bans, and immensely contributing to supporting the army during multiple wars, its disaster relief work has indeed been commendable and appreciable.

CHAPTER – 8

The Stalwarts of Hindutva &
Sangh Parivar

Introduction

The Rashtriya Swayamsevak Sangh, since its formation in 1925, has seen the contribution of many influential personalities, who have contributed to the ideology of Hindutva, Hindu Rashtra, and to the growth and development of the nation in almost every aspect. They have been associated with the Sangh and the movements of the Sangh Parivar organizations.

This chapter is based on such prominent personalities, leaders, and stalwarts of Hindutva and the Sangh Parivar; through this chapter, the reader will get an insight into the lives of the people who have been an inspiration for the nation and their contributions have been praiseworthy and most significant.

Swami Vivekananda
(12 January, 1863 – 04 July, 1902)

Sh. Swami Vivekananda was a monk, a philosopher, an author, a religious teacher, and the chief disciple of Sh. Ramakrishna Paramahamsa Maharaj. He introduced Ved Vedanta and yoga to the western world and bought interfaith awareness, he contributed to Hindutva by providing it an important status at the world level.

Swami Vivekananda became popular after the 1893 parliament of religions in Chicago, where he delivered his famous speech; he was so impactful at the world parliament that famous newspapers and senior journalists described him as an orator who possessed divine powers, through the years he delivered lectures about Hindutva, across Europe. He founded the Ramakrishna mission in 1897 for promoting Vedantic philosophy and carrying out charity, social work, and education.

Hindutva and nationalism were a prominent theme in Swami Vivekanand's thought; he believed that the country's future depends on its people, and his teachings focused on human development. The national youth day is celebrated each year on January 12, which is the birth anniversary of Swami Vivekananda, his quotes and teaching has always been a source of inspiration and motivation for youth and people across the nation.

In the Sangh, Swami Vivekananda is seen as a role model, and one cannot deny the fact that he remains one of the greatest figures of Hindutva in pre and post independent Bharat. The teachings and philosophy of Swami Vivekananda are taught in the Baudhik sessions of the Sangh shiksha vargas, even in major Adhiveshans and programmes of the ABVP. Swami Vivekananda is considered the main source of inspiration and a guiding light. He was a historic philosopher, and he will continue to inspire and motivate the youth in the Sangh as well as the people of the nation.

Sh.Vinayak Damodar Savarkar (Veer Savarkar)
(May 28, 1883 – February 26, 1966)

"सावरकर माने तेज, सावरकर माने त्याग, सावरकर माने तप, सावरकर माने तत्व, सावरकर माने तर्क, सावरकर माने तारुण्य, सावरकर माने तीर, सावरकर माने तलवार, सावरकार माने तिलमिलाहट... सागरा प्राण तड़मड़ला, तड़मड़ाती हुई आत्मा, सावरकर माने तितीक्षा, सावरकर माने तीखापन, सावरकर माने तिखट। कैसा बहुरंगी व्यक्तित्व! कविता और क्रांति"! – *Sh. Atal Bihari Vajpayee on Veer Savarkar.*

Sh. Vinayak Damodar Savarkar (Veer Savarkar) is regarded as one of the stalwarts of Hindutva in Bharat and across the world; he was a freedom fighter and a leader of the independence movement; he coined the term Hindutva, which is regarded as the core of the Hindu ideology.

Veer Savarkar began his political activity while he was a student; he was educated at Ferguson college Pune; he founded a secret society known as Abhinav Bharat society with his brother Ganesh Savarkar; the aim of the society was achieving Bharat's independence through revolutionary measures. Right from his childhood, he was a vocal advocate of Hindutva; he also served as the president of the Hindu Mahasabha from 1937 to 1943; little do people know that in his book (The History of the War of Indian Independence), he analysed the circumstances of the 1857 uprising, it was by his book and contribution that 1857 is regarded as the nation's first independence movement.

He went to the United Kingdom for his law education, and in London, he was involved in organization such as the India house and the Free India society; he was active in the movement aimed at overthrowing the British government from India. When he reached back to India in 1910, he was arrested on multiple charges, and he was then imprisoned for 50 years in 1911 at the infamous cellular jail in Andaman and Nicobar Islands. He was considered as a political prisoner by the British.[40]

He was a prominent figure of the Hindu Mahasabha; he wanted to establish a collective Hindu identity as the essence of Bharat; he developed the ideology of Hindutva while he was imprisoned. Savarkar wrote his ideological treatise 'Hindutva – Who is a Hindu', he promoted a farsighted new vision of Hindutva and Hindu social and political consciousness, he began describing Hindu as a patriotic inhabitant of the Bharatvarsh. He outlines his vision of the Hindu Rashtra as Akandh

---

40   https://organiser.org/2023/05/28/82575/analysis/contribution-of-veer-savarkar-to-
    national-life-

Bharat stretching across the entire Bharatiya subcontinent; during his lifetime, he wrote 38 books in English and Marathi, and out of these, the most important was the 'Essentials of Hindutva' in which he described Hindutva as bound together not only by a place but by a common fatherland and common blood which is the Bharatvarsha.

He was a true Hindu to the core; he was a real Bharat Maa ka Laal, and his contributions to Hindutva in the nation can never be disregarded; he was a statesman, a believer in the idea of Bharat and Hindu Rashtra, he was a visionary and a revolutionary patriot.

'Kranti Veer' Ganesh Damodar Savarkar
(G.D Savarkar) (13 June, 1879 – 16 March, 1945)

Sh. Ganesh Damodar Savarkar was a freedom fighter, Hindu nationalist, a revolutionary, he was the elder brother of V.D Savarkar, and he imparted excellent training at physical and intellectual levels and created an atmosphere against the British. His essay on nationalism, "Rashtra Mimansa" was abridged as the first systematic statement of the Rashtriya Swayamsevak Sangh ideology.

He single-handedly brought up his two brothers Vinayak Damodar Savarkar and Narayan Savarkar, and a younger sister after the family lost their parents when he was just twenty years old. He was a true nationalist and motivated the youth to rebel against the British Raj; he was the first to declare that "Hindustan is a Hindu nation." Ganesh Savarkar also established the Mitra Mela, a revolutionary secret society in Nasik in 1899. It was one among several such revolutionary societies functioning in Maharashtra at that time, which believed in overthrowing British rule through armed rebellion; the society grew to include several hundred revolutionaries and political activists with branches in various parts of the nation.

Sh. G.D Savarkar was an astute leader with exemplary organizational skills; his contribution to the independence movement and to the Sangh was exemplary.

Sh. Nanaji Deshmukh
(October 11, 1916 – February 27, 2010)

Chandikadas Amrit Rao Deshmukh, also known as Sh. Nanji Deshmukh was a brilliant social reformer and worked extensively in the field of education, health, and rural self-reliance. He was a leader of the Bhartiya Jan Sangh and was also a member of the Lok Sabha and Rajya Sabha.

Sh. Deshmukh was inspired by Sh. Bal Gangadhar Tilak, and from the beginning, he acquired deep interests in social service; Dr.Hedgewar inspired him to attend Sangh shakhas and it was by his inspiration that in the initial years Sh.Deshmukh became an active Swayamsevak of the Sangh.[41] He joined the Sangh in 1928, and became a full time pracharak of the Sangh, in the 1940's the then Sarsanghchalak Guruji Golwalkar had sent him to Gorakhpur for overlooking the activities of the Sangh in Uttar Pradesh.

Sh. Deshmukh was a visionary leader and had superb intellectual qualities, within three years of his induction in Gorakhpur he established about 250 shakhas of the Sangh, he also established the nation's first Saraswati Shishu Mandir at Gorakhpur in 1950.

---

41 https://organiser.org/2023/02/27/18774/bharat/nanaji-deshmukh-the-social-reformer-par-excellence/

Swami Vivekananda.

Sh. Veer Savarkar.

*Sh. Veer Savarkar, Sh. Narayan Savarkar,
& Sh. Ganesh Savarkar.*

Sh. Nanaji Deshmukh.

The Saraswati Shishu Mandir, is currently one of the largest chain of schools in the nation, he also founded the Deen Dayal research institute situated at Chitrakoot, Madhya Pradesh, and established the nation's first rural university, the Chitrakoot Gramodaya Vidhyalaya; he actively participated in the Bhoodan movement, he was a true patriot and personified compassion and service to people in the society.

In 1947 the Sangh decided to launch two journals, 'Rashtra Dharma' and 'Panchajanya', as well as a newspaper 'Swadesh'; Sh Atal Bihari Vajpayee was assigned the responsibility of the editor, and Sh. Deen Dayal Upadhaya was made the Marg Darshak, with Nanaji as the managing director. In 1978 in Chitrakoot, Madhya Pradesh, he created a self-sustainable model of development based on the concept of Gram Swaraj. He was an example of holistic development and wanted that development should reach the last man in line.

In an interview in 1997 with the India today magazine, Sh. Nanaji said 'if it had not been for the Sangh, I would not have thought of the country and devoted my life to it, whatever Nanaji Deshmukh is today is because of the Sangh, the Sangh is an inspirational and historic organization'.

Sh. Nanaji Deshmukh was a social reformer par excellence, and his contribution to the nation and the Sangh will always be revered and remembered. Nanaji was posthumously awarded Bharat Ratna which is regarded as the nation's highest civilian award in 2019 by the Government of India.

Sh. Eknath Ji Ranade
(19 November 1914 – 22 August 1982)

Sh. Eknath Ranade was a social activist and a senior leader of the Sangh. He joined the Sangh in 1926 only after a year of the formation of the organization, later in 1930, he became the Prant pracharak in Madhya Pradesh. He was deeply influenced by the teachings of Swami Vivekananda. From 1963 to 1972 Eknath Ranade is considered to have played an instrumental role in constructing the Vivekananda rock memorial and the Vivekananda Kendra at Kanyakumari.

He served as an important ideologue of the Sangh, and played a crucial role when Sangh was banned illegally in 1948; in the book written by M.G Chitkara, Eknath Ranade has been mentioned as the quint essential underground Sarsanghchalak for his unparalleled contribution for keeping the Sangh alive during the tormentous ban of 1948.

From 1956 to 1962, Sh. Ranade served as Sah Sahkaryavah, the general secretary of the Sangh; in 1962 he was appointed as the All India Baudhik Pramukh. In 1963 during the centenary year of Swami Vivekananda's birth, Sh. Eknath Ranade established the Vivekananda rock memorial committee for the construction of the Vivekananda memorial.

Sh. Eknath Ranade was instrumental in drafting the constitution of the Sangh, the management style and discipline of organising the cadre in the Sangh, the drills, sports, and the main purpose of the officer training camps, which are known as the Sangh shiksha vargs are some of his important contributions.

Sh. Ranade was a relentless and hardworking Swayamsevak who contributed his life to the Sangh, a documentary called 'one life one mission' was made by Vivekananda Kendra to pay respects to him. He was a perfect blend of nationalism, spiritualism, and Hindutva.

Sh. Dattopant Thengadi
(10 November, 1920 – 14 October, 2004)

Sh. Dattopant Bapurao Thengadi, was a senior Sangh ideologue, he was a ardent supporter of Swadeshi economics. He was born in Wardha district in Maharashtra in 1920. The kind of impact he left on the social and economic life of Bharat is unparalleled and unique and has inspired generations.

He was the foremost advocate of simple living, deep thinking, courage, and a missionary zeal for a goal. He did his LL. B from the law college at Nagpur. He was a lawyer as well as a philosopher, he actively took part in the freedom movement; he became a full-time pracharak in 1942. Dr.Hedgewar deeply influenced him; he was an ardent follower of Guruji Golwalkar and Pt. Deen Dayal Upadhaya. Sh. Thengadi was a highly spirited person, and he established various organizations affiliated with the Sangh; he was a vocal supporter of the core philosophy of Hindu Dharma.

He first founded the Bharatiya Mazdoor Sangh in 1955, which went on to become one of the largest organizations related to trade and labour in the nation; he also founded the Bharatiya Kisan Sangh in 1979, and later in, 1991 he founded the Swadeshi Jagran Manch; he was one of the founder members and mentor of the ABVP. In 1992 the Akhil Bharatiya Adhivakta Parishad was founded in Delhi and Sh.Thenagdi was one of its co-founders.

He was also elected as a member of the Rajya Sabha for two terms representing the Bharatiya Jan Sangh; he showed exemplary leadership capabilities by organising the anti-emergency movement in many parts of the nation in 1975. He was a widely travelled man. He travelled practically to almost every district in the nation; he is regarded as one of the most intellectual leaders within the Sangh and Hindutva paradigm. He was an amazing orator and an expert in social, economic, and political issues.

He was also critical of western development models such as socialism and capitalism; he propounded the third way of socio–economic development based on the ideology of Sanatan Dharma. Sh. Thengadi was one of a kind leader and an intellectual par excellence; he also wrote many books from his experiences and ideological conviction towards Hindutva.

Sh. Deen Dayal Upadhyaya
(September 25, 1916 – February 11, 1968)

Sh. Deen Dayal Upadhyaya was the founder and proponent of the integral humanism (Ekatmanata Manavavd) concept and was the leader of the Bhartiya Jan Sangh; he established the monthly publication known as the Rashtra Dharma in the 1940s to spread the ideals of Hindutva.

He was a profound philosopher, organiser par excellence, and a leader who maintained the highest standards of personal integrity; he has been the source of ideological guidance and moral inspiration for the BJP since its inception. His treatise integral humanism, which is a critique of both communism and capitalism, provides a holistic alternative perspective for political action and statecraft consistent with the laws of creation and the universal needs of the human race.[42]

Sh. Upadhyaya was associated with the Sangh since 1937; he also came in close contact with Dr. Hedgewar Ji, in the 1940s he became a lifelong pracharak of the Sangh. He was always regarded as an ideal Swayamsevak of the Sangh essentially because he reflected the main philosophy and ideology of the organization. In 1951, Sh. Syama Prasad Mukherjee founded the Bhartiya Jan Sangh and Sh. Upadhyaya was seconded to the party by the Sangh. In 1951, Sh. Golwalkar shifted him to the Jan Sangh; he was chosen as the organizing secretary at the party's first convention in 1952 in Kanpur.

---

42 BJP e-Library: Pandit Deendayal Upadhyay. https://library.bjp.org/jspui/handle/123 456789/433

The integral humanism concept of Sh. Upadhaya became the official doctrine of the Jan Sangh in 1965; the doctrine is based on the principles of progress of all, Gram Swaraj, affiliated with the cultural and national values of Bharat. Many newspapers and senior journalists in the 1960s-1970' described him as one of the most notable and credible leaders of that time.

Sh. Upadhyay was the first person in the Sangh to write extensively about the economy, he also wrote the 'Bharatiya Arth Niti' which contained economic analysis and specific policy aspects for growth of the nation, it also elaborates his vision for a domestic economic policy based on Bharatiya conditions and traditions, one of the key pillars of his view was the employment guarantee, he considered the right to work an integral part of democracy, minimum wage, equitable distribution, and social security system as an inalienable right of the citizen.

For Bharat, he visualised a decentralised polity and self-reliant economy, with the village being the core basis. The main motto of Sh. Upadhaya was to build a strong and prosperous nation on the foundation of Bharatiya culture, which guaranteed freedom, equality, and justice to all, and Sarvodaya and Antyodaya as a basis of life.

The nation lost Sh. Upadhaya on February 10, 1968; he was mysteriously found dead near the railway tracks at Mughal Sarai in Uttar Pradesh. Till date, his death has remained unresolved; the congress government of that time did not properly investigate the death of Sh. Upadhaya. The incident of death, was so meticulously planned that many senior commentators and journalists said that it was purely a political murder, at the time of his death Sh. Upadhaya was the president of the Bhartiya Jan Sangh; Bharat lost a great son of the soil on that day.

Sh. Eknathji Ranade.

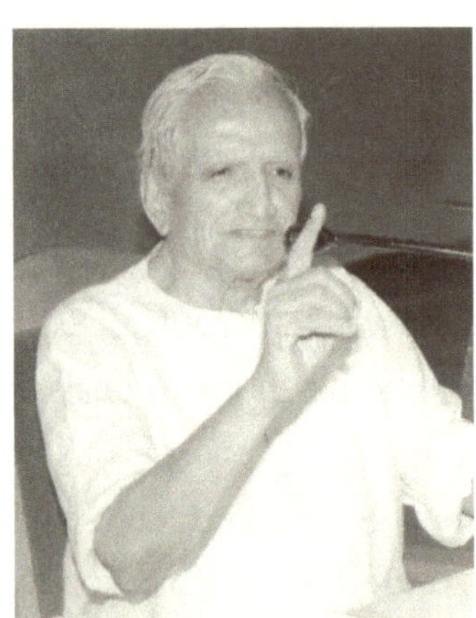

Sh. Dattopant Thengadi.

Sh. Deendayal Upadhyay.

He was a national treasure and an asset to the nation Pt. Deen Dayal Upadhyay is and always will be remembered in the hearts of every Swayamsevak.

Sh. H.V Sheshadri
(1926 – 2005)

Sh. H.V. Sheshadri was born in 1926 in Bangalore. He completed his master's degree in chemistry from Bangalore university. He was an author, social activist, and a senior Sangh pracharak; having been inspired by the ideals and principles of the Sangh from childhood, he became a pracharak of the Sangh in 1946.

He played a pivotal role in the growth of the Sangh in Karnataka. He held various responsibilities in the Sangh, such as Pranth pracharak and Kshetra pracharak, and finally became Sarkaryavaha in 1987. Due to his failing health, he retired as Sarkaryavaha in 2000 and was subsequently the organization›s Akhil Bharatiya Pracharak Pramukh, a post he held until his death. He was one of the most senior and respected leaders of the Sangh Parivar and inspired thousands of Sangh workers. He commanded respect throughout the Sangh; he contributed significantly to communicating nationalistic thoughts and Sangh ideology to the masses through his brilliant speeches and writings. He devoted his entire life to promoting Hindutva and the philosophy of the Sangh.

Sh.Sheshadri wrote articles for several decades for Vikrama weekly, Utthana monthly, Organiser weekly, Panchajanya Hindi weekly, and other periodicals; his writings were very popular. He wrote numerous books, his Torberalu, a collection of essays with social themes, won the Karnataka State Sahitya Akademi award in 1982. He wrote many articles, books, and booklets, and his writings have been deeply appreciated.

Sh. Syama Prasad Mukherjee
(July 06, 1901 – June 23, 1953)

Dr. Syama Prasad Mukherjee occupies a very important place in the national political landscape of Bharat. He was an astute leader, barrister, and legendary academician; he founded the Bhartiya Jana Sangh, the predecessor organization of the BJP, on October 21, 1951. He was also the president of Akhil Bhartiya Hindu Mahasabha from 1943 to 1946.

Dr. Syama Prasad Mukherjee after the nation's independence in 1947, focused on achieving the complete integration of Kashmir into India; he strongly opposed article 370, which provided autonomous status to Jammu and Kashmir. In the initial years of his life, he was associated with the congress, he was also inducted into the first ministry at the time of Nehru as a Minister of Industry and Supply but after certain experiences within the congress, he resigned for the cause of Hindutva and founded the Bhartiya Jan Sangh.

The ideology by which the Bhartiya Jan Sangh was created was with the object of nation building and bringing within people the philosophy of Hindu nationalism. Syama Prasad Mukherjee was a visionary leader who could visualise the far future and had set the foundation stone for the formation of the world's largest political party.

For the demand of accession of Jammu and Kashmir's to India, Dr.Mukherjee entered J&K on May 11, 1953, he was arrested upon entering Kashmir, in June 1953, he suffered from pleurisy disease; later on, 23 June 1953 he died of heart attack; his death was an impervious mystery that was never solved.[43] He was a veteran leader and was respected by all political classes for his knowledge and foresightedness; the nation lost a great son at a very early stage of the nation's independence.

---

43   https://theprint.in/india/how-syama-prasad-mookerjee-launched-first-nationwide-campaign-on-jk-and-paid-with-his – life/446397

Sh. H.V Sheshadri.

Sh. Syama Prasad Mukherjee.

Swami Chinmayananda.

Dr.Mukherjee will always be respected and remembered for his contribution to the nation's development, particularly in sectors of commerce and industry; he was a core nationalist and also a determined believer and follower of Hindutva. The nation will always be indebted to his contribution.

Sh. Swami Chinmayanada
(May 08, 1916 – August 03, 1993)

Swami Chinmayananda was a Hindu spiritual leader and a philosopher. He founded the Chinmaya mission in 1953 to spread the knowledge of Advaita Vedanta, the Bhagwat Gita, and the Upanishads, among other Hindu scriptures. The Chinmaya mission was founded with an aim to bring the timeless knowledge of Ved Vedanta closer to the people; at the same time, it teaches one about spiritual growth and contentment.

The mission spearheaded a global Hindu spiritual and cultural renaissance that popularised the Hindu spiritual text and values across Bharat and the world. The mission has built several of hospitals and schools around the world, and today, it has more than 300 centres in the nation and abroad.

Swami Chinmayananda was a historic figure in the context of the Hindutva philosophy; he founded the Vishwa Hindu Parishad in 1964 with Sh. Guruji Golwalkar and SS Apte; according to him, the objective of the VHP was to awaken Hindus about their morale and rights in the world. He was also a profound believer in the ideology of the Sangh.

He authored 95 publications in his lifetime, including forty commentaries on classical scriptural texts, eight compilations, 13 co-authored works, and 34 original works, he was a firm believer in the ideas of the Sangh. Also, he believed that Hindus must be politically empowered and that the revival of Hindu strength is very important for the rejuvenation of the nation; he also advised that every Hindu should raise a Bhagwa Dhwaj in front of each house.

On May 08, 2015, Prime minister Sh. Narendra Modi released a commemorative coin to mark his birth centenary. His contribution and commitment to Hindutva will always be remembered.

Sh. Ashok Singhal
(September 27, 1926 – November 17, 2015)

Sh. Ashok Singhal was a prominent leader of the Vishva Hindu Parishad and was the international working president of the VHP; he led the organization for about 20 years and was in charge of the Ram Janmabhoomi movement, he was born in Agra, and he belonged to an influential family of senior bureaucrats and businessman.

Sh. Singhal was an alumnus of the prestigious IIT BHU and received bachelor's degree in metallurgical engineering. He joined the Sangh in 1942 under Sh. Balasahab Deoras, soon he became a full-time pracharak, and worked extensively for the Sangh in Uttar Pradesh for many years; later he became the Prant pracharak for Delhi and Haryana.

In early 1980's, he was deputed to the Vishva Hindu Parishad as the joint general secretary, and he was one of the core members of the VHP. He was a key organiser of the first Dharam Sansad, which was held in 1984 at Vigyan Bhawan in New Delhi; the Dharam Sansad was attended by hundreds of Sadhus and notable eminent personalities, the movement to reclaim the Ram Janmabhoomi began here, Sh. Singhal is regarded as one of the chief architect of the Ram Janmabhoomi movement.

From the 1980s to 2000, he was considered to be the lifeline of the VHP. Balasahab Deoras, the third Sarsanghchalak of the Sangh, wanted the Sangh Parivar to be more assertive and active in the public arena; thus, Sh. Singhal was given charge of VHP in 1983.

Sh. Singhal is often regarded as Hindu Hridhaya Samrat because of his relentless devotion and work for Hindus; he expanded VHP's base through various innovative programmes surrounding the Ram Janmabhoomi. The Shila Poojan was one of the most important programmes of the VHP in which bricks for the foundation of the Ram Mandir were sent from across the country to Ayodhya. He was committed to make Hindutva, a household name across the nation. In an interview, he said that the Sangh is the university, and organizations like the VHP are branches of that university. He was a stalwart and legendary leader of the VHP and the Sangh.

Sh. Bhaurao Deoras
(November 09, 1917 – May 13, 1992)

Sh. Murlidhar Dattatray Deoras, popularly known as Bhaurao Deoras, was a senior Sangh pracharak and was the younger brother of the third Sarsanghchalak Sh. Balasahab Deoras. He was born in Nagpur and joined the Sangh at the age of eleven years; he was amongst the first batch of Swayamsevaks who joined the Sangh shaka started by Dr. Hedgewar at Mohite Wada, Nagpur.

He became a full-time Sangh pracharak in his early adulthood, and he worked for the Sangh in Uttar Pradesh extensively, he is also regarded as one of the leading ideologue of the Ram Janmabhoomi movement. He was a meritorious student in his college days; he was an LL. B by education. He is also regarded as being instrumental in establishing the nation's first Saraswati Shishu Mandir in Gorakhpur in 1952; he groomed very well-known leaders of the Sangh who went on to became stalwarts and leaders of the Sangh Parivar.

He was an organiser par excellence, and Dr. Hedgewar was quick to identify this important trait of his personality, from a Mukhya Shikshak of a shakha to the Sangh Karyavaha of Nagpur, with time he became an important figure in the Maharashtra circle of the Sangh.

Sh. Ashok Singhal.

Sh. Bhaurao Deoras.

Smt. Laxmibai Kelkar.

During the birth centenary of Sh. Hedgewar, in 1989, Sh. Bhaurao announced the creation of Seva Vibhag within the Sangh and launched more than five thousand service projects. He will always be remembered for his long-lasting contribution to the motto of social service, he was also at the centre of movements such as the Ram Janmabhoomi, and he aggressively pushed forward events like the Ekatmata Yatra and Prabhu Ram Shila Pujan; his personal assistant, Sh. Shrikant Joshi once commented that if Guruji was described as the heart of Dr. Hedgewar, Sh. Bhaurao was his soul and vision.

Smt. Laxmibai Kelkar (Mausiji)
(6th July 1906 – 27 November 1978)

Laxmibai Kelkar, affectionately known as 'Mausiji' was the pioneer who established the 'Rashtra Sevika Samiti' she was born with the name 'Kamal' in Nagpur to Bhaskar Rao Datey, a government servant, and Yashodabai, a homemaker. After her marriage, she was named 'Laxmibai'. Unfortunately, her marriage could only last for a span of eleven years.[44] She got widowed at the very young age, as her husband expired due to tuberculosis.

She single-handedly took care of the family. She realized that there was no school for girls in Wardha to admit her daughter, so she took the first step in laying the foundation of a girl's school, which was named Kesarimal Kanya Vidyalaya and established in the early 1930s.[44] Her milestone work paved the way for women's literacy in Wardha. She considered that a woman is pivotal for raising a family and a nation.

She was introduced to the Sangh through her sons in the early 1930s, as they were Bal Swayamsevaks; she was keenly observing the way of working based on individual contact, mutual respect, and voluntary discipline. It gave her the idea that such an organizational type of work amongst women could be significant as building character, creating a sense of patriotism, and discipline was necessary.

Fortunately, Dr. Hedgewar was to visit the Wardha shakha of the Sangh. With the help of local workers, including Sh. Appaji Joshi, she got an opportunity to meet him. In their meeting, Smt. Kelkar expressed the significance of organizing Hindu women on cultural and national basis.

Gifted with divine vision, Dr. Hedgewar was convinced and conceded to the proposal; Smt. Kelkar had the zeal that women should serve the nation, this motivated her to unite women who wished to perform 'Seva' for the nation. Moreover, this is how the Rashtra Sevika Samiti came into being with the determination of Laxmibai Kelkar and the guidance of Dr. Hedgewar. It was decided that although Samiti's ideology would be parallel to the Sangh, but it would be autonomous and independent. On Vijayadashmi day in 1936, the Rashtra Sevika Samiti was formally inaugurated.

She established the Grihini Vidyalaya in 1953 to provide vocational courses, training programs, and short-term courses to develop the natural talents of women. She also established the Bharatiya Shrividya Niketan to reorganize women's education based on Bharat's glorious culture.

She formed Bhajan Mandals to encourage the musical and devotional talents of the women and inspired them to compose the achievements of great women like Rani Lakshmibai and Jijamata in poetic form. She constructed the Devi Ahalya Mandir at Nagpur, the Ashtabhuja Mandir at Wardha, and many other temples.[44]

Smt. Kelkar embodies a Bharatiya Naari who was brave and taught others to fight their own battles. She did not let widowhood or other struggles pull her down. She is a true role model for every woman of Bharat. She struggled to establish the supremacy of the Hindu ideology of 'Vasudaivaka Kutumbakam,' meaning 'the world is one family'. She dedicated her life to the service and care of the motherland.[44] As the first head of the Sevika Samiti, she was the Pramukh Sanchalika. She retained the title until her death in 1978.[45]

Sh. Baba Saheb Apte
(29 April 1903 – 1971)

Babasaheb Apte, was a senior pracharak of the Sangh, in 1924 he moved to Nagpur and joined the press of the Udyam magazine and later formed a Vidyarthi Mandal (student society) for promoting revolutionary ideas.[46] Dr. Hedgewar visited the organization in 1925 and inspired Apte to merge his organization with the Sangh. In 1927, he became one of the first Swayamsevak to be a Sangh pracharak, even before the term itself was coined.

Sh. Apte was instrumental in spreading the network of the Sangh shakhas in Maharashtra in the early 1930s and, later, in the rest of the country.[46] He became an important associate to Dr. Hedgewar in coordinating the Sangh pracharak network. He travelled continuously and provided help to the pracharaks by meeting people in society to encourage their support for the Sangh shakhas.[46]

Sh.Apte also had significant interest in history and the Sanskrit language, thus to commemorate his keen interest in rewriting Bharat's history with the vision of Hindutva as well as popularising Sanskrit, Sh Moropant Pingley had set up Babasaheb Apte Smarak Samiti in 1973 for commissioning and publishing books on these topics. This organization in due course gave rise to the All-India Akhil Bharatiya Itihas Sankalan

---

44 https://organiser.org/2022/07/09/88896/bharat/lakshmibai-kelkar-jayanti-mausi-ji-the-nari-shakti-behind-rashtra-sevika-samiti/

45 How RSS inspired a young widow to build an all-women's organisation across India. https://theprint.in/india/how-rss-inspired-a-young-widow-to-build-an-all-womens-organisation-across-india/617386/

Yojana. The Sangh has also instituted a "Baba Saheb Apte birth centenary national Sanskrit award" given annually in recognition of efforts for promoting Sanskrit.[46]

Mahant Avaidyanath Ji Maharaj
(Sh. Kripal Singh Bisht)
(May 28, 1921 – September 12, 2014)

Sh. Avaidyanath Ji Maharaj was the Mahant of Sh.Goraknath Mandir, succeeding his guru Sh Digvijay Nath, he was also a leader of the Hindu Mahasabha and later was elected to the Lok Sabha from Gorakhpur for four times, representing the BJP. He played a significant role in the Ram Janmabhoomi movement.

He was a staunch believer in the idea of the Ram Janmabhoomi movement. In 1984 he founded the Sri Ram Janma Bhoomi Mukti Yagna Samiti (committee of sacrifice to liberate Ram's birthplace). The Samiti aimed to bring all the Hindu organizations and Sadhus associated with the Ram Mandir movement on a single platform.

In September 1984, the Samiti launched a "religious procession with Hindu nationalist slogans" from Sitamarhi in Bihar to Ayodhya to liberate the Ram Mandir. At the Dharam Sansad organized at Udupi, Karnataka, on October 31, 1985, Mahant Avaidyanath and Ramchandra Das Paramhans, a Mahant of the Digambar Akhara, demanded the opening of the locks of the Babri Masjid so that devotees could offer prayers to the Bhagwan Sh. Ram idol. Also, a committee known as the Akhil Bhartiya Sangharsh Samiti was constituted to give a push to the movement.[47]

---

46 https://www.rss.org/ Babasaheb Apte (RSS Archives). | https://www.archivesofrss.org/ Encyc/2014/1/16/Babasaheb-Apte.aspx

47 Tracing the role of Gorakhnath Math in Ram temple movement – Hindustan Times. https://www.hindustantimes.com/india-news/tracing-the-role-of-yogi-adityanath-and-gorakhnath-math-in-ram-temple-movement/story-0zaFhkWuRY62qic8FSuWsI.html

Sh. Babasaheb Apte.

Sh. Moropant Pingley.

Mahant Sh. Avaidyanath Ji Maharaj with Yogi Adityanath Ji.

Sh. Yadavrao Joshi.

In a rally organized in Delhi on September 22, 1989, Sh Avaidyanath Ji announced 'Shilanyas' at Ram Janmabhoomi on November 09, 1989. His contribution to the Ram Janmbhoomi movement was unprecedented, and he was a true believer in the philosophy of Hindutva and Hindu Rashtra.

Sh. Moropant Pingley
(December 30, 1919 – September 21, 2003)

Sh. Moreshwar Nilkanth Pingley was a senior leader of the Sangh. He is often called the "commander of Hindu awakening." he was among the few who were honed under the mentorship of Dr. Hedgewar and Sh.Guruji. After graduating with a bachelor's degree in english in 1941, he became a full-time Sangh pracharak in 1946.

At the age of 26, he was appointed as Sah Prant pracharak of Maharashtra and Vidarbha. He was associated with the Sangh for sixty-five years; he was also a lifelong Sangh pracharak and was also the Akhil Bhartiya Baudhik Pramukh of the Sangh. During the 1975 emergency, he played a very significant role in the underground movement of the Sangh. He was also called as the "field marshal" of the Ram Janmabhoomi movement. The conversion of hundreds of Hindus at Meenakshipuram, Tamil Nadu, in 1981 led the VHP to organize its first Ekatmata Yatra by 1983. Due to his excellent organizational skills, he was given the responsibility of planning, coordinating, and executing the Yatra.

Sh. Pingley played a vital role in the Ekatmata Yatra, the Yatra began in 1983 and was followed by the 'Ram-Janki Rath Yatra' in 1984. It was a precursor to the Ram Janmabhoomi movement. This yatra aimed to reunite the Hindus and kindle the feeling of pride among them. Seven chariots travelled through Bihar and Uttar Pradesh; his effective selection of routes for the Ekatmata Raths (chariots) magnified the impact of the yatra. Sh.Pingley was appointed as the convener and controller of this Yatra. During its planning, he travelled extensively around the nation.

Sh. Yadavrao Joshi
(September 03, 1914 – August 20, 1992)

Sh. Yadavrao Joshi was a senior leader of the Sangh; he became a Sangh pracharak in the 1930s. He was associated as a Bal Swayamsevak with the Sangh; in 1932, he completed his Tritiya Sangh shiksha varg, and in 1941, he became the Sangh pracharak in Karnataka. He is also regarded as the "Commander of the South" as he extensively worked in spreading the Sangh in states such as Karnataka, Kerela, Tamil Nadu.

The Sangh Prarthana 'Namaste Sada Vatsale Matrbhume' was first publicly sung by Sh.Yadav Rao Joshi on May 18, 1940, in the Sangh shiksha varg held at Nagpur.[48] During the bans imposed on the Sangh in 1948 and 1975, he served prison terms and returned from prison with redoubled vigour and zeal for Sangh activities.

The Rashtrothan Parishad was established through his inspiration in the year 1965; it is today not only running the biggest blood bank in Bengaluru for needy persons but it is also reported to be the largest blood bank in the state; it also runs free coaching centers for slum children. On Sangh, he said, "the world wants to see the ordinary side of extraordinary men, but Sangh wants to see the extraordinary side of ordinary men."[49]

In 1978 he was appointed as Sah Sahkarvyah, he pioneered the Sangh work in Karnataka, and soon Karnataka became the second state after Maharashtra to become a stronghold of the Sangh after its formation in 1925. He founded many regional newspapers and

---

48   https://www.sewagatha.org/sewadoot/yadavrao-joshi
49   https://samvada7.rssing.com/chan-8997128/article349.html

magazines which were widely circulated during the 1960s – 1970s; he organized three major spoken Sanskrit conferences (Shivirs) in the years, 1948,1962,1982. Sh. Joshi also prepared the first batch of pracharaks and Sangh Swayamsevaks, who led the Sangh in senior positions for decades. He was an incarnation of uncompromising devotion to the Sangh and was associated with the Sangh for almost six decades. He inspired many in the Sangh, and his contribution to the organization can never be forgotten.

CHAPTER - 9

The Sangh Parivar ~ Affiliated Organizations & Contribution

Introduction

The Sangh Parivar is a group of organizations, which follow the philosophy and the ethos of the Rashtriya Swayamsevak Sangh; the Sangh Parivar represents the Hindu nationalist movement in Bharat. The organizations are called Parivar because they share the same genealogy of ideas.

The Sangh worked as a sole organization during the first two decades of its establishment; there were no affiliated organizations, the Sangh changed its focus after 1945, and it expanded and consolidated to each part of the nation through establishment of various organizations which came to be known as the Sangh Parivar. In the 1960s, a decade after independence, Swayamsevaks of the Sangh joined many social and political movements in the nation. After independence the Sangh also supported the formation of organizations such as the Bharatiya Mazdoor Sangh, Seva Bharti, and the Akhil Bhartiya Vidyarthi Parishad among others.

The organizations of the Sangh Parivar have inherent linkages and mutual coordination, which results in a nation building vision, this is also known as 'Sangh Samanvay'. During the decades from 1960 until the 2000s, the Sangh Parivar and its affiliated organizations have had steady growth in the nation's socio-economic and political landscape. Events after independence led to many organizational changes inside the

Sangh; what important occurrence happened after independence was that the Sangh and its leadership was determined to play an important role in the nation's development.

The Sangh Parivar organizations are, professional, social, economic, religious, educational, and socio-ethnic. Apart from them, there is the Prasar Prachar division, which is the news and communication centre. Many national and international think tanks are also functioning under the umbrella of the Sangh Parivar. Apart from them, there are overseas organizations of the Sangh Parivar which are situated in different countries across the world.

The organizations in the Sangh Parivar draw their intellectual and behavioural templates from the Sangh, but are complete in themselves and firmly grounded in society. A common emphasis of all organizations is that no dimension of society should be left untouched; they should impact all in society. The Sangh Parivar organizations are people-centric, they engage with the government's political system and the administrative setup. The organizations function on 'Samvad' & 'Sangarsh' (dialogue and agitation)

The Sangh Parivar organizations are not linked to any political party; they are tied to people's interest; this ensures their high credibility. The activities and organizations have considerable social impact, not only nationally but internationally; the Sangh's philosophy and ethos are followed, the basic essence of the Sangh Parivar is social, economic and personal empowerment of each one in the society.

The Sangh remains the mentor and provides guidance, direction, and support to the Parivar organizations as and when the need arises. Technically all the Sangh Parivar organizations are autonomous in nature; they have a separate organizational structure and representatives. However, Sangh pracharaks, who are full-time workers of the Sangh, are also deputed to work in these organizations at different levels.

As time passes, there will be multiple Sangh inspired forums in all fields of society; there are no full stops for Sangh activities; the Sangh is always an early respondent to changing needs and stays ahead of time. Swayamsevaks and the Sangh Parivar organizations are hardworking, laborious, and disciplined in their efforts. This chapter elaborates the Sangh Parivar organizations, their role, functioning and contribution in the society.

Occupational & Professional Organizations
The Bhartiya Kisan Sangh
(Founded – 04 March 1979)

The Bhartiya Kisan Sangh is a farmers organization linked to the Sangh; it was founded by visionary thinker, senior Sangh ideologue & pracharak Sh. Dattopant Thengadi Ji with a motive to help and achieve holistic development of the farmers across the nation, the BKS has nearly one million members across 17,000 villages and 800 districts across the country.

It was the vision of Sh. Dattopant Thengadi Ji that he wanted the Sangh to build an organization for the welfare and needs of farmers; the aims and objectives of the BKS have been the welfare of farmers, and to help the farmers to turn around farming into a profitable economic model.

The Bhartiya Mazdoor Sangh
(Founded – 23 July 1955)

The Bhartiya Mazdoor Sangh was also founded by Sh. Dattopant Thengadi Ji on 23 July 1955, Sh. Thengadi called together a meeting of a group of Swayamsevaks and representatives from 76 trade unions in July 1955 to lay the ground work for a new labour movement inspired by the ethos and principles of the Sangh.

Today it has nearly 15 million members; and forms a quintessential part of the Sangh Parivar. The Bharatiya Mazdoor Sangh became active in 1963 when it collaborated with the Hindu Mazdoor Sabha, it grew from 30,000 members in 1963 to 4,25,000 members in 1969 the Mazdoor Sangh has an Bharatiya approach to the labour union activity.

The BMS came into existence at a time when the trade union movement was taking shape, and the emergence of BMS has played an immense role in shaping the trade union movement in the nation; the main task of forming the BMS was to build a strong organizational structure for the benefit and welfare of the labour and factory workers.

Sh. Dattopant Thengadi Ji was one of the most stalwart Mazdoor Sangh ideologue and leader who explained that an economic system must be devised which makes use of a person's natural aptitude and the system should not exploit the human power, the material conditions and welfare should be the main focus, the Bharatiya Mazdoor Sangh is one of the most important affiliate organization of the Sangh.[50]

The Akhil Bhartiya Adhivakta Parishad (ABAP)
(Founded – 7 September 1992)

The Akhil Bhartiya Adhivakta Parishad is the organization of lawyers and is known as the RSS lawyers' wing; it aims to work for a judicial system which is in harmony with the ethos of the nation and in consonance with the Bharatiya traditions.

It was founded in 1992 by Sh. Dattopant Thengadi Ji, the ABAP has grown immensely with time; it was formally constituted in Delhi in 2001 and was also registered as a society; the founding members of the ABAP included Sh. H. R Khanna, Sh. Venkatramiyya, Sh. Rama Joyice, Sh.Guman Mal Lodha, Sh. U.R Lalit.

The ABAP exists at the nation level, there is a national executive of the Parishad, and it is responsible for making all policy decisions, at the state level, there is a state executive body and also a proper system of executives has been established, at the district, and individual court level their separate units have also been established for the smooth functioning of the organization, every three years. A national conference of the ABAP is held in which thousands of advocates from all across the nation participate.

Activities of The Akhil Bhartiya Adhivakta Parishad

Nyay Kendra – It is one of the flagship programs of the parishad; they have been established as legal aid centers to make justice accessible to the socially and economically backward sections of society, **Legal Awareness Camps** – It also organizes legal awareness camps to inform people of their rights, **Study Circles And Symposiums** – Many study circles and research groups are formed at the state and national levels in which senior advocates work on matters of law and jurisprudence with the cooperation of junior advocates. The Parishad also publishes a quarterly bilingual magazine known as 'Nyay Pravaha.'

Akhil Bhartiya Vidhyarthi Parishad (ABVP)
(Founded – 9 July 1949)

After the independence of the nation the Sangh tried to widen its base and included students into the ambit of the organization. The first ban of 1948 – 1949 offered the Sangh an opportunity to organize students, the first student group was formed at Delhi university, and later similar groups were formed in Haryana and Punjab; Balraj Madhok, a young Sangh pracharak was one of the most influential persons who was successful in organizing students.

In October 1948, senior members of the Sangh met in Delhi, and later in 1949, on 9 July, the Akhil Bhartiya Vidhyarthi Parishad (ABVP) was formed as a new national body; the Vidhyarthi Parishad is one of the nation's prime student organization working very actively in university campuses across the nation.[50]

Yashvant Rao Kelkar and Balraj Madhok are considered to be the real architects of the ABVP; today it is one of the largest student organizations in the nation, lakhs of students are associated with it; it is an organization committed to Hindutva and the welfare and good being of each and every student, the ABVP provides free of cost college counselling to students seeking admissions and also organizes study circles for students.

By 1970, the Vidhyarthi Parishad had become a significant force in university campuses and in students union politics; the most important turning point in the Vidhyarthi Parishad activism came in 1974 – 1975 when ABVP was actively involved in the student agitations of Bihar and Gujarat, the Vidhyarthi Parishad in Gujarat participated in the Nav Nirman movement which ultimately led to the resignation of the congress state government in February 1974.[50]

When the emergency was declared on 25 June 1975, the Parishad and its top leaders, like Sh.Arun Jaitley, were arrested. The Vidhyarthi Parishad was involved in underground activities during the emergency and played a very significant role.

The ABVP's motto is to have a right perspective towards the need for holistic and all-round development of students. The ABVP has been very successful in student elections across universities in all parts of the nation; the organization is also significantly influenced by the ideals and teachings of Swami Vivekananda; it focuses on student power

---

50   Walter K. Andersen & Shridhar D. Damle – The Brotherhood in Saffron | Chapter – 4 (The RSS 'Family' Takes Shape), pg. 143 | 1987,2019 Reprint, Penguin Random House India.

which is also known as 'Chatra Shakti'. ABVP aims to build an ideal student movement which will work in the wider context of national reconstruction; the organization also organizes many study tours, career guidance programmes, and personality development workshop for students. The official ABVP magazine is 'Rashtriya Chhatra Shakti', which is published monthly in Hindi.

As of 2023, the membership of the Vidyarthi Parishad is nearly four million in number, and it is the nation's largest student organization committed to nation building and student welfare.

The Think India conference and summits for students, such as the Yuva Vikas Kendra, are some of the primary programmes of ABVP, which are very successful and fundamentally transforming students and their ideas for the nation; the ABVP has been one of the most influential and historic organizations of the Sangh Parivar. The motto of the organization is Gyan Sheel Ekta (knowledge, character, unity), Chhatrashakti (students power), & Rashtrashkati (nation's power)

Swadeshi Jagran Manch
(Founded – 22 November 1991)

The Swadeshi Jagran Manch, is an economic, cultural organization founded by Sh. Dattopant Thengadi Ji in 1991 in the backdrop of the liberalization reforms in the nation. It was founded in Nagpur, Maharashtra.

The Swadeshi Jagran Manch has been critical of the overt globalization of resources and is an organization which aims for indigenous growth; the motto vocal for local is inspired by the Swadeshi Jagran Manch, which pleads for the development and better growth of the local industries at the rural and urban level in villages and cities across the nation.

The Swadeshi Jagran Manch has an all-India network of sub units up to district level across the country. It is progressively reaching geographical and social spread of the country. The Swadeshi Patrika is published as a monthly magazine of the SJM in Hindi as well as in English. Swadeshi Jagran Manch has emerged as a successful organization, with a vision and action plan for a truly self-reliant Bharat and an equitable world order.

Sahakar Bharati
(Founded – 11 January 1978)

Sahakar Bharati is the Pan India organization of cooperatives founded in 1978, it works for the upliftment of small farmers, land less labourers, tribals, and rural craftsmen. Sh. Lakshman Rao Inamdar is regarded as the main motivational force in the formation of the Sahakar Bharati, he is also the founding father of the Sangh in Gujarat. The Sahakar Bharati is one of the most respected organizations of the Sangh Parivar.[51]

It is headquartered in Thane, Maharashtra; the Sahakar Bharati has been working relentlessly over the years for the development and revitalization of cooperatives across the nation; the Sahakar Bharati is in the forefront of the cooperative movement in the nation. It also works in the development of primary agricultural societies across states.

---

51   The Sahakar Bharati | https://sahakarbharati.org/

Akhil Bharatiya Adhikvakta Parishad.

Bhartiya Kisan Sangh.

Bharatiya Mazdoor Sangh.

Akhil Bharatiya Vidhyarthi Parishad (ABVP).

Swadeshi Jagran Manch.

Social Services Organizations
Bharat Vikas Parishad
(Founded – 12 January 1963)

The Bharat Vikas Parishad, also known as the Indian Development Council, was founded in 1963 on the birth anniversary of Swami Vivekananda; it is headquartered in Delhi. The primary purpose of the Bharat Vikas Parishad is to organize citizens of the society for philanthropic work; it is an organization where people from all walks of life join the motto for the development and growth of the nation, through promoting a sense of patriotism, national unity, and integrity, culminating in Swastha – Samarth Bharat which means, physically, economically strong nation.

Vanvasi Kalyan Ashram
(Founded – 26 December 1952)

The Vanvasi Kalyan Ashram is a social welfare organization and it works for the welfare of the members of the schedule tribes and schedule communities. It was founded in the year 1952 by Sh. Balasaheb Deshpande. It was inaugurated by Sangh Sarsanghchalak Sh.Guru Golwalkar Ji.

The main objective of Ashram is to eliminate the gap between Hindu community and their Vanvasi brothers with affection and good faith. It is working to develop a sense of belonging, among the Vanvasis, for attaining this aim, various projects, and several volunteers are working full time for the educational, health and developmental (social, religious, and spiritual) projects started by the Ashram. VKA has always made efforts on all fronts to bring Vanvasis in the mainstream of society and at the same time introduce the rich culture of the Vanvasis to society.

The Seva Bharti
(Founded – 2 October 1979)

Seva Bharti is a social service organization which was founded by the Sarsanghchalak of the Sangh Sh.Balasaheb Deoras Ji, it was founded in the year 1979. In April 1979, Sh. Deoras addressed a mammoth gathering of Swayamsevaks & volunteers at the Ambedkar stadium in Delhi, where he called upon them to start social service activities among the neglected sections of the society.

His speech was the first significant step that led to the idea of Seva Bharti. Although the volunteers of Sangh and other allied organizations had been informally working for the betterment of people in the society, it was opined that a formal structure would help coordinate the service programs all over the country. Thus, the organization was formally established on 02 October 1979 in Delhi.

The Seva Bharti functions on the motto of official community service and the Akhil Bhartiya Sah Seva Pramukh of the Sangh guides the organization. It is also represented in the Akhil Bhartiya Prathinidhi Sabha, the highest decision-making body of the Sangh Parivar.

The Seva Bharti has time and again proved that it is an organization that has always worked for the welfare of the society; the Seva Bharti did massive relief work during the 2001 Gujarat earthquake, the 2004 Tsunami, Kerala floods, and the 2013 Uttarakhand floods.

The organization is also known for its efforts to rehabilitate victims of terror also, the volunteers of Seva Bharti today are involved in more than 1500 service projects in remote areas of the nation. Apart from it the Seva Bharti is running nearly 19,000 projects in education; 14,000 projects in healthcare and nearly 9,000 projects in self-reliance.[52]

---

52   The Seva Bharti | https://www.sevabhartidelhi.org/

The Seva Bharti has established over 5,000 healthcare centres across the nation; it also works for the rehabilitation and empowerment of differently abled children; it runs orphanages named Matri Chaaya. During the Covid pandemic, the Seva Bharti distributed food packets, sanitary masks and basic medicines to people across the nation, almost 2.5 lakh Seva Bharti cadres were reaching out to people to remotest corners of the nation; only in Delhi nearly 79,000 people were being fed daily by the Seva Bharti and 47 kitchens were working round the clock. Seva Bharti has also developed vocational centres for women's empowerment in the field of handicrafts and cottage industry. The Seva Bharti has worked immensely in the establishment of environmental awareness programmes and awareness campaigns for clean drinking water.

'Seva' means serving people and the name of this historic organization suggest its true nature which is the welfare of people. The Seva Bharti is an historic organization of the Sangh Parivar. It has been a catalyst for sustainable development and social change. Little do people know that the Sangh is an organization for the welfare of each and every person in the society, many see, the Sangh only as a proponent of Hindutva but the Sangh, has brilliant contribution in every field of the society, the work of Seva Bharti is just a reminder of what actually the Sangh is.

Women Organizations
Rashtra Sevika Samiti
(Founded – 25 October 1936)

The Rashtra Sevika Samiti is the women wing of the Sangh. It was founded by Smt. Laxmibai Kelkar, it is an organization that is independent of the Sangh, but shares the same ideology. In the 1930s, Laxmi Bai Kelkar took inspiration from Dr. Hedgewar Ji, the founder of the Sangh for, the need to start a women wing in the Sangh. Dr. Hedgewar Ji advised Kelkar to establish the organization as autonomous and independent of Sangh. Still, he promised unconditional support and guidance for the Sevika

Samiti; following this, Laxmi Bai Kelkar founded the organization in 1936 (Vijayadashmi Day) at Wardha, Maharashtra.

Soon after its formation, the Rashtra Sevika Samiti became a nationwide phenomenon with thousands of volunteers. Several Sevika Samiti centres and shakhas were opened in different parts of the country, in which much importance was given to the overall development of the services with a particular focus on the physical development of women. Through a standardized structure, more and more women became empowered. Various programs are also undertaken by the Sevika Samiti, which includes recitation of Ramayan-Mahabharat, art, education, and historical accounts of important Bharatiya figures, among many others.

Today, Rashtra Sevika Samiti is one of the important organizations involving women actively in social awareness programmes. The Samiti currently operates nearly 6000 centres and has overseas branches in 10 nations across the globe; it also runs 500 plus service projects and Gaushalas, libraries, and computer training centres; also, shakhas are organised regularly.

Under the aegis of the Rashtra Sevika Samiti, Smt.Kelkar, began the publication of a journal, 'Sevika' in Marathi, which is now published in many languages as 'Rashtra Sevika.' Smt Kelkar remained the first head of the organization; she was called Pramukh Sanchalika.[53] She retained the title until 1978.

Religious Organizations
The Vishva Hindu Parishad
(Founded – 29 August 1964)

The divisions within the Hindu community were persistent even after a decade of independence, thus with this concern in mind, Guru

---

53   Laxmibai Kelkar – Personification of Indian Spirit – Vishwa Samwad Kendra, Mumbai. https://www.vskkokan.org/2021/07/19/6806

Golwalkar Ji invited a selected group of leaders in Bombay in 1964 and discussed ways in which different Hindu sects and movements could work more closely with each other, thus on 29 August 1964, the Vishwa Hindu Parishad was formed, the main founders were Guru Golwalkar Ji, Sh.Shivaram Shankar Apte & Swami Chinmayananda.

VHP was officially established in 1964 at Sandeepany Ashram, the headquarters of the Chinmaya Mission in Bombay and Swami Chinmayananda presided over the first meeting of VHP in which many other great saints of various Hindu faiths and sects were also present. Its theme was 'Dharmo Rakshati Rakshitah,' that is, Dharma protects those who protect it. Swami Chinmayananda was the first president of VHP.

The main objectives of the Vishwa Hindu Parishad is to: – Consolidate and strengthen Hindu society, to protect and spread Hindu values, to establish and strengthen the links among Hindus living in different countries. Organize, consolidate the Hindu society, and to serve and protect the Hindu Dharma. The VHP considers Buddhist, Jains, Sikhs, and the native tribal communities as part of the greater Hindu fraternity; it promotes education and involvement of members of the Hindu diaspora in their cultural duties and spiritual values; the VHP has a presence in 29 countries across the world. In early 1970's, the number of social welfare projects under the VHP increased dramatically; many state Kalyan Ashrams, Vivekananda medical missions, orphanages, and student hostels were established by the VHP.

By 1981 the VHP claimed to have 3000 branch units in 437 of the nation's 534 districts, nearly 850 full-time workers, and 442 hostels, including orphanages and vocational schools, with ten published journals. The VHP also played an important role in the Ram Janmabhoomi movement. It established a trust to rebuild the temple. It raised nearly 18 million rupees for the project.

Sahakar Bharti.

Bharat Vikas Parishad.

Sewa Bharti.

Vanyasi Kalyan Ashram.

Rashtra Sevika Samiti.

Vishva Hindu Parishad.

To establish solidarity among the various Hindu sections the VHP, in March 1981, formed the Margdarshan Mandal, a forum of religious leaders who would advise the Parishad trustees on Hindu philosophical thoughts and a code of conduct; the Mandal provides the VHP leadership a link to other Hindu religious establishments, in 1982 the Mandal established the Dharm Sansad, a deliberative body of religious figures who would formulate a Hindu perspective on social and political problems. In 1982, the conversion of Hindus to islam in Meenakshipuram (Tamil Nadu) had set a stir within the Sangh; it assisted the VHP to tackle the situation, the Sangh supported the VHP'S fund raising campaign, its Ekatmata Yatra (unity campaign), which sought to create pan Hindu symbols and unify Hindu religious establishment and its social welfare activities aimed at uplifting and saving vulnerable HinduS from the alleged conversions.

The **Durga Vahini** was also established under the aegis of the VHP; it is the women's wing of the Vishva Hindu Parishad. It was established in 1991, and its founding chairperson is Sadhvi Rithambara. The Durga Vahini aims to empower women and encourage more women to participate in spiritual and cultural activities.[54]

The Rashtriya Sikh Sangat
(Founded – 12 March 1986)

The Rashtriya Sikh Sangat, is an affiliate organization of the Sangh Parivar. It is headquartered in Delhi. It has nearly 500 plus units in the states of Rajasthan, Haryana, Punjab, Gujrat, Delhi, Uttar Pradesh, and Madhya Pradesh. The Hindu nationalist movement inspires the Rashtriya Sikh Sangat. It considers the ancestral lineage of Hindus and

---

54   https://vhp.org/durga_vahini/ | Durga Vahini.

Sikhs as one, the Sikh Sangat works towards bringing Samrasta (Social harmony) in the society.

The Sangh celebrates the birth anniversaries of all Sikh Gurus, and even in the Baudhik sessions of the Sangh shakhas, the sacrifices and inspirational stories are taught to Swayamsevaks.

Educational Organizations
The Ekal Vidyalaya
(Founded – 10 June 1986)

The Ekal Vidyalaya foundation is an organization of the Ekal Abhiyan trust. It is an affiliate of the Sangh. It is involved in providing free education and village development programmes in rural areas and tribal villages of the nation.

The Ekal Vidyalaya foundation was formed in 1986 in Jharkhand by Sh. Bhaurao Deoras, the younger brother of the third Sarsanghchalak of the Sangh Sh. Balasaheb Deoras. The Ekal Vidyalaya started as a movement to impart integrated education and holistic development of children in rural areas; the main activity undertaken is to run one teacher schools known as Ekal Vidyalays all over nation.

The movement aims to take education to every child; the main motto of the Ekal Vidyalaya was to develop better models of grassroot education in the nation; as of November 2023, there are more than 21 lakh students enrolled in the Ekal Vidyalays and the it currently runs more than 83,000 schools including 3,100 schools in the north-eastern states.

The Ekal Vidyalaya was also set up in the United States of America in the year 2002, and was also established in Australia in 2004; currently, the Ekal schools are run across ten countries around the world; the organization is very well recognised globally and is of the premier organizations of the Sangh Parivar.

Vidhya Bharti
(Founded – March 1977)

The Vidhya Bharti, also known as the Vidhya Bharti Akhil Bhartiya Shiksha Sansthan, is the primary educational wing of the Sangh; it runs one of the largest private networks of schools in the nation. It was established in the year 1977 and by the year 1990, it had a network of nearly 5000 schools across the nation; it also manages over 270 intermediate colleges and about 25 institutions of higher education.

As of September 2023, there are 12,828 schools with 3,465,631 enrolled students under the aegis of the Vidhya Bharti Akhil Bhartiya Shiksha Sansthan, it has its functional headquarters in Delhi, and in the year 2020, it became the official member of the Van Guard Cohort for its contribution to school education.

Dedication to the motherland with a Bharatiya spirit is inculcated in every child, and the will to develop his character and fulfil and serve the needs of the nation; this is the main motto of the Vidhya Bharti. It is a historic organization which is developing leaders for Bharat.

Saraswati Shishu Mandir
(Founded – April 1952)

The Saraswati Shishu Mandir teaching system has a very special place in the world of education system. The scheme was launched in 1952 in Gorakhpur with the inspiration of revered Sh. Bhaurao Deoras, Sh. Krishnachandra Gandhi and Sh. Nanaji Deshmukh. Saraswati Shishu Mandir became famous as the first lamp of the Vidya Bharti in 1952 in Gorakhpur Sh. Nanaji Deshmukh established the first Shishu Mandir.

The Saraswati Shishu Mandir model was quickly replicated across the nation, revolutionizing education across the nation; the Vidhya Bharti Sansthan officially manages the Saraswati Shishu Mandir schools. The main motto of the Saraswati Shishu Mandir schools is that from the childhood; each child should be instilled with a mindset of Bhartiyata; the focus is on the Vyakti Nirman and Rashtra Nirman.

The vision of Sh. Nanaji Deshmukh is highly appreciable and commendable in every aspect, he was a legendary personality, and his contributions to the nation will always be remembered and revered. Until 2022 the Saraswati Shishu Mandir and the Vidhya Bharti schools have nearly 42 lakhs students and a network of 1.76 lakh teachers, what is more, interesting is that more than 13,000 muslim and christian students are being taught in the schools, this showcases the inclusive nature of the organization.

Publications & Communication

Given the critical questions that arose after independence of the nation, the Sangh leadership wanted to communicate its views quickly and rapidly to the growing membership and to the larger Hindu community.

The Sangh was initially hesitant for publicity and mass communication, but in 1946 senior pracharaks of the Sangh established the Bharat Prakashan trust in Delhi; many Swayamsevaks and people from the society contributed, and nearly 4 lakh rupees were raised, and it began to publish the 'Organiser' an english language weekly published in Delhi, the Organiser magazine reached national audience and became one of the most influential and prominent forum of viewpoint of the Sangh.

In order to communicate the vast majority of the population, which was not well versed in english, pracharaks of the Sangh decided to establish newspapers and journals in the local vernacular languages, during the ban of 1948-1949 Swayamsevaks established two weeklies

'Panchjanya' in Hindi and the 'Rashtra Shakti' in Marathi, in the following years many trusts were also formed to publish newspapers and journals in 12 vernacular languages.

In the period of 1970s, the Sangh formed the 'Hindustan Samachar', which was the nation's first vernacular news service, it was an important element in the communication network of the Sangh, during the times of emergency the Sangh affiliated newspapers experienced a surge in circulation and the affiliated magazines and journals tried their best to showcase the dictatorship during the emergency.

The Organiser
(Founded – 3 July 1947)

The Organiser is an affiliated weekly publication of the Sangh; it was launched as a newspaper on 3rd July 1947, in the weeks before the partition of India; senior Sangh members and members of the BJP, such as Sh.L.K Advani, Sh.Seshadri Chari, and Sh.K.R. Malkani have been its editors, its first issue was published in 1947, and the Bharat Prakashan trust, Delhi publishes it.[55]

After the second world war, the leadership in the Sangh wanted to communicate its views quickly to the growing membership. Initially, the Sangh was not in favour of publicity and mass communication. However, after discussions, the Sangh establishment consented to allow the publishing of newspapers and journals. The Organiser has been one of the most independent and historic weekly magazines today in the nation. The Organiser is circulated across the nation, spreading views about cultural, social aspects, issues of defence, education, health, and policy implementation.

---

55   https://organiser.org/ | About.

Panchjanya
(Founded – 14 January 1948)

The Panchjayna is a weekly magazine published in Hindi, Pt. Deendayal Upadhaya Ji had launched it in 1948 in Lucknow, the first editor of the Panchjanya magazine was Sh. Atal Bihari Vajpayee Ji, the inaugural cover page carried a picture of Lord Krishna with its objective to pursue idealism based on patriotism and uphold Bharat's cultural heritage.[56]

It is considered as one of the best written magazines which is widely circulated across the nation; Panchjanya means the preserver of the supreme deity Vishnu Ji, and Panchjanya also symbolises the five elements of nature. The magazine has a vast readership base in Hindi speaking states of the nation.

Rashtra Dharma
(Founded – 31 August 1947)

Rashtra Dharma is a Hindi monthly magazine affiliated with the Sangh Parivar; the magazine has been in publishing for over seven decades since 1947. On August 31 1947, the first issue of the magazine was published; Sh. Atal Bihari Vajpayee Ji was the first editor of the Rashtra Dharma magazine; his poem *"Hindu Tan-Man, Hindu Jeevan, Rag-Rag Hindu Mera Parichay'* was quoted in the first edition. Pt. Deendayal Upadhyay Ji was the first 'director' of the magazine. The magazine is published in Lucknow.

---

56   https://panchjanya.com/rss | The Panchjanya

The Ekal Vidyalaya.

Rashtriya Sikh Sangat.

Vidya Bharti.

Saraswati Shishu Mandir.

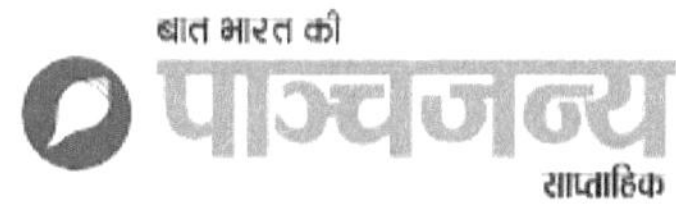

Panchjanya.

The Organiser.

Rashtra Dharma.

Sh Dattatreya Hosabale Ji, the Sarkarvayah of the Sangh in 2022, at the release program of 'Rashtriya Vichar Sadhana', the occasion of the diamond jubilee year of Rashtra Dharma magazine, said "That this magazine was started only to get out of the mentality of slavery. This magazine was started to wake up the country and the nation, he said that when we talk about the welfare of the whole world. We cannot go on ignoring the national religion and Hindutva."[57]

Think Tanks

**Bhartiya Shikshan Mandal
(Founded 27 March 1969)**

The Bhartiya Shikshan Mandal is an organization affiliated to the Sangh Parivar; it works in the field of education reforms across the nation. The Bhartiya Shikshan Mandal was founded on the auspicious day of Sh. Ram Navami in the year 1969, by Sh. Balasaheb Deoras, it is working with the objective of accomplishing national resurgence in the field of education.

According to the Bhartiya Shikshan Mandal, 'The goal of education should be the holistic personality development of students in the context of the national resurgence'. 'Bharatiya culture should be reflected in the personality of the students'. 'All the members of the teaching fraternity as teachers, administrators, alma-maters, and the parents, should get involved in this activity. We do not need to perform the task of reconstruction of the Rashtra; only reawakening is needed.'

---

57 https://organiser.org/2022/12/01/100362/rss-news/rashtra-dharma-magazine-was-started-to-emancipate-us-from-mental-slavery-dattatreya-hosabale/

Vivekanand Kendra
(Founded – 7 January 1972)

The Vivekananda Kendra is a social service organization affiliated to the Sangh Parivar and it aims upon nation building; it represents the legacy of Swami Vivekananda; it is headquartered near the Vivekananda Rock Memorial near Kanyakumari, Tamil Nadu; it was established in 1972 by Eknath Ranade Ji, a senior pracharak of the Sangh. The Vivekananda Kendra received the Gandhi peace prize in 2015 for contribution to rural development, education, and development of national resources.

The Kendra also provides, and imparts basic vocation skills to rural boys and girls; it organizes seminars and documentation projects on sustainable development, renewable energy, and Sanathan Dharma. The Kendra also runs Vidyalayas based on the teachings, philosophy, and principles of Swami Vivekananda. The schools are run under the Vivekananda Kendra Shiksha Vibhag. Approximately 68 Vivekananda Kendra schools are providing education to approximately 22,000 students across the nation.

Syama Prasad Mukherjee Research Foundation (SPMRF)

Dr. Syama Prasad Mukherjee Research Foundation has emerged in recent times as an important forum felicitating the conversion of ideas, visions that aspire to strengthen the nation, and preserve its unity, integrity and contribute towards its progress and integral development.

SPMRF is a platform for academicians, field experts, opinion makers who come together and exchange ideas on wider range of issues facing the nation with the objective of educating the wider public opinion.[58]

---

58 https://spmrf.org/spmrf/ | Dr. Syama Prasad Mookerjee Research Foundation.

The organization thrives for excellence and encourages the study and dissemination of the work and legacy of Sh. Syama Prasad Mukherjee, an educationist, a legendary statesman, and founder of the Bhartiya Jan Sangh, the predecessor of the Bhartiya Janta Party. The organization is working to uphold and sustain the vision of 'Ek Bharat Shresth Bharat', it regularly publishes, editorials, articles, and research papers and also works in vast fields such as foreign policy, defence, agriculture, heritage, and international cooperation, it is headquartered in New Delhi.

Public Affiliated Organizations
The Bhartiya Jan Sangh
(Founded – 21 October 1951)

The Bhartiya Jan Sangh was a right-wing political organization that existed from 1951 to 1977. The origin of the Bhartiya Jan Sangh can be traced when Dr. Syama Prasad Mukherjee, the founder of the Bhartiya Jan Sangh resigned from the congress government in 1950, and wanted to establish a nationalistic alternative to the congress party.

The ideology of the Bhartiya Jan Sangh was Hindutva, and it was closely related to the Sangh; many of the post holders of the Bhartiya Jan Sangh were members of the Sangh. Hindutva had always been a main focus of the Jan Sangh from the beginning. The Bhartiya Jan Sangh was succeeded by the Bhartiya Janta Party when it was founded in 1980.

The Bhartiya Janta Party
(Founded – 6 April 1980)

The BJP is the biggest political party in the world, with a membership of more than 20 million, it is a right wing political party, and it is connected to the nationalist Hindu ideology; it was founded in the year 1980 by Sh. Atal Bihari Vajpayee Ji & Sh. L.K Advani Ji, as successor of the Bhartiya Jan Sangh.

Bharatiya Shikshan Mandal.

Vivekananda Kendra.

SPMRF.

Bharatiya Jan Sangh.

Bharatiya Janta Party.

The official ideology of the BJP has been integral humanism, formulated by Pt. Sh. Deen Dayal Upadhyaya Ji in 1965, the party is considered ideologically close to the Sangh, the BJP has seen a meteoric rise in the number of political membership since its formation in 1980.

Overseas And International Diaspora Organizations
The Hindu Swaymsevak Sangh (Hindu Volunteer Association) (Founded – March 1940)

The HSS is a non-profit, social, educational, and cultural organization of Hindus living outside Bharat. It is affiliated to the Sangh Parivar.

It was founded in 1940 in Kenya; it is currently active in 158 countries and has an estimated 3389 branches across the world. The organization was initially named the Bharatiya Swayamsevak Sangh, later it was named as a Hindu Swayamsevak Sangh, senior Sangh pracharak Sh. Bhaurao Deoras played a very quintessential role in establishing the HSS. He spent several years abroad to develop the organization; the HSS was formed in the United Kingdom in 1966 and was established in cities like London, Birmingham, Stanford, and Bradford; in the USA, the HSS was formed in 1971.

The presence of HSS at a worldwide level suggests the inclusive nature of the Sangh Parivar; it is very amazing to see the level of public participation and influence that the Sangh has internationally and in the global sphere. The Sangh Parivar and the Sangh are not only respected and loved in Bharat but also across the globe.

The Hindu Students Council (HSC)
(Founded – June 1990)

The Hindu Students Council is a diverse community of student and young professionals, it was founded in 1990 and today is one of North America's largest pan Hindu communities. It is a registered non-profit organization working to provide a safe place for Hindu students on campuses all across the United States of America; it is working on the motto of knowledge, unity, and Dharma.

The HSC also works on youth advocacy to raise awareness for Hindu heritage, culture, and history; it also extensively works for youth empowerment, organizes international level conferences, and strives to create the leaders of tomorrow. It is associated with Hindu temples and organizations in the USA, including the Chinmaya Mission, Gayatri Parivar, Barsana Dham, and Ram Krishna Mission, with time it has expanded across USA and is considered as one of the most dignified Hindu organizations globally.

Other Important Organizations
Samskrita Bharti
(Founded – March 1981)

It is a non-profit organization working to revive the Sanskrit language; it is headquartered in New Delhi and was founded in 1981. The basic mission of the organization is to democratise and popularise Sanskrit language across Bharat and the world, it organizes conversations and language camps, and till 2023 nearly 8.9 million people have attended their programmes and conferences; it also works in the field of dissemination of Hindu traditions and languages, and it also works for the promotion of Sanskrit language in school education and in its curriculum.

Kreeda Bharti
(Founded – August 1992)

It was founded in the year 1992 with a vision to build a fit and hit Bharat; it envisages the participation of all citizens by promoting traditional sports along with established sports.

Hindu Swayamsevak Sangh.

The Hindu Students Council.

Samskrita Bharti.

Kreeda Bharti.

Akhil Bharatiya Gharak Panchayat.

The Kreeda Bharti is one of the most important organizations of the Sangh in terms of sports and physical games. Kreeda Bharti is considered as one of the organizations working to develop the spirit of sportsmanship, healthy body and mind, and proper mental values. The Kreeda Bharti organizes various conferences, and marathons, it also plays a very important in the world yoga day celebrations which are held across the nation. It works with the mission of promoting and developing youth for the service of the nation.[59]

The Akhil Bhartiya Grahak Panchayat
(Founded – September 1974)

The ABGP was founded in 1974 as a forum and organization working for bringing consumer awareness in all spheres of society; it works for consumer awareness, guidance, and it follows the ethos of the consumer protection act. It is headquartered in New Delhi. It was founded by late Sh. Bindu Madhav Joshi, who was a senior Sangh leader.

It was first established in Maharashtra; it is affiliated to the Sangh.[60] Today, it is actively working in 25 states and nearly 250 districts across the nation. The Grahak Panchayat also aims to inculcate Bharatiya ethos and values in consumerism in society. It looks forward to creating a well-informed consumer. It aims to make consumers aware and assist them in protecting their interest against unhealthy market practices and to help them achieve their social and economic welfare; it also runs research centres known as Bhartiya Grahak Niti.

---

59   https://kreedabharati.org/about-us/ | Kreeda Bharti.
60   https://www.abgpindia.com/ | Akhil Bhartiya Gharak Panchayat.

CHAPTER – 10

The 21ˢᵗ Century Bharat &
The RSS Perspective ~ Kartavya Kaal

Introduction

As the Rashtriya Swayamsevak Sangh is on the brink of completing hundred years in 2025, one can see the devotion and commitment in the Sangh to fulfil the vision of Dr. Hedgewar Ji & Guruji Golwalkar, the two Sarsanghchalaks of the Sangh who formulated the primary goals and ideals of the organization since its formation in 1925. Since 1925, It has been a long journey, and the journey of the Sangh has not been easy; it has been full of ups and downs.

The Sangh was born as an idea; it is a constantly evolving idea. It has a twin vision: individual perfection at the micro level and social cohesion and unity at the macro level. It has changed with time, adapted to things and to new situations.

In the past century, the Sangh, as well as the nation, has seen dynamic changes. The Sangh has always focused on building an organization that is involved in virtually every aspect of society, and the Sangh has been very successful in it. With each passing moment in the history of the organization since 1925, the Sangh has always focused on Service (Seva), Dedication (Samarpan), Organization (Sangathan), & Nation Building (Rashtra Nirman).

The Sangh has always been a dynamic organization, and its worldview and perspective have evolved with changing times. The Sangh's philosophy has been intact, and the vision and mission have always been the same. The twenty-first century Bharat and the perspective of the Sangh is an idea of development, growth, prosperity, happiness, and unity in the society and the nation.

This Chapter gives an insight into the Sangh's worldview, the goals and challenges of the 21st century, and its perspective and idea of the nation in the Kartavya Kaal, as Bharat will complete hundred years of its independence in the year 2047.

The 21st- Century Perspective & Dimensions

Bharat is today the world's largest democracy; the nation has witnessed tremendous growth and development in the 21st century. It has made significant strides in various sectors, including technology, education, healthcare, and the economy, transforming it into a global player. In the 21st century, the nation is, brimming with potential and teeming with challenges. It stands at the crossroads of tradition and modernity and rapid socio-economic changes.

Despite challenges, the nation's growth in the 21st century is commendable. It continues to evolve, promising a bright future. To introspect multiple dimensions is very important in the context of the nation, such as economy, technology, environment, health, education, and society.

Economy: – The nation's economy has witnessed remarkable growth, shifting from agriculture to a services and industry-oriented economy. However, the challenge lies in achieving inclusive growth, addressing income inequalities, and improving living standards. The nation has seen significant social changes. Economically, it has become one of the fastest-growing major economies in the world. Introducing reforms to facilitate the ease of doing business has brought growth. Increased literacy rates, a growing middle class, and greater gender equality are reshaping societal norms, but there is still a need to address issues like unemployment and income inequality.

Technology: – The advent of the 21ˢᵗ century has marked a technological revolution in the nation. The country has emerged as a global IT hub; the surge in digitalization, fuelled by initiatives like 'Digital India,' has improved governance, increased transparency, and provided a boost to the digital economy. In the space arena, The Indian Space Research Organisation's feats, such as the Mangalyaan, Chandrayaan have further showcased Bharat's technological prowess on the global stage.

Healthcare: – The nation has made commendable progress in healthcare. The government has successfully eradicated many diseases and significantly reduced maternal and child mortality rates. Schemes like the Ayushman Bharat provide health insurance to over 500 million people, which is a substantial step towards universal health coverage. Vaccinating a populace of 140 crore during and after COVID-19 has been an achievement of the nation's healthcare system.

Environment: – While the nation's growth story is impressive, it has been accompanied by environmental challenges. Rapid urbanization and industrialization have led to increased pollution levels and biodiversity loss. In the 21ˢᵗ century, the nation is grappling with issues like air pollution, water scarcity, and climate change, which pose a challenge. Thus, these issues need sustainable solutions.

Education: – Education in the nation has recently witnessed a paradigm shift. The world is changing at an inconceivable pace. We must now understand that we are preparing our children for challenging times.[61] Therefore, 21ˢᵗ-century education must teach students how to

---

61 https://indianexpress.com/article/opinion/columns/india75-looking-at-100-what-indias-education-system-needs-8203245

deal with rapid change. The Sangh has been actively working in the field of education, and with the introduction of the New education policy of 2020, which lays the aspect that "No education system can succeed without moral values, the new policy is built on moral values which are inherent to Bharat. Students will be taught the fundamental rights and duties through the education system, which is borrowed from ancient texts and cultural practices.

The New education policy also talks of "curriculum and the method and practice of teaching, especially as an academic subject or theoretical concept to develop a deep sense of respect towards citizens fundamental duties, living closely with one's country, and conscious awareness of one's roles and responsibilities in a changing world," Thus, the focus on creating an inclusive education model is hence significant for the growth of the nation and harnessing the potential of the youth in the 21st century.

Brotherhood & Harmony: – To promote harmony and brotherhood among every citizen, first, we must refuse and resign to any act degrading our society's fabric. Then, we need to pass on our ancient culture and heritage to our upcoming generation so that it remains well preserved and maintained as well. In the 21st century, it is essential to maintain a spirit of brotherhood in society that involves treating one another metaphorically or symbolically, referring to something considered to have a relationship. Thus, a spirit of brotherhood can be attained by encouraging patriotism and maintaining unity; the Sangh has always maintained its ideology and focus on harmony and brotherhood.

The nation is striving to balance economic growth with social equity and technological advancement with environmental sustainability. The journey has been challenging, but the potential is immense. The 21st century could indeed be Bharat's century if it successfully navigates the perspectives and emerging challenges.

Challenges in the 21ˢᵗ century

The path ahead for the nation in the 21ˢᵗ century includes many concerns and challenges; Bharat has achieved many milestones in different spheres, but challenges remain that need to be addressed. Important issues include: – population explosion. urbanization, gender equality, unemployment, drinking water scarcity, unhealthy lifestyle, poverty, income inequality, and the confluence of modernity and tradition.

Population: – India is on its way to becoming the most populous nation. Population imbalance cannot be ignored; the Sangh has, on numerous occasions, underlined the need for a population control policy in the nation; the unprecedented population boom in the country is a serious matter of concern.

Urbanization: – More than one-third of Indians live in cities. It is estimated that by 2050, as many as 900 million people will live in urban centres. Meeting their needs while safeguarding the environment will require innovative models of urban development.[62] Developing sustainable cities and conserving the environment is a significant issue that needs to be addressed.

Gender Equality: – There is a need for the nation and the society to ensure gender equality and the equality of opportunity for everyone. The gender gap holds back economies all around the world. Any society that does not create equal opportunities for women as much as men is not reaching its full potential.[62] Though gender equality has improved in recent years through the initiatives and programs of the government, there is still a lot more space for betterment. The Sangh has been a vocal proponent of gender equality and equality of opportunity.

62 Secure Synopsis: Nov 08 2018 – Insightsias. https://demolive.insightsonindia.com/2018/11/13/secure-synopsis-08-november-2018-2/

Drinking Water Scarcity: The nation's large population severely strains its natural resources, and most of its water sources are contaminated by sewage and agricultural run-off. While progress has undoubtedly been made, but still gross disparities in access to safe water remain. Many researches have estimated that 21% of communicable diseases in India are related to unsafe water.[62]

Unemployment: – As the nation progresses to become one of the largest economies of the world, there is an inherent challenge that emerges in the face of unemployment; there is a need to tackle unemployment aggressively and equal attention to creating jobs and entrepreneurship opportunities for those who are among the most disadvantaged should be the focus. The Sangh in its Akhil Bharatiya Pratinidhi Sabha has specified that a 'Bhartiya Economic Model' should be implemented to ensure sustainable employment and end joblessness among the youth.

Unhealthy lifestyle: – While the nation might be growing in terms of socio-economic development parameters, in terms of lifestyle and health, the nation faces many challenges; lifestyle diseases like cardiovascular, diabetes, hypertension, asthma, and respiratory, as well as cancers, are on the rise. The nation has the highest number of diabetics at 50.8 million, according to the World Health Organization; twenty-five million suffer from cardiovascular diseases, which amounts to 60% of the global figure. The Sangh as an organization focuses on creating a healthy mind and body for everyone; the Sangh also emphasizes following the Bharatiya traditions for maintaining a healthy lifestyle.

Poverty & Income Inequality: – Poverty and income inequality are some of the biggest challenges today in the nation. The Sangh has flagged

---

62 Secure Synopsis: Nov 08 2018 – Insightsias. https://demolive.insightsonindia.com/ 2018/11/13/secure-synopsis-08-november-2018-2/

issues of poverty, unemployment, and rising inequality in the country and batted for creating a robust environment for entrepreneurship so that job seekers become job providers.[63] Sarkarvyah Sh. Dattatreya Hosabale Ji recently said, "The poverty in the country is standing like a demon in front of us. We must slay this demon. he also mentioned that the 'faulty' economic policies of the earlier governments for the "ills" in the economy."[63] The Sangh has acknowledged that several steps have been taken in the last few years to address this challenge. The Sangh has also been vocal about reviving cottage industries and more initiatives in the skill development sector to increase its penetration in rural areas further.

Modernity and tradition: – As society progresses with time, newer concepts and ideas emerge and lead to change and modernity. The Sangh has always been an organization that has kept itself with the pace of time, but overt westernization at the cost of disbelieving the traditions and culture of Bhartiyata is a challenge today; creating a positive balance between both is the goal.

Within the broader contours of the society, the Sangh is striving to infuse various sectors like education, governance, jurisprudence, and social systems with nobler Bharatiya ideas. The youth of the nation, the majority of its population, are proud nationals at one level and globalized citizens at another. Modernity and prosperity are the mantra for them. Sangh is the only force that has the potential to become the epicentre of their hopes and aspirations.

The Rashtriya Swayamsevak Sangh has always created a vision for the nation's growth and prosperity. In the Kartavya Kaal, the role of

---

63 RSS general secretary Dattatreya Hosabale raises alert on poverty, joblessness, inequality (Indian Express) – Hindutva Watch. https://hindutvawatch.org/rss-general-secretary-dattatreya-hosabale-raises-alert-on-poverty-joblessness-inequality-indian-express/

the Sangh has become more significant; the 21st century demands and requires the Sangh to lead the Bharat of the future with its philosophy and ideas for the nation.

The Goals for 21st century

As the nation navigates through the twenty-first century, it is very significant and essential to ponder upon and focus on the goals that are to be achieved and which are most pertinent in nation-building and bringing growth, development, and prosperity.

There are some challenges that the nation faces in terms of addressing the economy and society, setting the country on a sustained growth path, benefiting from the demographic dividend of a young population who seek remunerative employment, and finally building a united country with peace and tranquillity is essential.

Basic amenities should be guaranteed to everyone. No one should go to sleep hungry. No life should be lost because of lack of access or affordability of healthcare. The quality of life should see a significant uplift.[64] This will need more public-private partnerships in all segments; only government participation will not suffice, civil society must be an active participant in achieving the goals of the nation.[64]

The Broader goals that the nation should aim to achieve can be summarised as: –

1. Free from Poverty, Full of Prosperity (Garibi Se Mukt, Samriththi Se Yukt).

2. Free from Discrimination, Filled with Equality (Bhedbhav se Mukt, Samanta se Yukt).

---

64 Road to India@100: Envisioning the India of 2047 – Business Today – Issue Date: Feb 19, 2023. https://www.businesstoday.in/magazine/columns/story/road-to-india100-envisioning-the-india-of-2047-368958-2023-02-

3. Free from Injustices, Ensuring Justice (Anyay Se Mukt, Nyay Se Yukt).

4. Free from Filth, Ensuring Cleanliness (Gandagi Se Mukt, Swachchhta Se Yukt).

5. Free from Corruption, Ensuring Transparency (Bhrashtachar Se Mukt, Pardarshita Se Yukt

6. Free from Unemployment, Enriched with Employment (Berozgari se Mukt, Rozgari se Yukt).

7. Free from Despondency, Full of Hope (Nirasha se Mukt, Asha Se Yukt).

In line to achieve these goals, many policy initiatives and steps have been taken by the government with the active participation of civil society, such as the Beti Bachao, Beti Padhao, which aims to address the issue of declining child sex ratio and ensure proper care & education for the girl child, revolutionizing the Jan Dhan, Aadhar and GST which are ensuring transparency in taxation, subsidies, and money transfers to people making them fiscally more prudent, a new approach to rural development has been undertaken in the face of the Sansad Adarsh Gram Yojana, On the economic front there has been a push for India's entrepreneurial growth by the Make in India policy.

The Namami Gange program has been launched for a clean environment and river system. To empower farmers for a prosperous nation, The PM Kisan Samaan Nidhi program has been undertaken to provide money transfers to all farmers in the nation. To ensure last-mile connectivity and building infrastructure for a resurgent Bharat, schemes such as the Sagarmala and Bharatmala have been launched. Thus, the dream of Atmnirbhar Bharat (self-reliant India) in every field and sphere can be fulfilled with the proper policy implementation and a proper mindset to achieve and deliver.

The country has completed 75 years of independence with appreciable progress in the economic and social upliftment of large masses of the population. Its poverty reduction efforts, growth and development, and improvements in human development indicators are impressive. However, there are gaps to be addressed in sectors like education, health, water and sanitation.

For Bharat to be a developed nation, we need to harness the full potential of our current demographic dividend.[64] Pioneering a knowledge economy, a system of consumption and production based on intellectual capital, is necessary for a better tomorrow.

Bharat @ 100

Kartavya Kaal means 'The Era of Duty.' 'The Amrit Kaal will also be Kartavya Kaal for citizens to prioritize their duties.' Kartavya should be Bharat's priority, leading to 100 years of independence in 2047. It endorses the duties of citizens as a priority, As the nation looks forward to economic growth over the next 25 years through rapid development, higher living standards for everybody, infrastructure, and technological achievements, and reinvigorating global confidence in the nation. People should undertake The Panch Pran (five pillars) of Amrit Kaal, which will be making the nation developed, removing every trace of bondage, taking pride in the nation's heritage and unity, and fulfilling their duties.

Thus, setting a Mission 2047 is significant to achieve the target and to make Bharat a developed nation; the next twenty-five years will be crucial to ensure that the country's aspirations are met by the time it celebrates 100 years of independence. A nation-first approach

---

64   Road to India@100: Envisioning the India of 2047 – Business Today – Issue Date: Feb 19, 2023. https://www.businesstoday.in/magazine/columns/story/road-to-india100-envisioning-the-india-of-2047-368958-2023-02-

is also required by everyone. Demography, Democracy, and Diversity collaboratively can help the nation power its development journey. The convergence of these three can fulfil the country's dreams. The nation should also act against evils of corruption, dynasty, and appeasement, which are hurdles to its goals. There is also a need to deliver solutions through peace and focus on enhancing cooperation and collaboration.

Elaborating on the goals for 2047, the nation should aim that *'Jan Bhagidari'* through *'Sabka Saath & Sabka Prayas'* is essential and delineated in the Saptarishi principles: inclusive development, reaching the last mile, infrastructure and investment, unleashing the potential; green growth; youth power & financial inclusion.

The '4 S' principles can be emphasized to stress the need for prosperity growth to be matched by **social progress**, **shared** across all regions within Bharat, environmentally **sustainable**, and **solid** in the face of external shocks. Bharat is well on the path to becoming one of the two largest economies in the world by 2047. As predicted, by 2047, the nation will be a global powerhouse with an economy of around $35 trillion.[64]

The seeds we sow today will define the fruits reaped in the future. To achieve the above-mentioned transformational objectives of *Viksit Bharat* envisioned for 2047, the country must continue to focus on ***"Sabka Saath, Sabka Vikas, Sabka Vishwas, and Sabka Prayas."*** Let us pledge to make efforts, individually and collectively.

By 2047, we must build a nation that will be connected to the pride of the past and which will have all the golden chapters of modernity. We have to make a Bharat that is self-reliant and can fulfil its humanitarian

---

64   Road to India@100: Envisioning the India of 2047 – Business Today – Issue Date: Feb 19, 2023. https://www.businesstoday.in/magazine/columns/story/road-to-india100-envisioning-the-india-of-2047-368958-2023-02-

obligations. A Bharat with no poverty and where the middle class is also prosperous, a Bharat whose youth and woman power will be at the forefront to give direction to the society. How the nation addresses these issues will determine its trajectory in the coming years. The 21st century holds immense potential for Bharat, and with the right policies and initiatives, the country can achieve sustainable and inclusive growth.

Yesterday was difficult, but today is better. However, tomorrow should be the Bharat of our dreams. The Bharat of 2047 should be a leading voice and thought leader globally and play a significant role in shaping the geopolitical order.[64]

Way Forward – The Sangh's Idea of Bharat

As an organization, the Sangh is unique. No other body has shown such enormous voluntary service for the nation. For decades, generation after generation it has instinctively chosen austerity and devoted itself to the national cause; as the Sangh completes its hundred years of establishment in 2025, the Sangh's idea of Bharat and its perspective becomes most significant.

The Sangh outlines the broad and multiple aspects and believes that social justice, social harmony, self-reliant society, promotion of Hindu culture, promotion of Bharatiya languages, Parivar Prabodhan (awakening about the family system), resurgence of the Bharatiya knowledge system, Dharam Jagran and Samrasta (social harmony), popularization of Sanskrit studies, Paryvaran Vikas (environment conservation) and Gram Vikas (rural development) are the significant ideas and perspectives for the twenty-first century.

---

64   Road to India@100: Envisioning the India of 2047 – Business Today – Issue Date: Feb 19, 2023. https://www.businesstoday.in/magazine/columns/story/road-to-india100-envisioning-the-india-of-2047-368958-2023-02-

The Roadmap for the twenty-first century is also focused on specific social and academic aspects, such as identifying and eliminating falsehoods and misrepresentations about the Sangh and emphasizing its role and contributions to the nation; the inclusion of important events, developments, and personalities who have contributed immensely to the nation, with the suitable weightage and attention that they deserve but have not been given, the other is the reclamation of the Bharatiya history through reforming academic curriculum and university researches.

The Sangh also believes that the nation needs several new museums to show the "real history" of the country, and the existing museums to be turned around entirely as several important aspects about the lives of national heroes – like Shivaji, Maharana Pratap, Chanakya, Chandragupta Maurya. Distorted history should be replaced by correct history so that the countrymen can take pride in their heritage. Art, literature and other expressions of creativity should reflect contemporaneity.[65]

Writing about the revamp plans, Sh. Sunil Ambekar Ji, the current Akhil Bhartiya Prachar Pramukh, in his book RSS: The Roadmaps for 21st, century describes the Sangh's vision "The revamp of existing museums is necessary as many untold histories have to be made known.

In Sangh's perspective on education, the Sanskrit language also occupies a very important place. The Sangh considers Sanskrit as the great unifier and part of a grand heritage. Sanskrit is both the culture and civilization of Bharat. Leaders of the nation, from Aurobindo to Ambedkar, considered it the genius of Bharat.

Sangh sees the Crumbling down of the family as an institution and the weakening of social bonds in society as a challenge. Hence,

---

65 https://theprint.in/india/ram-mandir-to-ram-rajya-rss-begins-work-for-its-roadmap-for-next-25-years/784403/

it notes that we need to make special efforts to achieve the objectives such as strengthening the family institution, creating a fraternity-based harmonious society, and developing entrepreneurship with a Swadeshi spirit.

Problems like technological progress, insatiable hunger for consumption, depletion of natural resources, extinction of vital species, and threat to the economy will endanger human life. Under these circumstances, a model of life following the Hindu Philosophy must be presented to various countries. Sangh is working with all its strength and resources in preparing the Hindu Society for this purpose. The Sangh's approach follows the footsteps of Adi Shankaracharya and Swami Vivekanand, as well as hundreds of saints and sages right up to the present century. Only when we build institutions will we see the material and spiritual progress due to the people of this country. This can happen when the power of Dharma is fully explored.

At the Sangh Pratinidhi Sabha, which was held in March 2023, the Sangh Sarkaryavyah Sh. Dattatreya Hosbale Ji emphasized that Sangh aims to bring transformation through social harmony, family values, ecological conservation, Swadeshi (Bharatiya) conduct, and awareness about civic duty. He said, "At a time when Bharat is taking bold steps on the path to global leadership, the citizens need to be vigilant of those looking to impede the nation's progress."[65]

The Rashtriya Swayamsevak Sangh and the entire society will continue to work to remove all the obstacles coming in the way of the nation's resurgence.[65] He added that the narrative about the country should change as we march ahead in this Kartavya Kaal, and answers to questions on Bharat should emanate from Bharat only.

---

65   https://theprint.in/india/ram-mandir-to-ram-rajya-rss-begins-work-for-its-roadmap-for-next-25-years/784403/

Going forward, 2025 will be the year of the Sangh centenary; as newer platforms germinate and grow to full stature and as its activities permeate multiple layers, coordination and cooperation will be key features. Param Pujnaiye Sarsanghchalak Mohan Bhagwat Ji said "That as the organization will turn 100 in 2025, the Swayamsevaks should reach every household with the extension of branches in all villages," The Sangh was born out of a 'Desh Bhava' a Meditative experience about Bharat, forward planning, meticulous designing of initiatives and inspiring rich contributions from Swayamsevaks is a Sangh speciality and the 21st century Bharat will see a lot of it.

In the twenty-first century, important aspects that have been achieved are the reconstruction of the Sh. Ram Mandir in Ayodhya, an active debate of the uniform civil code, and the abrogation of article 370 of the Indian constitution as they have been significant Hindutva concerns and have been linked to the identity of Bharat.

In the twenty-first century, the Sangh's emphasis is on establishing a way of social life and polity that follows the principles of 'Ram Rajya' within the Constitutional framework and the spiritual traditions of Bharat. Ram Rajya, in the Bharatiya context implies an ideal governance and social system where the goals and activities of society, rulers, and individuals are in perfect synergy, resulting in peace and prosperity for all.

Elaborating on the 25-year plans, Sh. Arun Kumar Ji (Sahsarkarvyah) of the Sangh said: "As the construction of Ram Temple has begun, it seems that now the society is prepared to build the Bharat that we want to make. The journey from Ram temple to Ram Rajya has to take place in the next 25 years." In the next 25 years, Prabhu Sh. Ram must be established in the heart of every person in the nation. Moreover, every individual must be inspired and motivated to live their personal and family life according to the principles followed by Prabhu Sh.Ram."

The Sangh believes that in the next 25 years, the nation will have to be built to reclaim its position of *'Vishwa Guru'*. However, it should not be based on power and materialistic success. Instead, it should primarily be guided by the age-old spiritual traditions of Bharat.[65]

"It is our dream to see *'Bharat Mata'* sitting on the worlds highest pedestal of *Vishwa Guru'* in the coming 25 years. For us, there is a picture of a Bharat endowed with ultimate splendour and power but full of spirituality for which we all must work," Overall, the Sangh is preparing to begin the journey from Ram temple to Ram Rajya, which will span over the next 25 years and probably be at the centre of the national discourse.[65]

The cause of Hindutva is, therefore, the cause of Ekatmata and Vasudhaiva Kutumbakam. In the twenty-first century, Hindutva is a bold vision for truth and oneness. It defines the Sangh. In the years and decades ahead, Hindutva will be Bharat's greatest cultural export, the chief instruments of which will be the Sangh and its Swayamsevak's.[66]

"जय हिन्द, जय भारत."

---

65   https://theprint.in/india/ram-mandir-to-ram-rajya-rss-begins-work-for-its-roadmap-for-next-25-years/784403/

66   Hindutva to be our greatest cultural export: ABVP leader | Latest News India – Hindustan Times. https://www.hindustantimes.com/india-news/hindutva-to-be-our-greatest-cultural-export-abvp-leader/story-LIDA87wDeCOXiMnGmB9pOL.html

Quotes & Sayings

The Sangh does not want to exist anyhow like any organization for centuries, the Sangh has a desire that Hindutva spreads rapidly throughout the nation.

– Dr. Keshav Baliram Hedgewar.

It is inevitable, therefore, that in order to be able to contribute our unique knowledge to mankind, in order to be able to live and strive for the unity and welfare of the world, we stand before the world as a self-confident, resurgent, and mighty nation which is Bharat.

– Sh. Guruji Golwalkar.

RSS is a revolutionary organization. No other organization in the country comes anywhere near it. It alone has the capacity to transform society. I have great expectations from this revolutionary organization that has taken up the challenge of creating a new Bharat.

– Sh. Jayprakash Narayan.

'If it had not been for the Sangh, I would not have thought of the country and devoted my life to it, whatever I am is today is because of the Sangh, the Sangh is an inspirational and historic organization.'

– Sh. Nanaji Deshmukh.